The Science of Language *LF*

and the Art of Teaching

The
Science
of
Language

and
The Art
of
Teaching

Henry F. Beechhold
and
John L. Behling, Jr.

CHARLES
SCRIBNER'S
SONS

New York

A–3.72[C]

Printed in the United States of America
Library of Congress Catalog Card Number 75–162781
SBN 684–12596–X (College paper)

Acknowledgments

Acknowledgment is gratefully made to the following publishers who have permitted the use of their materials in copyright:

HARCOURT BRACE JOVANOVICH, INC.
   For the chart from *The Five Clocks* by Martin Joos, published by Harcourt Brace Jovanovich, Inc. Reprinted by permission of Harcourt Brace Jovanovich, Inc.

HOLT, RINEHART AND WINSTON, INC.
   For the table from *Man's Many Voices: Language in Its Cultural Context* by Robbins Burling. Copyright © 1970 by Holt, Rinehart and Winston, Inc. Reprinted by permission of Holt, Rinehart and Winston, Inc.

Contents 165883

Foreword

This book is mainly for teachers and prospective teachers of the language arts. In it we have tried to bring together a sound introduction to linguistics (the science of language) and techniques for using linguistics in the classroom. Our educational philosophy is essentially that of Jerome Bruner, and the method we urge, therefore, is that of inquiry/discovery/problem-solving. The questions, problems, and projects in which the book abounds are for the most part open-ended and not designed merely to elicit *informational* responses. They are designed rather to put student (and teacher) in the position of the worker at the frontiers of knowledge. Every one of man's questions had to be struggled with a first time, a time when there were no books in which to look up the answers (indeed when there *were* no answers). Someone had to make the initial assault. We have tried to put the inquirer into that frame of reference with respect to many areas of language study. To read a chapter and repeat the data presented there does not in our judgment make for genuine learning; and while there may be some types of academic work where that approach is valid, we feel that it is only minimally so in the exploration of language. Yet wherever the language arts

teacher addresses linguistic matters it is at the level of *read and memorize*, mainly, it seems, grammatical definitions and "rules"; and what is perhaps the most intrinsically exciting of all things to study—language—becomes for the student the hallmark of academic dullness. (Who remembers his "grammar" lessons with pleasure?) It need not be thus as we hope we have shown in *The Science of Language and the Art of Teaching*.

Debts in an undertaking such as this are many and are owing in various ways to our teachers, colleagues, and students. We wish, however, to particularly thank Professors Albert H. Marckwardt of Princeton University, H. A. Gleason, Jr., of the University of Toronto, Louis Levine and Allan F. Hubbell of New York University, and Bruce Fraser of Harvard University. Their advice, encouragement, and intellectual stimulation over the years has been invaluable. To our wives, Irene Beechhold and Mary Jane Behling, who patiently endured this extra trial, go our special thanks. We are deeply grateful, likewise, to the editorial staff of Charles Scribner's Sons for their dedicated labors on a difficult manuscript.

H.F.B.　　　　J.L.B., Jr.

Trenton, N.J.　　Danbury, Conn.

Preface

The problem posed by the title of this book is an old one and to a considerable extent inherent in the relationship between knowledge and education. Almost any aspect of the complex world we live in can be understood only in terms of organizing and systematizing the observed facts about it. Any other procedure would lead only to absolute chaos. This is especially true of the human aspects of our world, and of course nothing is more essentially human in character than language. To this extent, the concern here is with science.

At the same time, knowledge is not necessarily transmitted most effectively in the neat packages into which it is bundled by the scientists. Any consideration of the practices of the greatest teachers, from Socrates on down, tells us this. The teacher does more than transmit knowledge. He inculcates attitudes, among which the two most important are a passion for inquiry and a spirit of open-mindedness. These have little to do with taxonomies or with packaged bundles of knowledge. Although we speak of the person at the front of the classroom as a teacher, and of his day to day activity as teaching, his real concern is with learning; that is, with stimulating his students not only toward the acquisition of facts and skills but toward the development of something approaching common sense, and beyond this, wisdom. This is an art. In it, intuition and sensitivity play larger roles than technical virtuosity.

All of this is implicit not only in the title but in the approach that Professors Beechhold and Behling have taken in this book. This is difficult to do with the content of any of the school subjects, but especially so with language. Whether we like it or not, most people in this country, teachers included, with a few notable exceptions, possess a deep-seated uneasiness about language study. The very same parents who, in a PTA meeting, will loudly demand that their offspring be given a sound training in the fundamentals of grammar, will also be the first to purchase a set of foreign-language records that promises a command of the language without recourse to grammar. The presentation of language and of language study to be found here should go a long way toward correcting this unhappy and curiously contradictory situation.

ALBERT H. MARCKWARDT

Princeton University

ix

1
English Is
a Language

Language study is not important for what it finally allows one to do with language; it is important for the questions it asks and the freedom it opens up to one in answering them.

(Wayne O'Neil, "Foreword" to N. R. Cattell, *The New English Grammar*, Cambridge, Mass.)

To be thoroughly prepared for his work, an English teacher will need to familiarize himself not only with the contents of [*Linguistics and English Grammar*], but also . . . with a standard treatment of general linguistics, three or four good English grammars of as diverse approaches as possible, a solid history of the language, an introduction to English phonology (and the general phonetics usually included in such books), and a sampling of the professional literature on the application of linguistics to English teaching. In addition, . . . experience with exploring the system of the language beyond the limits described in the reading. This is not a course of preparation for specialists . . . [but] the *minimum* necessary for a rank-and-file teacher. For specialists . . . a great deal *more* is required.

What do you need to teach Shakespeare? A literary history, a social history of England, a critical introduction to Shakespeare, fundamentals of English poetics, introduction to the drama, and a sampling of professional literature on Shakespeare, plus some first-hand experience with his plays.

(H. A. Gleason, *Linguistics and English Grammar*, New York.)

Perhaps the root problem of "English" teaching is the ill-defined nature of *English*. Let us resolve this problem at once by taking "English" teaching to be *language* teaching, for English is a language. If, then, we direct our teaching energies toward English-as-language, we thereby give our subject a shape and will, perforce, be far less frustrated in our tasks than we must be with the current amorphous "English." Not that teaching English-as-language is without either its problems or its challenges; but the problems are shapelier and the challenges more meaningful. Hence solutions are more likely, and challenges are more satisfyingly met.

There is, however, little in our educational background that gives us true and useful insights into the nature and operations of English. The usual "English" teaching is a farrago of no truth, little truth, and half truth about the language and is calculated, it would seem, to madden the guilty, appall the free, and bore everyone else. The plain fact is that after having undergone twelve or more years of "English" teaching the student knows virtually nothing to the point about language or about the English language and precious little of consequence about anything else. It is not too much to say that dropping the present "English" program from our curriculum and replacing it with nothing would lose us nothing. It might, quite possibly, gain for us at least a neutral attitude toward English instead of the prevalent proclaimed distaste of Americans for their mother tongue—which, of course, means a distaste for the *study* of their mother tongue. There is no point in picking over the reasons for the pitiful return on the education hour and dollar. The only conscionable thing is to do something about it.

If we take *English* to be the English language, we easily conclude that literature, composition, and the other odds and ends that are traditionally subsumed under English are simply the English language in its several uses. And if language is the heart of the matter, then we must use the techniques and insights of the science and philosophy of language as our teaching tools. We must, in short, become practicing *linguists* (not to be confused with *polyglots* or people skilled at speaking several languages).

The *discipline* of the English teacher is *linguistics*, more particularly, *applied linguistics*; and becoming an English teacher means becoming a specialist, or expert, in the English language. Language is the basis of our humanness, the *sine qua non* of thought, the prime mechanism of acculturation. Literature is a way of using language, but the nature of language must be explored deeply before we can hope that artful uses of language can be grasped and appreciated.

Of course, the English teacher doesn't really *teach* English, for the child is already linguistically well developed when he starts school. The language center of the cerebral cortex is already well programmed, and little any teacher can do will have much effect on that basic programming. The teacher's job is one of stimulating, drawing out, encouraging, enlarging, and so on. Presenting data to be memorized and repeated is not only useless but counterproductive. That is, traditional "English" lessons are inhibitory and reaction-forming. Hence that "hatred" of English that so many Americans proclaim and that ineptitude in using the language, outside of the day-to-day conversational uses, that both the commercial and academic worlds endlessly point out.

The only reasonable way out of the mess is to thoroughly ground the prospective English teacher in both the science of language and its applications in the classroom, and the purpose of this book is to provide the materials for such a grounding. Not that there is any lack of books currently available on linguistics, the "new English," or "modern grammar." The special value of the present book is its combination of message and method. The prospective teacher will explore not only language but also ways of using those explorations in the classroom. The experience of the authors convinces them that teaching linguistics and "methods" as separate courses (often in separate departments) is without value to the student. The linguist generally knows little or nothing about the problems of teaching below the university level, and the teacher of methods courses almost invariably knows nothing of linguistics (or what he knows is superficial and dated). Furthermore, the usual approach to methods teaching is to offer separate courses in Kindergarten-Primary (K-P), elementary, and secondary methods and thereby to maintain the educationally unsound balkanization of the school program. (On this point, see H. Beechhold, *The Creative Classroom*, 1971.) Thus we have split content from method and disrupted the organic unity of the educational process. We shall try here to put the pieces together.

Linguistics is a term in great currency these days. No language arts series, basal reader series, or anything else to do with English in the school program can afford not to use the term. Unfortunately, the word is more often than not an advertising slogan, so as a first step in preparing to teach, let us put aside all those tempting (but highly suspect) sets and series of textbooks and look carefully at *linguistics*.

Linguistics is the scientific study of language. That is, it is the study of language (through specific languages, of course) carried out according to certain methodologies paralleling those used in the other sciences. The linguist means to take language as an object of study and to describe, with as little whimsy and personal prejudice as possible, its shapes and its operations. But there is a philosophical dimension to language study that carries the modern linguist beyond the narrowly objective views that characterized the science in its post-Bloomfield, pre-Chomsky period.* Despite the existence, however, of sometimes competing schools of linguistic thought and of acrimonious academic debates, linguistics is properly the *science of language*.

This means, for example, that language features are identified through observation or demonstrable inference and that language descriptions represent the realities of language use. A curious furor erupted upon the publication of the G. & C. Merriam *Webster's Third New International Dictionary*. The detractors of that admirable piece of lexicography were

---

* Leonard Bloomfield is said to be the father of *structuralism*, the most methodologically rigorous of the modern linguistic "schools." Noam Chomsky is widely credited with being the father of the current "revolution" in linguistics, the profoundly philosophical *transformational-generative* school of linguistics.

to greater or lesser degrees exercised, even outraged, by this dictionary's refusal to assign rhetorical and social values to its words. The lexicographical philosophy of the dictionary, as it is clearly stated in the introduction to the work, is to offer the reader a *description* of the current *English vocabulary*. (The designation "unabridged," incidentally, should not be misunderstood for "complete"; there is really no way of knowing the extent of the English—or any natural language—vocabulary; hence no dictionary can be truly "complete.") The defenders of the faith, as it were, felt betrayed by this prestigious "authority"; and much polemical nonsense was written by these "purists," as they fancied themselves. One should read the exchange between Wilson Follett (*Atlantic Monthly*, January 1962), *contra*, and Bergen Evans (*Atlantic Monthly*, May 1962), *pro*. The former article was entitled "Sabotage in Springfield: Webster's Third Edition"; the latter, "But What's a Dictionary For?"—the precise question to ask, after all. The point is that the makers of the *Webster's Third* were guiding themselves with pertinent principles of the *science* of language. They were taxed, however, by their detractors for avoiding pronouncements that may be subtended under the *art* (or even the *whimsy*) of language. In the case of the lexicographers, it was a matter of linguistic *fact* taking precedence over authoritarian *opinion*. As Dr. Evans reminds the critics

> The most disturbing fact of all is that the editors of a dozen of the most influential publications in America today are under the impression that *authoritative* must mean *authoritarian*. Even the "permissive" Third International doesn't recognize this identification—editors' attitudes being not yet, fortunately, those of the American people. But the Fourth International may have to. (p 62.)

What we are trying to do is to establish a set or frame of reference for the study and teaching of linguistic matters, for the study and teaching, that is, of English. We are, alas, all too familiar with the *authoritarian* approach to the subject. We have all committed many "rules" and prohibitions to brief memory, and they have done little except to turn us away from a serious interest in our language.

> In the schools misconceptions of Standard English have produced "schoolmarm English," taught as if it were a dead language, like Latin. In particular teachers have treated spoken English as simply an inferior form of written English, instead of a properly different form, and assumed that "colloquial" means corrupt. They have taught their students never to write in the natural ways they talked; they have even tried to make them talk more in the way they were supposed to write.
> (Herbert J. Muller, *The Uses of English*, p. 59.)

The fact is that our traditional, essentially unscientific approaches to the study and teaching of English have bored us, inhibited us, and left us with little or no useful knowledge *about* our language. The study of grammar from the point of view of linguistics should be a study that is in many ways like the study of physical phenomena (physics) or the heavens (astronomy), or rocks and minerals (geology), not like the impressing of doctrine and dogma. We must understand the vast difference between finding out what something is, how it works, and what it's for, on the one hand, and the art of using it on the other. Traditional "grammar" study (among its numerous faults) failed to make this vital distinction. It also gave one to believe that there was in most cases only one "right" or "correct" way of expressing oneself; that is, that there is a "pure" and "proper" English (known to grammar book writers and English teachers and, it would seem, virtually no one else) and "impure" and "improper" English (the language of the great unwashed and nearly everyone else). This is, to be sure, nonsense. There are many "Englishes" and each serves its speaker, for every language and dialect of language is, as linguists say, "approximately adequate to the needs of its speakers." This means that wherever language is used, it works; it does reasonably its job of social intercourse. Without doubt there are failures in particular situations (hence "approximately" above), just as there are individual failures in the human physiology; but overall it seems to work quite well. Those speakers of English, for example, who do not speak the "Queen's English," are, within their own speech communities, in no jeopardy of somehow failing linguistically to get on among themselves. What an outsider may think of the aesthetics of this or that dialect is of no practical consequence. Each of us does in fact speak a dialect—it is false to think that there is a "pure" form of the language somewhere; that is, a non-dialect, except in the most abstruse philosophical sense. In those parts of the English-speaking world where people use the pronunciations of -ir- that are commonly (and inaccurately) rendered into print as -oi- (bird/boid; third/thoid, etc.), there are no problems in communication because of this "corruption." It is, in fact, no corruption at all but one of several widely used variants.

We wish, then, to take language as a complex and fascinating subject for study, and the science of language will give us tools and methods.* We wish further to learn how we can apply our knowledge in the classroom. Here we are pushing into new territory, for little substantive work has been done, though what has been done is suggestive of the value of linguistics to the teacher. The result of our explorations will make of "English" a whole new thing: A subject that for both student and teacher will have the vitality and excitement of, say, subjects related to the space program, a subject that will help both

* The science of language is actually composed of a number of disciplines including historical and comparative linguistics, grammatical theory, neurolinguistics, psycholinguistics, anthropological linguistics, ethnolinguistics, sociolinguistics, computational linguistics, and stylistics.

student and teacher to discover more about themselves and, in consequence, more about the world around them. We think with language, we filter our experience through the universe of language within us. We are quite literally creatures of language.

> Language is everywhere. It permeates our thoughts, mediates our relations with others, and even creeps into our dreams. The overwhelming bulk of human knowledge is stored and transmitted in language. Language is so ubiquitous that we take it for granted, but without it, society as we now know it would be impossible.
>
> (R. W. Langacker, *Language and Its Structure*, p. 3.)

Let us go further: *Human* society would be impossible.

The teacher must never forget that whatever he teaches he always teaches language, because he uses language to teach and he draws on the linguistic programming of his students to complete the teaching-learning circuit. And, of course, no subject can be taught *directly*. A lecture on physics is a linguistic reality not the physical reality that the Second Law of Thermodynamics is supposed to describe. To teach *directly*, we would have to sort out the linguistic mechanisms and get at knowledge strictly through some kind of direct neural contact. This is not only generally impossible, it is not desirable because it isn't really useful. We'd be too close, as it were, to the reality to have any functional grasp of it.

Compared with language, achievements like moon walks and high-speed computers are paltry indeed. No invention of man's past or present can approach the magnitude of language. One merely need try to imagine our world without it to appreciate its significance. Of course, such an exercise in imagination could not be carried on without language!

> To insist upon the importance of language may seem like battering at an open door. But there are times when it is necessary not to flinch from the obvious. In the society to which we belong, talking and listening, reading and writing, are so constantly present that familiarity blunts perception of the extraordinary character of such activities. Yet it really is remarkable that arbitrary sounds or marks should be able to convey accurate or misleading information, arouse fear, gratitude, or any other passion, set machines in motion, topple governments, or consign men to the firing squad. How extraordinary that revolutions or wars can be started by words!
>
> (Max Black, *The Labyrinth of Language*, pp. 5–6.)

The implications are far reaching. As we learn language we learn with language. Numberless human problems arise from language, and as many are resolved through language. Many arguments, for example, turn on the question of what this or that word means, and many of these arguments are of national and even global import. How often have we turned aside wrath by application of the proper linguistic formula? John the Evangelist derives creation itself from "the Word" (*logos*), making of the Creator something of a divine magician. And what is any magician's performance without its *abracadabra* and *hocus pocus?* Indeed, the widespread existence of "word magic" of many kinds has been of immense interest to anthropologists. (See, for example, B. Malinowski, *Magic, Science and Religion,* 1948.)

Though the uses of language are evident enough, what of the uses of linguistics? Linguistics on the one hand provides us with techniques for discovering the nature of language and on the other hand with insights into the operations of the human mind. Thus, as we learn more and more about language, we learn more and more about ourselves as users of language in particular and as human beings in general. We learn, therefore, about thinking, about communication and its problems, about the physical and psychological and spiritual worlds we build with language, interpret with language, and live in with language. Some of the most exciting and insightful work in psychology is being done by psycholinguists. Increasingly, sociology and anthropology are drawing on linguistics in their efforts to understand the workings of human culture and society. The study of literary style has been revitalized by linguistics, and linguistics has caused radical changes in the teaching of foreign languages. And, as we hope to demonstrate in this book, linguistics can make a new and exciting field of study out of one that is well nigh moribund.

We have so far given only the broadest definition of *linguistics* and no definition at all of *language.* If we understand, even broadly, what *science* means (not forgetting the philosophical dimension of science), then linguistics offers no great difficulty. But *language* is altogether another matter. One could easily put together a sizeable volume merely of definitions of language. (Indeed, the present volume constitutes in some sense a definition of language.) Of course, for most of us language is so much a part of our existence that we hardly give it a thought, except superficially when we are "at a loss for words" or caught in one kind of linguistic bind or another. To say that "language is the characteristic form of human communication" is to say little and imply much. Yet such definitions have their merit, for the implications demand of us that we inquire further. Still, as laymen our questions are likely to be badly framed or off the target, and we will lack the techniques for finding useful answers to such questions as prove productive. It is perhaps fair to ask whether we need bother to define language at all, since we all do know what language is in a very practical way. To speak, to communicate, we need not bother, any more than we need bother to define breathing in order to breathe or living in order to live. But if we are to know language as professionals know their subjects, then definitions are in order.

In the seminal work of modern transformational theory, *Syntactic Structures* (1957), Professor Noam Chomsky defines language as "a set (finite or infinite) of sentences, each finite in length and constructed out of a finite set of elements" (p. 13). Professor W. Nelson Francis (*The Structure of American English*, 1958) puts it rather differently: "A language is an arbitrary system of articulated sounds made use of by a group of humans as a means of carrying on the affairs of their society" (p. 13). A somewhat more elaborate version of the latter is offered by Professor Harry Warfel (*Language: A Science of Human Behavior*, 1962): "Language is a structured system of overt, learned, and therefore non-instinctive, sequentially produced, voluntary, human, symbol-carrying vocal sounds by which communication is carried on between two or more persons" (p. 29). Each of these definitions has the merit of making a good beginning but the defect of telling us too little. Despite the wealth of definitions available, the plain truth is that we do not yet know all there is to know about language and are therefore in no position to enunciate a final and "complete" definition. Language has not really been fixed and formulated, though the students of language are attacking in force on all fronts. Perhaps we are well into our subject if we appreciate that language has two properties that distinguish it from the language analog in non-human species. First, language has a bilateral structure, which is to say that it is syntactic and phonological. Syntactic structures are the complex strings of structured units ("words," "phrases," "clauses") that represent the predicational core of human communication. Everything we utter can be taken to be sentence or predication, either entire or reduced. The syntactic component is the one that is directly involved with meaning. The phonological (sound system) component allows the syntactic component to be expressed but is taken to be, in and of itself, meaningless. The second of the two properties of language is its productivity or "open-endedness." In simple terms this means that any human language is potentially capable of producing an infinite number of new utterances, as opposed to merely repeating a limited number as in the case of animal communication. Any human language may have a finite number of basic structures and distinctive sounds and rules for their manipulation, but these sets of finite entities can generate sentences without end. The animal, on the other hand, commands a severely limited repertoire of sounds and strings of sounds; once through that repertoire he must, as it were, go back to the beginning. He cannot "make up" any new strings. That this seems clearly to be the case (with the possible disturbing exception of the bottle-nosed dolphin, *Tursiops truncatus*) leads modern theorists (notably among them, Professor Chomsky) to suggest that human beings are distinguished from the animals primarily in virtue of having a genetic inheritance specifically for language. Thus the *human* brain is inherently a language-producing device, and the implications of this idea are far reaching indeed.

English is a language. English (and Russian and Haitian Creole and Tamil) are manifestations of that human phenomenon known as language. What any individual utters is *speech*.* The only empirically demonstrable reality is the individual speech act (*la parole*). It is this and only this that can provide us with the data upon which to build our descriptions of language and our theories of language. (Let's for the moment keep writing out of the picture, for writing is after all a type of *displaced* speech.) "Existence," as it were, "precedes essence." This is a cardinal point in language study and must always be kept before us in our considerations.

To make this book as useful as possible to the student as prospective teacher, we have included in each chapter a section called "Implications for Teaching." These "Implications" are mainly questions, projects, and problems designed to lead the student more deeply into the materials of the chapter than can be achieved merely by one's attempting to memorize those materials. Answers are not provided for these questions, for in most cases perfectly valid alternatives may be arrived at and, more importantly, student and teacher *alike* should explore them. The classroom must cease being a data supermarket and start being a laboratory. From the former we end merely by "buying" tidbits for the garbage pail of information, in the latter we learn how to think, how to search, how to solve problems. If the study of language is not to degenerate to the dull vacuity of the old "grammar" class, we must not treat it as 1001 facts to be memorized, but as an intellectual safari into the exciting unknown.

---

* Ferdinand de Saussure made these same distinctions at the beginning of this century—his terms were, respectively, *la langue, le langage, la parole*.

2
Language, Culture, and Reality

Language is so much a part of our lives that we seldom stop to think about it. We take it for granted that our words are mere passive tools, means of self-expression and of communication. But there is another way of looking at language. Words certainly are the vehicles of our thoughts, but they may acquire an influence of their own, shaping and predetermining our processes of thinking and our whole outlook.

(Stephen Ulmann, "The Prism of Language," *The Listener*, Vol. 7, July 22, 1954.)

Were we able somehow to excise language from the rest of life and lock it away someplace, there would be, we would quickly discover, no life at all as we now know it. The conduct of human affairs, however trivial, requires the medium of language. And while there have been small communities (e.g., the Trappists) who have abrogated *talking*, they have not ceased to use language; they have simply stopped uttering language with the vocal apparatus, substituting hand signals and the like (in fact, *displaced speech*) for necessary daily communication and losing not a jot of their interior language programming.

Despite endless speculation on the subject, no one knows when and how language came into being. It is amusing to imagine what the conversations in Eden may have been like, for man of course was not put together like a doll in Santa's workshop and was not provided with a set of language tapes. Like man, language must have grown into being through a long process of evolution. Perhaps there were from time to time "great leaps," but nobody knows because no direct evidence exists. The most ancient of hieroglyphs and other evidences of language are latecomers on the language scene.* And going to "primitive" sources today is useless because, regardless of what we, as members of a highly technological society, think about "primitive" peoples, the languages of these people are every bit as ancient, complex, and developed as ours. Some indeed are so complex that linguists have yet to unravel their mysteries. The verbal system of the Cree language (an American Indian language) is a case in point. There are apparently four verb classes, fifteen verb modes, and a bewildering variety of affixal (*i.e.*, pertaining to prefixes, infixes, and suffixes) manipulations. The system is so subtle that the linguist is hard pressed even to identify the boundaries of root

---

* The oldest extant written—or incised—examples of man's language go back perhaps no more than 6,000 years. They reveal fully developed languages that must have been in development many times that number of years.

(*i.e.*, the basic verbal element) and affix. The point is that people who may be primitive by our technological standards are far from being linguistically primitive. None of the languages of our own family (the Indo-European, which includes the Germanic languages, the Romance languages, the Balto-Slavic languages, and so on) offers the overt structural complexity of any number of exotic, "primitive," languages, for example, those of Black Africa or the Melanesian highlands.

But if we are ignorant of beginnings, we do, none the less, know a great deal about language. Since it is the predominant mode of intraspecific communication its overriding function is social. Were man a solitary creature he would have no language. (Whom would he speak to?) Conversely, were there no language, man would very probably be a solitary creature. Of course most animals, solitary or not, use some sort of phonation for purposes of communication; but it is reasonably certain that without language man could not have developed anything resembling "human civilization."

The question of whether language precedes culture or *vice versa* is one of those chicken-and-egg non-questions that used to occupy the pages of popular magazines. Language is both a manifestation of culture and a contributory factor in cultural processes. There is no precedence (or if there were at some remote time, it is now quite irrelevant). For any person at any moment, language provides the framework through which he views culture and by which he enters society. We see the world, so to speak, through language-colored glasses. To be sure, there are certain human experiences that transcend particular languages, and it seems to be true that all languages share (by a diversity of means) certain experiential and linguistic meanings. But there is no question that, for example, Eskimos and Frenchmen "compute" the realities around them in quite different ways. A Frenchman in the Arctic is a Frenchman, and an Eskimo in Paris is an Eskimo—at least until each has learned (really *learned*) the other's language. Only then will the Arctic begin to look to the Frenchman like the world of the Eskimo, and Paris to the Eskimo like the world of the Frenchman.

Much can be learned about these differing ways of organizing experience merely by examining a good bilingual dictionary. Any two languages will do. Even languages from the same general cultural and linguistic tradition show curiously different ways of relating language to experience. Consider these examples of English *vis-à-vis* French:

1. apply for [as a job]	1. *poser sa candidature à*
2. as	2. *au fur et à mesure que*
3. a tenant farmer	3. *un fermier*

4. glimmer	4. *d'une lueur faible et tremblotante*
5. gleam	5. *d'une lueur pâle*
6. glow	6. *d'une lueur rougeoyante*
7. glisten	7. *avec le luisant d'une surface mouillée*
8. glint	8. *avec le luisant d'une surface sombre*
9. ride a horse at breakneck speed	9. *étripe-cheval*
10. an elegant but immoral woman	10. *une horizontale*

The differences here are obvious, but a few comments may be helpful. In the *glimmer* series, 4–8 (matched, incidentally, quite precisely in German, one of the close cousin languages of English: *glimmern, scheinen, glühen, glitzern, glänzen*), the French phrases (syntactical units as opposed to lexical units in the case of English here) are all built around the verb *luire*, "to shine." Hence, the phrases speak of various ways of shining (*i.e.*, weakly and flickeringly; palely; reddishly; from a wet surface; from a dull surface). Lest, however, we fall into believing that French is somehow inferior to English in this respect, we should remember that in English we cannot, through lexical units, make these distinctions: *cloche, clochette, sonnette, grelot,* and *timbre,* which are all rendered in English simply as "bell." Likewise, *dimensions, taille, grandeur, pointure, module, format* are for us, "size." And so on. Of course, the differences signalled to a Frenchman by these various words can be expressed in English, but only in the same roundabout way that the *glimmer* series is expressed in French (unless we simply borrow the French word and its special meaning; thus, in place of an elaborate explanatory translation, we use *preciosité*). Example 9, "ride a horse at breakneck speed" is an illustration of a French equivalent of our *glimmer* series but brings out the idea in quite a different way. The French verb *étriper* means "to gut," "to eviscerate." Hence, "to ride at breakneck speed" (presumably it is the *rider's* neck which will be broken) in French means "to gut the horse": *étripe-cheval. Horizontale* needs no coment other than to remind the reader that in French (as in many languages) one can show gender by the modification of the word, in this case the adding of a suffix. *Horizontal* is an adjective (*horizontal*), and when modifying a masculine plural noun it is spelled *horizonteaux. Horizontale* is a feminine singular noun. This example reminds us too that given lexical units can in various languages carry greater or lesser semantic loads. In the French phrase, *bonne à toute faire* ("maid of all work"), *bonne* is a feminine noun that is rooted in the adjectival meaning *good* (*bon*). Thus, *bonne* represents the meaning, "a good [useful] female." The word then shows singular number, feminine gender (by formal marking: -[n]e), noun-ness, and adjectival-ness, the latter fused into what we might call an *adjectival noun* (not to be confused with a *noun adjunct*, or a noun that modifies a noun, as in *aircraft carrier*). A rather far-fetched way of deriving the same sort of word in English would be to go from something like, "good girl" to "goodette."

These examples from Japanese *vis-à-vis* English hint at greater cultural differences than those between the English and French speaking worlds:

1. *chōsei-boshi*

2. *daidō-shōi*

3. *gosatsusuru*

4. *henrei*

5. *izumō*

6. *kasei*

7. *kōkōsuru*

8. *shasō*

9. *shii*

10. *ukekuchi*

1. birth at morn and death at eve; the ephemeral nature of human existence

2. substantial similarity with minor differences

3. to kill the wrong person

4. a present given in return for a present

5. wrestling in a sitting position

6. to wait a hundred years [as in the expression: "One might as well *wait* a hundred years for the Yellow River to run clear," which is to say, "You'll wait 'til Hell freezes over before. . . ."]

7. to practice filial piety

8. funeral sponsored by the company (*i.e.*, business firm) of the deceased

9. the barbarians outside the country in the four quarters of the world

10. a mouth with a protruding lower lip

Since we are able to find some rough equivalence from lexicon to lexicon, one might assume that once this equivalence is established, the linguistic-*cum*-cultural differences will vanish; and all we need do to gain entrance to another language and another culture is memorize a sufficient number of lexical items (words, though this term is by no means linguistically well defined). The issue, unfortunately, is not that simple. Lexical entities (words) are merely part of the language enterprise. Even memorizing entire dictionaries, if that were all the information used, would leave one virtually tongue-tied in an attempt at conversation with the natives. Words find their function only in a matrix of phonology, syntax, and an incredibly complicated system of meanings —a system barely hinted at by the dictionary.

Some sense of this semantico-cultural universe can be gotten by trying to contrive a clear and objective description of American kinship terminology. (Kinship terminology is one of the prime areas of anthropological linguistic research because, as the anthropologist Robbins Burling puts it, "kinship terms occupy a peculiarly strategic position among the various sets of lexical items that one can try to extract from a language, and many of the possibilities and the problems of semantic analysis can be seen with special clarity in kinship terms," *Man's Many Voices*, p. 18). Of course, one's immediate consanguineal relations present no great problems (at least to a native), but as we move out into the collateral and affinal ("in-law") relationships (e.g., second cousin once removed; the second husband of your mother's sister, etc.), things get fuzzy. The mutual interaction of language and culture can, however, be clearly seen. The nature of our society's family system provides us with a system of terminology (which is not, alas, always well defined), and that system of terminology determines what kinds of relationships we can recognize. For example, there is in English no unequivocal base term (*i.e.*, a single distinctive term as opposed to an explanation) for the relationship of bride's parents to groom's parents. The groom can speak of his mother-in-law, brother-in-law, etc., as can the bride of hers. But how does each set of parents refer to the other? They cannot use the term *in-laws* without confusion, for they already have their in-laws of the preceding generation. So the best they can manage is something like "the parents of my son-in-law." This lack of a special term suggests (and predicts) the lack of a strongly felt relationship. In some (perhaps many) cultures such a term does exist; and the sense of relationship, in consequence, exists as well. In Yiddish (representing a fairly coherent Eastern European cultural group), one has available such terms as *machutén* and *machutaynéste*, which mean broadly, "in-laws," but commonly "the father of the boy (or girl) my girl (or boy) is going to marry," and "the mother of the boy, etc." The term *machuténim* is the general (*i.e.*, without regard to sex) term for in-laws (the *-im* indicates plurality, as it does in Hebrew). Kinship terminology can be extraordinarily involved, as in the Australian aboriginal Njamal tribe, wherein the terms can signal degrees and types of relationship that place one in a network of relationship that finally includes the whole tribe. This will, of course, give any member of the tribe a sense of his identity quite different from that, say, of an American. "Alienation," "identity crisis," and similar discontents of civilization are impossible in the linguistic-cultural environment of the Njamals. Of course the cultural situation of a tribe numbering perhaps a hundred isn't remotely akin to ours, so the semantic formulas are totally unlike. Likewise, the semantic formulas *predict* the sense of relationship. (See Burling, pp. 18–33, for a detailed analysis of both Njamal and English kinship terminology. But before doing so, try making your own analysis of the English and perhaps one or two other systems—French and German, let us say.

Our ultimate goal is to assimilate the culture, but to do this we must have the language. And as we have seen, merely learning the "meaning" of the words is not enough. Every language has a *lexicon* (word stock), *phonology* (a sound system, which is comprised of a relatively small number of classes of sounds, such as the class of phonetically similar sounds called the *phoneme* t, /t/),* and a *grammar* (which can be roughly and broadly described as a set of rules for producing understandable and structurally acceptable utterances). In a literate culture, the phonology provides the base for a *graphic* system, "letters" (in the case of European languages) representing phonemes. These representations can be quite inaccurate (English, French, and Irish offer good examples of the bad fit between the phonological and graphic systems), but this fact does not gainsay the principle that the spoken language precedes its written forms, which serve simply to make the spoken word more or less permanent. (At least, that was the reason for writing in the first place.)

Attempts to relate phonology to cultural, climatic, and even physiological differences among the several linguistic communities have come to nothing. On the example of the dialects of the American South, people have falsely concluded that a warm climate produces slow speech ("drawl"). And there are those who believe that at least some of the distinctive characteristics of black speech can be charged to physical characteristics (e.g., lip size, nose formation, etc.). This likewise belongs to the history of nonsense. The phonology of any dialect or language at

---

* The sounds represented by t in take (aspirated), steak (released), outdoors (unreleased), battle (lateral release), cotton (nasal release), latter (flap), mutton (glottal stop), and hit (simultaneous glottal stop and [t]) are literally different. Speakers of English, however, consider them to be the "same." This sense of identity among the t-sounds warrants them being grouped as a single class of sounds. Such a class is called a *phoneme*. The various actualizations of the phoneme (*i.e.*, the actual sounds, such as those illustrated above) are called *allophones*, literally, "other sounds." In English there are 24 consonant phonemes (/p b t d k g č ǰ f v e ð s z š ž m n ŋ l r w y h/), 9 simple vowel phonemes (/i e æ ɨ ə a u o ɔ/), and three semi-vowel phonemes (/y w H/). These are called segmental phonemes. For a detailed description of the English phonemic system, see H. A. Gleason, *An Introduction to Descriptive Linguistics*, rev. ed., pp. 14–50.

any moment in time is dependent upon the phonology of the preceding moment, and so on as far back as we can trace. In other words, phonology influences phonology. It is the interaction of contrasting phonologies that create certain "accents," such as, West Indian English, East Indian English, and so on. The prehistoric period of language is beyond our techniques for discovery, and anything we might conclude must be speculative. Of course, no linguist speculates on the thickness of lips, for example, as a factor in phonation. When, however, two cultures (each with its own language and hence its own distinctive phonology) meet, linguistic, including phonological, change is inevitable. The cultural question here becomes one of dominance. In the case of England, for example, at the time of the Norman Conquest, the native Germanic language of Anglo-Saxon ultimately "won," but not before it had been radically changed by the impact of Norman French. So phonological as well as other differences in English between the Old English (Anglo-Saxon) and Middle English (post-Conquest) periods are largely the result of cultural change; *i.e.*, the introduction into England on a relatively large scale of a new culture and its language. Phonology, then, doesn't reflect culture so much as it can reflect cultural change over a period of time. This is very clearly seen where two cultures (and languages) come together. Where we are dealing with the history of a language that has been subjected to no significant outside influence, cultural influences on phonology are difficult if not impossible to determine. Occasionally, specific phonations are modified radically by individuals and for one reason or another catch on with the language community at large. Prior to the seventeenth century, the French r was generally pronounced in the Italian fashion (that is, as a fronto-palatal trill). But during the seventeenth century the trill slipped further back in the mouth to end as the "characteristically French" uvular trill that it is today. This shift apparently started in the Île-de-France (Paris and environs) and finally, because of the dominance of Paris in the cultural life of France, became the national standard. The folk speech of the southern provinces, especially around Marseilles, retains the "Italian" r; but educated speech requires the Parisian. In somewhat similar fashion, Received Standard British is historically the language of educated Londoners. The cultural and political importance of London made the speech of culturally and politically important Londoners the prestige speech of the country. (An interesting phenomenon today is the rising status of English provincial dialects, especially that of Liverpool, the provenance of the Beatles and their cultural progeny. For a number of Englishmen today, the "Establishment" dialect is out, just as the Establishment is out. One wonders what the national British standard will be in a hundred years.)

Lest we appear to have overstated the effects of overt cultural influences on phonology, it should be understood that the prime reason for phonological change is the "natural" process of *phonetic drift*—"natural" in that it seems to occur regularly in all languages and dialects. This is the process that makes several languages where once there was one language. If we split up a speech community and keep the groups thus formed in isolation from each other, in time people who in aggregate spoke a single non-dialect-differentiated language will be speaking a set of distinct dialects. And if these new dialect communities are kept in isolation, they each will in time be speaking full-fledged "new" languages; that is, each group will be linguistically more or less unintelligible to the other. The great diversity of languages in our own family came into being rather in that way: From the parent language that scholars call *Indo-European* came (over thousands of years and by slow degrees) Sanskrit, Persian, Greek, Gaelic, Russian, Lithuanian, French, English, and so on.

A frequently cited example of the interrelationship of language and the non-linguistic cultural world is that of the *grammatical* (rather than the purely phonological) habits of the Navajo language of the American Southwest. In the Navajo world view, man is a natural part of the ongoing universal processes. Man does not really make things happen so much as he takes part in their happening. Navajo is a verb-centered language in contrast the noun-centeredness of our European languages. The arrow which the European would grammatically credit himself with shooting ("I shot an arrow," *i.e.*, I worked my will upon some*thing*: actor/action/thing *acted upon*, the dominant European sentence type), becomes in Navajo something like "I have taken part in arrowing"). The Navajo way of saying things predicts his attitude toward life. His language defines his world view. The Navajo sees himself as a small element within the natural process. The European, in distinct contrast, sees himself in command of nature, governing, as it were, a world of things.*

Thus, despite the possible existence of a core set of linguistic universals ("case," for example), each language is unique at the level of its users' consciousness. This uniqueness can be traced through phonology

---

* On the relationship of language and reality, see Benjamin Lee Whorf, *Language, Thought, and Reality*, passim. It should be noted that the Whorfian (or, more properly, Sapir-Whorf) hypothesis has come under attack. In the authors' view, however, the arguments thus far presented *contra* Whorf are not conclusive. Those who wish to examine the controversy at first hand should start with S. Lewis Feuer, "Sociological Aspects of the Relation between Language and Philosophy," *Philosophy of Science*, Vol. 20, pp. 85–100 (1953), and Eric H. Lenneberg, "Cognition in Ethnolinguistics," *Language*, Vol. 29, pp. 463–471 (1953). An eminently fair overview of the controversy is presented by Hans Hörmann in *Psycholinguistics, An Introduction to Research and Theory*, pp. 310–328. In addition, see Whorf, *supra*, and Lester Sinclair, "A Word in Your Ear," in *Ways of Mankind*, ed. Walter Goldschmidt. This was originally written as a radio broadcast and can be got on an LP record from the National Association of Educational Broadcasters, University of Illinois, Urbana, Illinois 61801. The record includes a passage in Navajo, spoken by a Navajo Indian.

(and its realization phonetically), lexicon, and grammar. Where language is in touch with the non-linguistic universe (*viz.*, in its lexicon and its complex of meanings), the interactions of language and culture can most clearly be seen. A society (represented linguistically by a *speech community*) will proliferate vocabulary around non-linguistic things and events of great concern to it. Arabic is supposed to have 1001 words for *camel*. English has but one (or two, if we include *dromedary*). In the history of the Arabic-speaking people, the camel played an important role; in the history of the English-speaking people, virtually none at all. On the other hand, what many cultures would be content to call an "automobile" and have done with it, we have proliferated into a large and bewildering variety of names (Ford, Chevrolet, Chevy, Mercedes 230S, Mustang, Vega, '71 Toronado, '69 Roadrunner SST, etc., etc.). We cannot be expected to notice the subtle differences among camels denoted by the Arabic camel lexicon, nor can a stranger to our world of wheels be expected to do the same with our automobile lexicon.

Lexical differences are relatively easy to detect, but the cultural differences implied (and predicted) by differences in grammatical strategies are much less obvious and much more difficult to codify. The temporal and aspectual meanings, for example, that attach to Hopi verbs are of an entirely different order than those that attach to ours. We are speaking here not of the *lexical* meanings, "running," "swimming," "walking," etc., but of the *psycho-grammatical* meanings, the meanings that arise from the "communal" or "tribal nature," so to speak. (And, as we insist, the meanings continue to form that nature.) Hence, we associate with our verbs such meanings as *past, present,* or *future time; complete* or *incomplete action, definiteness* or *conditionalness,* and so on. In Hopi, the verbal system is built around what Benjamin Lee Whorf calls *validity,* in which *duration, intensity,* and *tendency* are categories of experience that infuse the verb, rather than *temporality.* (See Whorf, pp. 102–159.) This means that grammatical categories are structural analogs of human experience. Prior to the influence of the European consciousness the Hopi lived for all practical purposes in a "timeless" world. Not that time didn't "pass," but that the sense of time did not enter the tribal awareness as it does so forcibly for the European.

> In this Hopi view, time disappears and space is altered, so that it is no longer the homogeneous and instantaneous timeless space of our supposed intuition or of classical Newtonian mechanics. At the same time, new concepts and abstractions flow into the picture, taking up the task of describing the universe without reference to time and space—abstractions for which our language lacks adequate terms. These abstractions, by approximations of which we attempt to reconstruct for ourselves the metaphysics of the Hopi, will undoubtedly appear to us as psychological or even mystical in character.
>
> Whorf, p. 58.

Just as it is possible to have any number of geometries other than the Euclidean which give an equally perfect account of space configurations, so it is possible to have descriptions of the universe, all equally valid, that do not contain our familiar contrasts of time and space. The relativity viewpoint of modern physics is one such view, conceived in mathematical terms, and the Hopi Weltanschauung is another and quite different one, nonmathematical and linguistic.

Whorf, *loc. cit.*

Linguistic ethnography can be descriptively resolved into mechanism/function/situation where *mechanism* represents language; *function*, the purpose of language (broadly, *communication*); and *situation*, the occasions of speaking along with their contextual requirements ("levels of discourse," social contexts, etc.).

Language as mechanism can be represented by this schema:

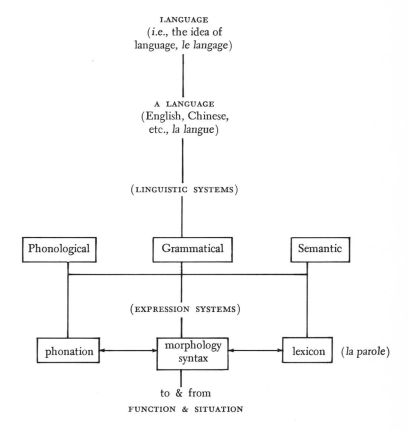

At any given moment, this is a closed, recirculating process.

Our primary concern in this chapter is with language in relation to culture (rather than with linguistic systems as such, the classic domain of the "pure" linguist). Hence, our attention is directed towards *function* and *situation*.

We have said that the function of language is communication. But "communication" covers several communicative intentions, whose particular linguistic shapes are dictated by social context (*situation*). Thus we can speak to *inform, inquire, direct* (command), *express feeling, contend* (argue), *ritualize,* or merely *make contact.* Any extended discourse may by turns do all of these, but each is nonetheless a definable and identifiable type of communication.

Informative communication has its grammatical analog in the declarative sentence:

1. Dinner will be ready in an hour.
2. Mt. Brandon is approximately 3300 feet high.
3. I do not like tea.
4. Germany surrendered in May 1945.

These declarative sentences happen to be cast in that *level of discourse* which can be labelled as *standard* (written or spoken, in this case; though *standard written* can differ from *standard spoken* in degree of *formality;* that is, the avoidance or use of contractions, and so on). This is the most generally useful of the levels in that it largely transcends regionalisms and educational differences. It is the level of discourse most likely to be used in more, rather than less, formal situations. If we add *phonation* to what on the page *looks* like standard American English, we can move through a wide spectrum of pronunciations representing all the distinctive regional dialects. The general American standard of pronunciation (the least "idiosyncratic" to our ears) is what we may call the "radio-TV norm." This dialect approximates the natural speech of the northern Great Plains (let us say Nebraska in particular), but with all identifiable localisms dropped. The value of such a "colorless" dialect is its "transparency." There is nothing in it to trigger unfavorable responses from its hearers. There were, on the contrary, many people who were chary of John F. Kennedy strictly on the basis of his sharply localized East-central New England speech. We do seem, however, to be growing more tolerant of regional pronunciations than was formerly the case as evidenced by the relaxation of network standards. It is apparently no longer necessary for a radio or TV news correspondent to smooth his native dialect to conform with the general American that for so long was the *only* acceptable speech on the air (Walter Cronkite, a native of Texas, exemplifies this older standard).

The grammatical form of the *inquiry* is any one of the question types. Questions that ask for some version of a *yes/no answer* are made by transposing declarative sentence elements.

1. He is hungry.	1. Is he hungry?
2. I am happy.	2. Am I happy?

A dummy auxiliary (*do*) is required when the verbs are other than forms of *be*:

3. I need a new car.	3. Do I need a new car?
4. He looks miserable.	4. Does he look miserable?

Questions requiring nominal answers and adverbial answers (*i.e.*, answers concerned with time, place, manner, etc.), use interrogators:

5. Who is missing?
6. Where are we going?
7. Why are we going?
8. When are we going?
9. How are we going?
10. What time is it?

And, finally, we can form questions simply by intonational changes:

11. This is a beautiful painting. (statement)
12. This is a beautiful painting?

This question type is situation-bound in ways that the other question types are not, for the intonational pattern (the rising terminal intonation) signals sarcasm or jocosity or (in most cases) a combination of both. This means that while most inquiries seek informative responses, there are forms of the inquiry that themselves convey information, feelings, etc.

An interesting case of social-context sensitivity is the ostensible question:

13. Can you close the door?
14. Will you hand me that book?

The intention here is obviously not to inquire but to direct. The social context mandates such question-directives. That is, to our social equals, we phrase our commands as requests, which are normally cast in the question pattern. To those over whom we exercise some social dominance, we can safely say, *Please close the door*, etc. The sociology (and psychology) of the directive can get extraordinarily subtle. If we say, *Would you mind opening the window*, with only a light stress on *mind*, we are being acceptably polite in all contexts. If we intensify the stress on *mind* so as to draw attention to the word, we are being sarcastic, even obnoxiously so. We generally know how to adjust the intonations to the situation without much forethought. All languages have such signals, though they may be manifest through different linguistic mechanisms.

In Japanese there is an elaborate system (both grammatical and lexical) for keying oneself to the social situation, wherein one understands his own place in the society and the place of those with whom he is conversing. Paralleling the linguistic system is a *kinesic** system, in the case of Japanese a regular and predictable system of bows, from very slight to very deep. Thus, when one studies Japanese, one must at the same time learn the proper uses of "plain speech," "elevated speech," and "honorific speech" (along with, if one intends to speak Japanese in Japan, the appropriate kinesic patterns). And one should be able to ascertain from the transcript of a conversation such matters as the sex and social stratum of each speaker. In other cultures, the coordinates may be even more closely drawn. The Nootka Indians include in their complex cultural signalling a special way of talking to left-handed men and men who are circumcised. And though English no longer uses the second-person pronoun (*you-thou/thy/thee*) to signal status, the device is very much alive in most European languages. In French, for instance,

> *Vous* and *tu* are power pronouns that give away class status and reflect a society that believes in social inequality as natural and beneficial, a rigidly structured society where everyone has an appointed place and everyone also says *vous* to the powerful state as angels say *vous* to God, who says *tu* back to them, and as Corneille's nobles say *tu* to their valets. *Vous* evokes titles and inequalities, while *tu* is the egalitarian pronoun.
> (Sanche de Gramont, *The French, Portrait of a People*, p. 267.)

It was at a time when this system obtained in England that the Quakers attempted to democratize the language by using the familiar forms (*thou*, etc.) in all social contexts. Curiously, when the democratization did finally occur, it was the "subservient" you (*vous*, in French) that became the democratic standard, the intimate forms being reserved for liturgical uses. Another footnote to the story is the ultimately exclusive use in Quaker "plain speech" of the accusative form *thee*, the nominative *thou* having been lost somewhere along the way.

There are many ways of *expressing feeling* in English, but the only formally distinctive devices are intonational (an emotive intonation can be imposed on any utterance: *Go to bed*/GO TO BED!) and lexical (in particular those "words" that we call *interjections*: Oh! Wow! Ow! Damn! etc.). These exclamatory utterances are linguistically conventionalized grunts of pain and pleasure and other emotional states and when used spontaneously should perhaps be considered sub-linguistic. Of course, when the writer or story teller uses them, he does so for effect and is then choosing signals that predict certain generally agreed upon responses. One might argue that at least some literature, poetry especially,

---

* *Kinesics* is the technical term for what has recently been popularized as "body language," a set of overt physical signals that are used in a consistent way and are keyed on one hand to the language and on the other to psycho-social phenomena.

is the artistic elaboration of the exclamation. Here the speaker (singer, writer) mines a particular "exclamatory experience" for all of its ore, and because he is an artist, he localizes and specifies the emotion that called forth the exclamation in the first place. The fact that this may have been called forth only in the imagination of the artist is of no moment. The point is that he turns language to the end of expressing feeling rather than of *informing*, etc. The intent of even so lengthy and detailed a work as "L'Allegro" is surely not "informative." Had Milton merely wanted to pass along some information (or to move the reader to action), he would have done what he frequently did, namely, write a tract.

In daily discourse, we are hedged in by cultural expectations in the way we express feelings in words. It is said in Ireland that life's difficulties (financial, familial, climatic, etc.) "can always be worse"; the same difficulties in Germany are always "the worst possible," "catastrophic." Or consider the recounting of some strongly affective experience by children as against adults. We have in each linguistic community certain expectations, and the person who deviates is noticed and may even be ostracized until he conforms. The voluble middle-class New York kid in the "uptight" linguistic context of a New England prep school will soon find himself the butt of his peers. But these differences seem to be fading. The cross-generational linguistic gap is perhaps more isolating than the cross-class linguistic gap.

Contention or *argumentation* (not to be confused with emotionally charged verbal wrangling, shouting, and so on) has no distinctive grammatical analog. Function in this case is signalled over a more-or-less extended discourse. The classic forms of argumentation are debates and legal actions, but any discourse that aims to persuade or dissuade is properly included here—hence, advertising pitches, sales talks, political speeches. Social restraints are evident in the length and complexity (or simplicity) of sentence structure and in the characteristics of the lexicon. These linguistic adjustments are equivalent to the New York mayoral candidate's eating *blintzes* in Jewish neighborhoods and *manicotti* in Italian neighborhoods. To an audience of construction workers, one does not indulge in the linguistic niceties that one must indulge in for an audience of academics. The substance of the argument may be precisely the same in each instance, but the forms are different. Reduced to essence, the political argument says, "*If* you vote for me, *then* these benefits will accrue." (Or the contrary, "*If* you vote for my opponent, *then* these disasters will befall us.") Likewise the advertising argument: "*If* you use this product, *then* these benefits will accrue." "*If* . . . *then*. . . ." is the timeless argument. Of course, the variations within the framework are endless, and many ancillary devices are used to arouse the audience to action. Hence, the advocate will try to frighten us, anger us, soothe us, amuse us, flatter us, and so on. Each device has its characteristic shapes and each is predicated on predictable responses rooted in our cultural experience. Thus, patriotic appeals are potent for large segments of our society but ridiculous for, let us say, our disaffected youth. The linguistic formulas (i.e., the lexicon of God, country, flag, etc.) work in a culture that can relate emotionally appealing non-linguistic experiences to them. And fail where the non-linguistic experiences are negative, "uncool," etc. The strength of the linguistic-cultural interlock is evident from the effectiveness of the verbal formulas in triggering often very powerful responses. The phenomenal success of American advertising is sufficient proof. Even our political candidates are being merchandised in accord with tested advertising principles. (On this point, see Joe McGinniss, The Selling of the President 1968.)

Prayers and other liturgical formulas, inaugural addresses, Fourth-of-July orations, and similar highly stylized, predictable, and intellectually empty utterances represent ritual uses of language. Regardless of the speakers' pretense to substance, these rituals serve not the mind but the emotions and usually do it in a way that is expected, hence comfortable. Even the preacher's harangues to abjure sin are comfortably familiar and free of intellectual demand. And while there is no grammatical analog for the ritual use of language, there are discourse characteristics that suit the use very well, the most obvious ones being rhythmical repetition ("we cannot dedicate, we cannot consecrate, we cannot hallow this ground") and alliteration (Mr. Agnew's "pusillanimous pussyfooting," "nattering nabobs," and other empty but somehow appealing phrases). The proximate major sources for this kind of rhetoric (for the English-speaking world) are the King James Bible (rhythms, archaisms) and the grandiloquent periodic style of the eighteenth century. The Declaration of Independence as well as the Gettysburg Address reveal these influences quite clearly. The vaguely Biblical tone of much of our ritual language lends to it a kind of (often specious) dignity and even at times sublimity. The Kennedy Inaugural Address is a good example of the successful management of the technique: The banal content of the speech went largely unnoticed in the coruscations of its rhetoric.

Despite the vacuity of most ritual language, it serves a valuable function. It has been said, for example, that if any single agent can be credited with England's will to survival during those grim war days, it must be Winston Churchill's great wartime speeches. The ringing phrases, such as "Never have so many owed so much to so few," "blood, sweat, toil, and tears," bound the nation together in its determination to prevail whatever the cost. Likewise, the Kennedy Inaugural, though it informed us of very little, set the special tone and style of the Kennedy presidency and for "one brief shining moment" brought the nation together. "I don't know what he's talking about but it sure sounds good," is a comment made of ritual language and one that the speaker should be pleased with, for it demonstrates the success of his "ritualizing." One doesn't go away from one of Mr. Agnew's alliterative speeches with facts but with feelings. Indeed, facts are anti-ritual and counter to the aims of ritual speech.

Contactive language resembles ritual language in its formulistic character ("How are you," "What's new?" etc.) but differs in its tone and purpose. The everyday speech rituals verge on being paralinguistic in that they serve primarily as tribal noises that signal our presence as one human to another. When we say, "How are you?" we are following an established formula for making contact. We expect nothing from the addressee other than "Fine. How are you?" And if we are in fact regaled with recent medical history, we judge that the speaker is either ignorant of our contact formulas, obtuse, or having a little fun at our expense. If we are *really* interested in the addressee's state of health, we signal that by special emphases, facial expressions, and the like. The point of contactive speech is that of merely making contact. No one expects substantive content. A simple demonstration of the importance of this type of speech can be had by answering the telephone and *not* saying anything to the caller; that is, greet him with silence instead of the usual formulas. The unnerving effect of this is one of the things that the nuisance caller counts on. We want to know that there is a person at the other end. We want to announce our presence and have our announcement acknowledged. The extensions of contactive speech, "small talk," can make whole evenings bearable. And nothing is so distressing in a social situation as those moments of dead silence when we seem to have run out of small talk. And it *is* sn all talk that we generally want in these social situations, not substance. I֝ fact, the party bore is often the person who, instead of small talk, gives us lectures.

The set of linguistic-cultural parameters we have called *situation* directs the *style* of the utterance, within the limits imposed by the grammar; that is, by the structural habits of the language, and within the limitations of the speaker. Thus we do not talk to a two-year-old in the same style as we talk to an educated adult; or if we do, we are in some fashion being humorous or we are addled. Age, then, is a situational constraint. At a certain point, age is joined by sex, though the former constraints of "mixed company" seem to be rapidly vanishing. Nevertheless, they are still quite strong in some segments of the population (which brings *class* and *education* into the picture) as evidenced by the reaction of the Chicago police to traditional male vulgarisms being uttered by females during the 1968 Democratic Convention's riots. Of course, as taboo forms find broader acceptance and use they will cease to be taboo and new taboo forms will have to be created. These need not be associated with sexuality and bodily functions, but until we overcome the neuroses that generate the taboo vocabulary, they will probably be so associated. Taboo words to be taboo require that some part of the society think of them as taboo. If one can convince people that *glurk* is a "naughty" word, it will then be a naughty word. But it really cannot be one's private naughty word, for language is finally communal not personal.*

One can think of the societal entities of *age, sex, class,* and *educational level* as *in-groups* (of which *family, neighborhood, town, state, nation, social circle,* and *religion* are additional examples), each with its acceptable and unacceptable linguistic behavior. Within the group a certain linguistic license is allowed that is not allowed to non-members. Likewise, when one finds himself in what for him is an *out-group* he will feel linguistically inhibited until he gets hold of the group's idiom, thereby becoming in some sense a member. Up to that time, he will use as neutral a kind of speech as he can manage. A simple example is the use of *ain't*, which may be quite heavily used within the intimate family group (even by highly educated speakers) but is eschewed in other social contexts.

In *The Five Clocks*, a brilliant examination of English usage levels, Joos writes

> English-usage guilt feelings have not yet been noticeably eased by the work of linguistic scientists, parallel to the work done by psychiatrists. It is still our custom unhesitatingly and unthinkingly to demand that the clocks [*i.e.*, usage levels] of language all be set to Central Standard Time. And each normal American is taught thoroughly, if not to keep accurate time, at least to feel ashamed whenever he notices that a clock of his is out of step with the English department's tower-clock. Naturally he avoids looking aloft when he can. Then his linguistic guilt hides deep in his subconscious mind and there secretly gnaws away at the underpinnings of his public personality. Freud or Kinsey may have strengthened his private self-respect, but in his social life he is still in uneasy bondage to the gospel according to Webster as expounded by Miss Fidd17ch [*i.e.*, the archetypal schoolmarm]. (p. 4).

We have all felt Miss Fidd17ch's chill breath on our speech and writing, but she would mean less than nothing to us were it not for the fact that we are willing to let her ride herd on our language. Here is social control gone haywire. Miss Fidd17ch's notions of correctness, after all, have little or nothing to do with the aptness and vigor of our expression; indeed, the contrary is commonly true: Miss Fidd17ch is the great sterilizer.

---

* This latter point is clear enough from the charge levelled at various writers that their writing is too "personal," that their use of language is so idiosyncratic as to make it virtually incomprehensible. Occasionally a writer is able by the vigor and special aptness of his idiom to make his personal language public. Joyce, Dylan Thomas, and a few others of our time have managed this to some degree.

At any rate, Joos views English usage under this schema:

Age	Style	Breadth	Responsibility
senile	frozen	genteel	best
mature	formal	puristic	better
teenage	consultative	standard	good
child	casual	provincial	fair
baby	intimate	popular	bad

These four scales are essentially independent; relations among them are not identities. (But isn't the best English genteel?— That must be Miss Fidditch talking.) (p. 11)

The scale that approximates the schoolmarm value system is the one called *responsibility*. This is, conversely, the scale that linguists have tended to steer clear of on the theory that such value judgments are outside the range of linguistic inquiry. This may be so from a narrowly linguistic point of view, but from a sociolinguistic point of view it is useful to know what types of usage are approved and disapproved by what segments of the population. One may hazard the conclusion that those cultures that are most coherent and compacted (small tribal societies perhaps) make the fewest distinctions of the kind listed under *responsibility*. Contrariwise, large, loosely agglomerated societies tend to proliferate these distinctions. Class differences seem to be the primary agents of this proliferation. Although, as the society grows more and more diverse, more and more elements enter into the equation. The mass media, for example, in our own highly diversified society seem to be exerting a strong levelling influence.

By *breadth*, Joos means breadth of linguistic experience, which broadens up to *standard* and narrows again to *genteel*—the broadening is a matter of growth, the narrowing a matter of choice. The schoolmarm English we have been speaking of is perhaps best characterized (from Professor Joos' analysis) as *senile–frozen–genteel–best*. But such English probably doesn't exist except as an "ideal." Even Miss Fidditch doesn't actually use this brand of English. Anyway, as Joos points out, there are no direct equivalents between items from scale to scale.

Living language, however, is slippery, and it is difficult to find samples that precisely fit the categories. Perhaps we can be satisfied merely with the general tendency of a discourse. In this respect we are not very different from the theoretical scientist, whose formulas represent ideal— which is to say, non-existent—conditions. Thus we can predict that an average of all utterances in a given cultural context will exemplify the usage categories. Any randomly chosen sample might not, for we are never (or hardly ever) so consistent in our behavior as to be wholly predictable. Nevertheless, we are consistent enough to react predictably to gross deviations. In the cocktail party context (let us say *mature–casual–popular–fair*, which might be informally labelled, "light banter, adult"), one's shift to *formal–puristic* ("stuffy") would be noticed and very possibly resented and even ridiculed, unless the shift was intended to be humorous. "Talking down" to someone is simply a failure to understand the context, as is "talking over the listener's head." The same mistake is made by resolute purists, those compulsive neurotics who must "correct" the speech of others. In the foregoing examples, language is shown to be used contrary to its essential purpose. Instead of uniting people, it is dividing them.

Professor Robbins Burling's analysis of the linguistic-cultural universe offers yet another schema (and one equally valid):

Grammar (= syntax +) phonology	Meaning		
	Referential	Situational	Personal
Syntax-Phrase Structure — Most of conventional grammar	Introduction of optional categories such as (adverb)		Individual style of sentence structure
Lexicon — Obligatory lexemes such as *do*	Most ordinary lexical choices	Javanese "levels"	Favorite words
Transformation — Obligatory transformations	Negation transformation	Passive transformation	
Intonation — Question intonation when required by the syntax	Varying intonation as in "He's here" and "He's here?"		
Phonological Opposition — Conventional phonology		-ing/-in'	A lisp which overrides a contrast
Phonetic Detail — Conventional phonetics		Phonetic effects of shouting	Individual voice quality

(*Man's Many Voices*, p. 8.)

The Javanese "levels" parallel the Japanese honorific system of which we have already spoken, though the Javanese is rather more complicated in that it allows of finer social distinctions. We have nothing in English that is so formally keyed to social stratification, but our rich collection of lexical doublets and triplets does allow us a great deal of stylistic flexibility in achieving just the precise tone for the occasion. Thus we can choose among vocabularies that are native (Germanic) or borrowed (French, Latin, and Greek). English in fact has borrowed from many languages, but the doublets and triplets we speak of derive from native, French, and Latin or Greek sources:

Germanic	French	Latin or Greek
kingly	royal	regal
rise	mount	ascend
fire	flame	conflagration
time	age	epoch
ask	question	interrogate

And so on. The choices we make among these resources are not so much directed by our sense of "place" in society as by other dimensions of *appropriateness* (rhetorical context, formality of context, etc.). This particular range of lexical choice is probably somewhere between Burling's *referential* and *situational* meaning; though *age* and *epoch*, for example, can have *different* referents, selection of one over the other may simply be a matter of making the proper *referential* choice. Likewise, one may choose *time* over *age* as a purely *personal* choice: "this is an *age* of progress"/"this is a *time* of progress." If all this seems rather shifty and uncertain, one must remember that certainties in language are hard to come by. We must be willing to settle for probabilities in the best scientific tradition.

Dialect

Every speaker of a language speaks one or more dialects of that language. There is no such thing as dialect-free speech or writing. One's habitual dialect is so natural a part of one's life that it is thought of as "normal." Concomitantly, the speech of those outside one's dialect area is thought of as strange or even, somehow, "incorrect." The definition of one's cultural selfhood is deeply rooted in one's linguistic patterns. The most immediately noticeable differences between ourselves and others as we cross cultural borders is linguistic. G. B. Shaw's St. Joan is a linguistic xenophobe. She wants the "godams," who speak English, out of her French-speaking land. Had England simply been a province of France, that is, a French-speaking province, Joan presumably would have been content to tend to her duties as a milkmaid. In *Pygmalion*, Shaw, who was deeply fascinated by language, gets at the same underlying issue via another route. Here, dialect is made a function of class and a means of leaping the walls between classes. In learning how to talk like a duchess, Eliza passes for a duchess. And once having stepped out of the bondage of her Cockney dialect, she is unwilling to return. Of course, Eliza commands greater social mobility than even the duchesses she has learned to ape, for she can speak Cockney and they cannot. This ability, if we move imaginatively beyond the confines of the play, could be of considerable use to her. Among the problems of ghetto blacks in America is the bondage of ghetto English, though this dialect is developing a sort of *cachet* of late; and among the problems of white teachers in dealing with ghetto blacks in the classroom is the inability of the former to use the ghetto dialect.

Among the sorrows of working-class immigrants to America is the abandonment by their children of their ancestral language (though this urge to reject the past is much less prevalent among the grandchildren). Or the dialect change of, say, the children of New York's Lower East Side. The desire to change speech habits bespeaks a desire to "rise." It also represents from the standpoint of the parents a visible and outward sign of alienation from the family. One can hear the parents talking about the "high and mighty ways," "big talk," etc., of their children. The most obvious mark of foreignness, of course, is the foreign "accent"; *i.e.*, dialect.* It is perhaps revealing of the English-speaking world's linguistic provincialism that *outlandish* (*cf.* German, *ausländisch*, "foreign") connotes *grotesqueness; i.e.*, what comes from outside is strange indeed. One might argue that the failure of Lon Chaney, Jr., to horrify us in his Dracula roles can be charged to his plain American speech. Bela Lugosi, on the contrary, chilled us to the bone with his "Transylvanian" English, for us quintessentially foreign—outlandish.

At the same time, it is these very dialects that give their speakers a special sense of identity, of belonging. And one's assimilation into a group can never be complete until one has mastered, in every subtle detail, that group's dialect. Of course, there are factors other than linguistic that can affect assimilation. Notable are race, religion, and education. The more educated the group, the more cosmopolitan its outlook —usually. The tolerance that says, as a matter of general principle, "*vive la différence*," can be born only of a cosmopolitan society; and, these days anyway, cosmopolitanism is the result of education. Religious differences can and do inhibit assimilation, as do racial differences; but a common dialect can help. Conversely, dialect differences exacerbate the problem.

An interesting exception to the urge toward linguistic conformity is the *status dialect*, a dialect different from one's own toward which one aspires, or, at the very least, which one admires. For many if not most

---

* To linguists, accent means *loudness*, as in the differences in pronunciation between CONduct and conDUCT, the former a noun, the latter a verb; the former bearing its main stress or loudest accent on the first syllable, the latter on its second.

Americans, Received Standard British (*i.e.*, the "Queen's English") is such a dialect. Yet when we wish to ridicule the British, it is that very dialect that (in a grotesquely exaggerated form) we choose as the butt of our humor. A not too difficult exercise in ethnolinguistics is to attempt to determine *why* Received Standard British is for us a status dialect.

The dialect of the classroom (the "schoolmarm English" of which we have spoken) is meant to be a status dialect that all "well educated" people should speak. Unfortunately for the teachers who have taken on or been given this thankless (and largely fruitless) job, the dialect is rootless on the one hand and fraught with contradictory prohibitions on the other. It is detached from the language as it is used in the world outside the classroom and tied down by myriad thou-shalt-nots that not even English teachers and "grammar"-book writers can agree on. For the student it is one more bit of evidence to support his conviction that formal education is both boring and irrelevant.

The logic of the concept of dialect leads us finally to the individual speaker and his own distinctive ways of speaking, his idiosyncratic dialect or *idiolect*. This is the linguistic composite of all the elements that bear significantly on his life. His vocal physiology directs the character of phonation: pitch level and quality (vocal bands or "cords"), resonance (size and shape of buccal cavity, nasal passages, and sinuses), and quality of articulation (structure of lips, teeth, tongue, and palate). His psychology directs other dimensions of his idiolect (the rapidity with which he speaks, for example), the speech habits of his family, friends, and community, which are in turn products of geography (*i.e.*, *regional* dialects), educational background, and class background. One's trade or profession likewise offers a dialect influence (professional jargon), as well as one's age and sex, as we have noted. It is not too much to say that our dialect forms for us a kind of social contract. Broadly, it tells the world a great many things about us; that is, it *identifies* us. More narrowly, our idiolect identifies us specifically to those we know. Rarely do we make radical changes in our speech habits. As we mature, we add to our linguistic skills, but our idiolect changes little. Indeed, we become conscious of dialect only when we are faced with speakers of dialects strange to us. Our reactions (initially at any rate) to these new speechways are commonly those of distrust or ridicule or (at least) edginess. We are always initially more comfortable in social situations with people who speak as we do.

Implications for Teaching

There is a "gee-whiz" element to revelations about the relationships between language and culture, and this can be profitable to the teacher looking for ways of arousing the universally latent interest in language. But it is pedagogically unwise to give in to the easy successes of the "Did you know that. . . ." technique of "teaching." Productive teaching aims at discovery on the part of the student rather than revelation on the part of the teacher. The basic discovery procedure is that of gathering data and building hypotheses. But there are antecedents to data gathering that must themselves be discovered. The teacher's role is to stimulate the student to an awareness of a problem to be solved and to possible ways of solving it or at least examining it. In a realm of human experience so immediate and eminently relevant, it takes but a few well-posed questions to start the student on his way. Questions such as those following can be used, with variations, at all educational levels. And the teacher must accept the principle that he cannot be looking for "right/wrong," "correct/incorrect" answers. Education like language is preeminently process not product.

1. Make a list of things (objects, events, people) for which there is more than one word; e.g., policeman, officer, cop, patrolman, fuzz, dick, flatfoot, peace officer, pig, etc. Try to explain what each of the different words for the same referent means to you beyond its function in merely designating the referent. Try to develop a questionnaire that you can use to determine how other people respond to each word. Perhaps you can devise something like an *intensity* scale—if, of course, intensity of response is worth measuring. (You must decide.) Test your questionnaire on a reasonable sampling of people. Think carefully about your sampling technique: Will you include *age* levels, *educational* levels, *occupational* varieties, and/or what (and why)? After you've worked through the problem, try to write an informative summary statement on the subject of vocabulary and the objects it describes.

2. Make one list of words that give you a *positive* feeling. Make a second list of words that give you a *negative* feeling, And make a third list of words that are for you *neutral*. Solicit similar lists from several other people. (On what basis will you choose these informants?) Do these lists reveal anything to you? Try grading your positive and negative lists from *most positive* to *least positive*, and from *most negative* to *least negative*. Do these gradations tell you anything about you and your language? Try collating all of the lists. Are there some words that people seem generally to feel good (or bad) about? Are there some that seem to be strictly individual reactions? Can the *neutral* words be ranked according to degrees of neutrality? Try writing a report of some recent local event in three ways: (1) with words from the positive list, (2) with words from the negative list, and (3) with words from the neutral list. What is the effect of each version? Try your versions on others and solicit

their reactions to each, but don't lead them to a pre-determined response. Try rather to elicit a response uncolored by anything but the text you have given them to read. (Why do you think you should proceed in this way?) When you have finished the project, write a report on your findings. Discuss the role of vocabulary in shaping our view of the world, and the role of societal experience in shaping our attitudes toward vocabulary.

3. "Tune in" to language for a week or so and try to listen, among other things, for differences in the way different people talk. Include radio and TV in your listening. Try to set up an informative "blueprint" (design, schema, chart, or whatever) for revealing these differences. Try to discover the general principles that seem to be operating. For example, you may detect certain differences in pronunciation that recur regularly, hence predictably. A person from northeastern New England, for example, will say something like *bahk* for the word that is spelled *bark*. And if he says *bahk*, we might tentatively conclude that he will say *pahk*, *caht*, *cah*, *paht*, etc., for the words that are spelled *park*, *cart*, *car*, *part*, etc. If in fact he does, then we have discovered a predictable recurrence in his speech. But these distinctive phonetic differences are only part of the picture. Listen closely and thoughtfully and see what else you can discover. Then organize your discoveries, for random (*i.e.*, unorganized) data is of little use. Your organization will then suggest a way of schematizing it. Your schema will represent an hypothesis or theory about language differences among speakers of the same language.

4. *Levels of discourse* is a term given to various modes of expression such as those that distinguish utterances like "Hey, ya got change of a buck?" and "Pardon me, but may I trouble you for change of a dollar?" These levels of discourse seem to play a role in the social process. How many distinctive levels can you detect in your everyday linguistic experiences? Try to characterize each one (*i.e.*, give examples and describe the context that seems to call for it). Contrive appropriate terminology. Is there any value in identifying these various ways of using language? Is there any value to the society in having these levels available to it? Try speaking with only one level of discourse for an entire day to everyone you meet (friends, relatives, adults, boys, girls, etc.). Discuss the results of your experiment.

5. Segregation of Negro and white may be seen in aspects of linguistic behavior quite distinct from the phonological [sound] system. Our investigation of New York City speech includes a number of semantic studies: one of the most fruitful of these concerns the semantic structures which revolve about the term *common sense*. This term lies at the center of one of the most important areas of intellectual activity for most Americans. It is a term frequently used, with considerable affect; its meaning is often debated, and questions about common

sense evoke considerable intellectual effort from most of our subjects. Negroes use the term *common sense*, but also an equivalent term which is not a part of the native vocabulary of any white speakers. This term is *mother-wit*, or *mother-with*. . . . For a few white speakers, mother-wit is identified as an archaic, learned term: but for Negroes it is a native term used frequently by older members of the household, referring to a complex of emotions and concepts that is quite important to them. Yet Negroes have no idea that white people do not use *mother-wit*, and whites have no inkling of the Negro use of this term. Contrast this complete lack of communication in an important area of intellectual activity with the smooth and regular transmission of slang terms from Negro musicians to the white population as a whole.

(William Labov, "The Reflection of Social Processes in Linguistic Structures," *Readings in the Sociology of Language*, pp. 248–49.)

Labov points to the implication of language in the operations of society. The implications in this example spring from the use by two identifiable communities of different terms for approximately the same range of meanings. Use this example as the basis for a study of your own that deals with the "reflection of social processes in linguistic structures." You may wish to read Labov's entire article as well as his very detailed study, *The Social Stratification of English in New York City*; but remember that the purpose of this project is not to report on Labov's findings but to set up your own study. Among other things, you will have to identify key terms (as Labov uses *common sense* and *mother-wit*), determine both who uses them and how they are used, and draw at least tentative conclusions about the social processes involved. You may wish to expand your study to include pronunciation factors and grammatical factors. If actually getting out in the field is not feasible, you can construct a potentially workable model for the study. Or you might do your study on a small scale within the classroom or school. With respect to the utility of this kind of research, Labov writes

It is hoped that the main achievements of linguistic science, which may formerly have appeared remote and irrelevant to many sociologists, may eventually be seen as consistent with the present direction of sociology, and valuable for the understanding of social structure and social change." (p. 251.)

This is of course a statement of general principle. Try to think of more immediate, "relevant," applications.

6. Imagine that a visitor from a totally alien culture (perhaps someone from a flying saucer) were trying to understand all the subtleties of English as a tool for social interaction. At the moment he is confused about utterances like *er, um, ah, oh, aha, hmm, eh, tsk, mmm, uh-uh, uh-huh, wow, zap, whee, whoopee, ugh*, etc. Attempt to explain to him the ins and outs of these——whatever they are. (Are they "words"?) He

is very logical and will need an orderly explanation. Explain why they are used, when they are used, how they are used and what actual sounds the spellings, which are simply conventions, represent. Do we all use all of them? Our alien friend is also curious about expressions like "it might be said," "so to speak," "as it were," "of course," "and so on," and so on. Tell him all you can about these and any other expressions of this kind you can discover. What seems to be the social function of all these expression (including er, um, etc.)?

7. Try getting through one entire day without using language, neither speech nor writing. This experiment might be especially interesting if you do it with a few friends. Write a report describing how you managed to communicate, what problems and frustrations you ran into, what you thought about as you attempted to "say" something without language. From time to time people assert that since language is an "imperfect" means of communication we should try to develop another, better means. Try. Write a report discussing the problems involved in creating such a system.

8. Try to spend an hour or two in which you exclude language from everything you do including *thinking*. What kind of thinking can you do without language? Does this non-language thinking serve your intellectual and emotional needs adequately? Explain. Try to describe the type of society we might have if we did away with language. Try to imagine the characteristics of human society had there never been language. What problems do you have in even trying to imagine such a situation?

9. Have you ever liked or disliked a person because of his manner of speaking? Can you explain your reactions? Can you explain how you modify your manner of speaking according to the person with whom you are trying to communicate? Can you recall an occasion in which you did not succeed in making the necessary adaptations? Discuss.

10. How is your telephone conversation different from face-to-face conversation? If you can recall no differences, try to "observe" yourself and others in both situations. Describe what, if anything, you discover.

11. Try writing a paper that clearly explains to a foreigner, who can read English but who doesn't really know much about the English-speaking world, the concepts of "good" and "bad" English, "correct" and "incorrect" English, "appropriate" and "inappropriate" English, "levels of discourse" in English. Then write a paper discussing the problems you had in writing the paper and the techniques you used for solving these problems.

12. Examine a variety of newsstand publications and attempt to determine the audience for each on the basis of the type of language

each one uses. Which publications do you feel most "comfortable" with? Why?

13. Are there any aspects of the language that adults use in speaking to you that you find objectionable? If so, what are they and why do you feel as you do? (Try to concentrate more on the way things are said than on the *explicit content* of the communications.) Try writing a dialogue that accurately imitates the conversation of two people who are ten or more years older than you. Describe how you went about preparing to write the dialogue. Point out what distinctive features of speech the listener or reader should discover from what you wrote. Now try the same experiment with children several years younger than you. And with very old people. With people from totally different backgrounds than yours. And so on.

14. Would you judge that your language provides you with adequate resources for expressing everything you wish to express? Do you ever have feelings or perceptions for which your language apparently has not given you sufficient expressive materials? Here is a simple example: Suppose you fall and scrape yourself about midway between your elbow and your wrist on the part of your arm that is on the same side as the palm of your hand. What do you call this place? Note what an elaborate description is necessary to locate it for you. Compare: I scraped my kneecap. Look around and try to find some things or events for which your language gives you no simple word. Invent some words for these things and try to make your words according to a rational principle (as opposed to nonsense words like *ikkle*). For example, when something that wasn't quite *smoke* nor quite *fog* but a combination of both was identified, it was called *smog*, a *blend* of *smoke* and *fog*. Likewise, a person of European and Asian descent is called a *Eurasian*. Another type of word formation is exemplified by words like *television, automobile*, etc. Check the *etymologies* of these and of words like *bonfire, neighbor, household, excavate, transmit*, etc., for some guidance in word creation.

15. It is said that a culture creates its vocabularies in accordance with its needs and values. Thus the Trobriand Islanders of the South Pacific have a large and complex vocabulary relating to the yam or sweet potato, the food staple of the Trobriand culture. From the evidence afforded by vocabulary, what seem to be among the more important items and events of our culture? Here's an example to get you started: Although we have a relatively small number of standard terms in the *automobile* vocabulary (*car, motor car, motor vehicle, automobile*), we have a fairly large number of slang terms (*heap, rod, buggy, unit, load*, etc.) and a huge number of trade names like Ford, Chevrolet, Plymouth, Fiat, *Corvette, GTO, Mustang, Cougar, Eldorado*, etc., all applied to essentially the same physical object (a "four-wheeled, self-propelled vehicle for personal transportation"). Discuss the implications of our automobile vocabulary and then go on to any other segment of our culture that we lavish vocabulary on. Discuss and interpret your findings.

16. Brand names and company names may afford some interesting insights into the character of our culture. Make an extensive collection of brand and company names (automobile names may be a good place to start) and the products associated with each. Do any patterns emerge? Ask yourself questions like "What does *Maverick* have to do with automobiles?" "What does *Homelite* have to do with chain saws?" And so on. Try to develop a sociology and a psychology of commercial names. Discuss the effectiveness (or ineffectiveness) of the various names. Explain the basis of your judgment in each case. Do names seem to be aimed at various special markets (age, education, race, etc.)? What seem to be the principles that lie behind the various choices?

17. Every culture seems to have a set of diminutives for use in intimate speech; for example, *babykins*, *sweetie-pie*, etc., in English. Make a collection of English diminutives, describe their structure, and explain (again, for that flying-saucer man) how each is properly used. Explain, further, what function these diminutives serve in the society. If it is feasible, make a collection of diminutives from other languages (French, German, etc.). Do they seem to work pretty much as ours do? Are they formed in pretty much the same way?

18. We use terms like *pompous, sarcastic, brash, supercilious, aggressive, dull-witted, awkward*, etc., to characterize the speech of various people at various times. What are the features that prompt each designation? What is your response to each way of speaking. Try to write a short address in each manner (pompous, sarcastic, etc.). Does there seem to be more-or-less complete agreement in the speech community on each label; that is, does everyone respond pretty much the same way to a speaker who is being "pompous" or "sarcastic" or "supercilious," etc.? How can you determine this? If there seems to be substantial disagreement on whether a certain style is "pompous" or whatever, try to account for the disagreement. Can you draw any useful conclusions about the degree to which it is necessary that a society agree on its various dimensions of language use. This is a complicated issue and requires a good deal of observation and reflection. Write a paper discussing the issue.

19. One usual function of language, sociologically speaking, is to cement the social fabric of the culture; that is, to bring people together. Thus, we feel a certain kinship with all speakers of English. This is especially noticeable and important when we find ourselves in a context in which there are no speakers of English but one, who then is our "brother" no matter what other social differences may separate us. But dialect differences of all kinds can work against this overriding unity. Generally this is not a planned effect but one "natural" to human social behavior. There are cases, however, in which we consciously use language to exclude "outsiders." Parents not wishing their children to understand what they are talking about will perhaps use an elaborate vocabulary or develop some kind of linguistic shorthand that they hope the children will not be able to puzzle out. Various subcultures likewise develop an "in" jargon that is supposed to keep outsiders outside. But in this day of instantaneous mass communications, these jargons don't keep their secrets very long. Items of teenage patois, for example, reach the advertising industry within days, it seems, of their coinage. Your task is to seek out some "secret" languages in current use ("pig latin" was invented as just such a secret language), describe them and the groups using them, explain how they deviate from ordinary English, and try to write a handbook for acquiring and using them. In some cases, like pig latin, the only deviations from normal English are in word formation (pig latin = igpay atinlay). But there may be quite different deviations in others. When you have finished, try concocting your own "secret" language built on the base of English. Make it sound odd enough and behave strangely enough to fool an outsider but easy enough to learn that it can be quickly picked up by the in-group that presumably will use it. Write a report discussing the motivations for secret languages. You may find it interesting to track down the origin of terms like hocus-pocus, mumbo-jumbo, abracadabra, etc., and to find out why the writing symbols of ancient Egypt are called hieroglyphs. (An etymological dictionary will get you started.)

20.   English is, for all practical purposes, a "universal" language; that is, some form of English is understood and spoken nearly everywhere on the earth. How can you account for this? After all, French used to be the international language of diplomacy, and Esperanto was specifically designed to be a universal language. Some years ago, Charles Ogden contrived a type of English called Basic* English that was meant to make the language quickly available to those who wished to learn it. One of its features is its very limited vocabulary (850 English words and a few non-English words), with which, it is claimed, one is able to express a vast number of ideas. This capability (within the limits of a very small vocabulary) would seem to make it an ideal universal language, and the perfect regularity of Esperanto would seem to make it an ideal universal language. Yet, neither one, nor any of the other

---

* The term Basic is an acronym for British American Scientific International Commercial.

"artificial" languages—e.g., Ido, Volapük, etc.—has been adopted on any scale for international use. Either "normal" English or spontaneous *contact vernaculars* based on English ("pidgin"—*i.e.*, "business"—languages) have made the natural English language the universal language. Can you account for the failures of the artificial creations? Attempt to create your own version of Basic English, limiting yourself to a vocabulary of one thousand words. (The average high-school graduate has a vocabulary of about twenty-five thousand words.) Explain how this vocabulary is to be used; that is, what rules or instructions are needed to make the vocabulary work effectively? Explain the basis upon which you made the choices you did. Attempt to teach your Basic to someone else and then attempt to communicate exclusively in your Basic. Write a report discussing the problems you encountered. What did you have the greatest difficulty in expressing? Try writing a story, a poem, a news report in your Basic. Try translating a few pages from a book you are reading into your Basic. Finally, get hold of Ogden's Basic and compare yours with his. How are they alike? How different? Try some of the preceding experiments with the original Basic. Discuss the results.

These are only a sampling of the kinds of projects that can be derived from the relationship between language and culture. Once the student has got into the habit of thinking as these exercises require him to think, he will—and should be encouraged to—come up with numberless questions and projects of his own. It is of paramount importance that the teacher appreciate that the aim of these projects is not to arrive at "right" answers. Many solutions are possible. Some will be more apt or trenchant than others, but the value at this stage lies in the doing, not in the answers. Indeed, what we really want is a spawn of new questions and the promise of new roads to explore, new doors to open. This will not effectively result from a pedagogy that relies on praising some students and humiliating others. If the student concludes, as he must if "right/wrong" is the game we play, that the idea is to give the teacher "what the teacher wants," then we are not educating but imposing. We want the student to learn how to recognize, evaluate, delimit, and explore problems. We want *him* to *discover* the world and *discover how to discover* and understand the world. The teacher must likewise be involved in discovery. Teachers don't know everything and shouldn't be required to conduct their classes under the tacit assumption that they do. There is much for the teacher to learn from the student. Education is (or should be) a working together to find out. Any teacher who believes that he knows all he need know about what he is teaching is a fraud. Indeed, teaching is learning. Knowledge grows daily. The physician who thinks he can do a proper job by using no more than he took from medical school is in the wrong line of work. Surely the case is the same for the teacher. Of course, the teacher does have a greater stock of information than the student and a greater skill at using his information (at problem-solving, that is). He is not simply another student in the classroom, but neither is his knowledge absolute. His real job is to generate learning not to impose data.

A particularly valuable kind of language project is the very complex one of devising a whole new language—a project perhaps best handled on a committee-of-the-whole basis. This task is not the same as the "secret" language project suggested above, but one that requires a close study of the phonological, grammatical, semantic, and cultural dimensions of language. Esperanto can be briefly studied as typical of the artificial language. The project can be ramified by asking the students to devise regional dialects and various cultural dialects paralleling those we find in English. Little of course will be gained by producing a "language" that is merely English with a new and exotic-sounding lexicon, though this may be a place to start. The project demands a good deal of linguistic sophistication on the part of the teacher, who must be able both to stimulate thinking, generally by raising questions regarding grammatical structure and process, psycho-socio-linguistic behavior, and so on, and to act as a resource. And the student must be at a learning level where he will willingly question and test and manipulate and, in general, act like a researcher, not a hopper into which the teacher pours a daily ration of information.

However, the first steps should probably be discussions of the role of language in communication in general and in societal cohesion, or lack thereof, in particular. It might be valuable for the student to attempt to define language. Then it would seem reasonable to spend some time trying to discover at least the main features of language (see Chapters IV and V). And the ways in which these features convey meaning and what kinds of meaning they convey (see Chapter III). The student should begin to perceive the facts of linguistic relativity and linguistic diversity; that is, various groups of people within a language community use their language—dialects and idiolects—differently one from the other, and various language communities have distinctively different phonological and syntactic systems, each of which is as "good" as the other. The Chinese, for example, have a system of pitch levels that is used in a way quite different from our pitch-level system. French has a marked subjunctive while English doesn't, and so on. Further, each language gives each culture a special set of tools for describing the world. Different verb systems convey different moods, aspects, tenses, etc.

In developing a new language, the student will want to explore at least some of the possibilities that lie outside of the usual (for him)

English way of doing things. He might, for example, want to try working out verbal elements that deal with modern scientific (and science-fiction) notions of *space-time* or with degrees of validity. Or we might want to fabricate unitary words that convey complex but holistically perceived realities (states of mind, newly observed physical realia, etc.). In short, the student should eventually find himself thoroughly immersed in the mechanisms of thought, perception, and acculturation.

Because this is a project that is more concerned with problem-solving processes than with answers and because language is so complex, one has to be prepared for a certain "messiness"; that is, there will be loose ends, misdirections, unsatisfactorily soluble problems, and a general incompleteness. The teacher cannot work against an answer sheet or "teacher's guide," but the situation is not greatly different from that faced by the professional linguist or any other scientist. We never can know more than a bit of the truth, and frequently there are alternate solutions to the same problem, each making an equally powerful claim to our intellectual allegiance. The burdens on both teacher and student are heavy, but the results in intellectual engagement are worth any of the messiness and any of the burden. In learning about the workings of language, the student will be learning how to learn.

Further dimensions of the language-making project will include developing ways of teaching the language quickly and efficiently, developing ways of describing the language (in order to have a base from which to teach it), producing a dictionary (which requires careful exploration of existing dictionaries and the lexicographical principles that govern their production), developing an orthography, writing stories in the language, and so on. All of this may seem a long way from a consideration of language in relation to culture and reality, but perhaps the old saw "the longest way round is the shortest way home" has relevance here. By getting sufficiently inside language to find the materials for building a language, the student is in the best possible position to grasp the nature of the complex interrelationships between language and culture. A human culture can properly be considered as largely the product of language. Man creates language and with it makes the rudiments of social behavior—which in turn lend force to the development of language—and welds them into the delicately articulated mechanism we call society. Withdraw language from society and we are reduced to loosely agglomerated herds lacking virtually every feature of culture. In coming to grips with the manifold nature of *meaning*, the student must inquire into both individual behavior and group behavior. Thus, the very process of mining one's own language for clues to the nature of language will help in working through the putative project and will perforce turn up vast quantities of associated materials. And the student will end not only with much new knowledge, but with new problem-solving expertise and, perhaps, a new language; that is, a creation of his own.

The first significant attribute of a pattern is that you can remember it and compare it with another pattern. This is what distinguishes it from random events or chaos. For the notion of random . . . implies that disorder is beyond comparison; you cannot compare one chaos with another chaos; there is no plural of the word. Pattern is a quality of familiar things and familiar things are comparable. It is much nearer to the truth to say that man abhors chaos than to say that nature abhors a vacuum. . . . Broadly speaking one may say that the sciences derive from pattern-seeking, the arts from pattern-making, though there is a much more intimate relation between the seeking and making of patterns than this would suggest.

(W. Grey Walter, *The Living Brain*, p. 69.)

3
Meaning

Meanings are in persons' minds, not in words, and when we say that a word has or possesses such and such meanings, we are really saying that it has evoked, or caused, those meanings. Until it gets into a mind, a word is only puffs of air or streaks of ink. What a word, sentence, or other expression means to hearers or readers is mainly what it makes him think or feel or do as a fairly direct consequence of hearing or seeing it, and, more narrowly, what it makes him think of as the direct and most immediate consequence of hearing or seeing it.

(Edward L. Thorndike, "The Psychology of Semantics," *The American Journal of Psychology*, Vol. 59, October 1946.)

It is probably impossible to say what meaning is, but we can say, with some hope of success, what kinds of meanings there are. The question of meaning (the general, all-inclusive term) lives in the midst of the tantalizing mystery of thought. Neither can be dealt with except in respect of their effects. Thus what we label meaning is the effect of meaning, what we label thought is the effect of thought. At the present state of the neurological-psychological art, what thought and meaning absolutely are cannot be known; that is, revealable, definable, objectifiable, etc. in the scientific sense of knowing. We are not stymied, however, for we can talk about species of both thought and meaning. Our prime concern here is with that dimension of thought we call meaning.

Let us posit two worlds: a linguistic world, the world of language and language events, and a non-linguistic world, the extensional world of non-language things and events. ("Reality" can of course be cut up in a variety of ways, our choice of cuts depending on what we are trying to do.) There is no *necessary* connection between these two worlds. That is, nothing in the phenomenal world "calls forth" language. Man has developed language as his basic tool for organizing the non-language world. Language resides not in the world but in man. Still, man has made connections between language (an activity of man's mind) and the world. Language reaches into the world and enables man to bring back to his mind the world (or bits of it) in a form he can process. The invisible thread between language and the world is meaning. But the meaning proceeds from the mind not from the world. Eventually, it is true, man comes to think of language as external to himself and to think that the meanings he notes are inherent in the world. And because language is a social (rather than a private) mechanism, there is a certain kind of truth in this view. Likewise, man comes to believe that linguistic units (e.g., "words") "contain" meaning. But as Professor Thorndike points out, they merely prompt meanings, though the belief that words are *meaning-full* governs our use of language, and it will seem to the everyday speaker that Thorndike's view is a kind of academic hairsplitting.

The general anthropological function of language is, as we have noted, to cement culture and to connect man productively to his environment. It is possible to say that the sense of form and structure and repetitive process that underlies language also underlies the rest of man's structured activities (farming, city building, etc.) and that as language emerged, man as fabricator emerged. Prior to language, the manlike creatures of the earth lacked the insight to do more than simply survive according to instinctual animal patterns. (It may be that language—that is, the human language potential—is "instinctual," genetically transmitted, but this does not vitiate the point we are making.)

Meaning is what "happens" when we speak, that is, when we consciously use language. (For the parrot, no meaning happens when it squawks its imitations of human speech.) Between sender and receiver messages flow on the language channel and leave behind the residuum of meaning. In the strictest sense, human beings cannot make *meaningless* utterances. There is always a species of meaning in any utterance contrived by man. "Nonsense" words, "gibberish," and the like, are all rich in meaning, though it may not be the kind of meaning we expect to get when we ask what time it is, or read a newspaper, or read an instruction booklet.*

Between the world of language and the world "out there," flow meanings which relate directly to one's experience with the non-language world, and which can be grouped under the heading of *referential* meanings. However, meanings also arise between elements of the language world. These intra-language meanings can be called *structural*, though they ultimately have some referential value, for language is not concerned merely with itself but with the non-language world. Nevertheless, the *referential* value of *structural* meaning is indirect and only weakly felt.

Referential meaning can be examined under the three headings of *lexical* ("word") meaning, *sentence* meaning, and *discourse* meaning. Lexical meanings are the sort of meanings we get from a dictionary. The definitions are descriptions of those fractions of the world the various

---

* We should appreciate the fact that while any linguistic utterance carries some semantic freight, meanings of several kind can be signalled without language. Cries of pain and pleasure, animal mating calls, "body language"—whether animal or human —all communicate meanings. For the present, we shall confine our considerations to meanings that come to us through language.

words are meant to designate. Essentially, a dictionary definition tells us that a particular thing in the non-language world is generally labelled by this or that lexical item.* In a sense, one can argue that *all* referential words are nouns, for they all "name" bits of reality. Of course, those bits may be objects, qualities, events, activities, functions, etc. (The "grammatical" definition of *nouns* as *names*, incidentally, has long since been discredited in linguistic circles. The most obvious reason is the point just made.)

One of the aims of contemporary linguistic theoreticians is to develop a rigorous semantics, one that will contribute to developing theories of grammar (transformational-generative, case, stratificational, etc.) so as ultimately to give us a "unified field theory" of language. A step in this direction is the *distinctive feature* concept, which in semantics means the construction of matrices of distinctive meaning features for each lexical unit. Thus, as a simple example, *girl* might look like this in its semantic matrix:

+human		−non-human
+animate		−inanimate
+female	___	−male
+pre- pubescent	*girl*	−adult
.		.
.		.
.		.

The feature matrix schema is meant to reveal at least those syntactically critical semantic values that each of us (presumably) associates with each word of the lexicon. The evidence for the actual existence of these sets of features seems to reside in our rejection of such anomalous utterances as

> Tillie wrote a canal
> The elevator smiled apples
> Girls are boys

And so on. The fact that none of these "sentences" expresses a rational idea can be accounted for by the incompatibility of semantic features among the referential words. Note that in no case is there a "purely" grammatical problem. The sentences are correct in terms of syntax alone. But semantic features are clearly a part of the syntax if the sentence is to communicate some sort of communally agreed upon sense.

---

* In the case of articles, prepositions, conjunctions, and the like, the words themselves are the things being labelled. This is why these are called *structure* or *function* words and belong primarily under *structural meaning* and only secondarily under *referential meaning*. This language about language is sometimes called *metalanguage*.

The matrix for any particular word could become extraordinarily complex as we tried to place the word in only those semantic environments in which it commonly occurs and in none of those in which it never occurs. We are really just at the threshold of semantic theory and there are at this writing no final words on the subject. The distinctive feature matrix, incidentally, is an important and reasonably well-developed dimension of transformational-generative grammatical theory, though its precise place in the theory is still an arguable issue among grammarians. Noun matrix features (for example) at the *grammatical* level include oppositions between *common* and *proper*, *concrete* and *abstract*, *animate* and *inanimate*, and *mass* and *count*, all of which can be moved into a *semantic* matrix but for somewhat different purposes.

In addition to *literal* (*denotative*) reference (*cat* denotes a member of the feline species of animals; that is, the word *cat* is a linguistic signifier for a non-linguistic entity), most referential words carry associative (*connotative*) references (*cat* connotes a stealthy and untrustworthy animal) and *metaphorical* references (a woman who gossips maliciously is a *cat*; an attractive, quick-witted person—male or female—is a *cat*, etc.). Denotative meanings approximate "scientific" meanings; that is, they are devoid of emotional content, though because we rarely operate in an atmosphere free of emotion, many words are rarely used in a purely neutral way. Since of course our own emotional states are in constant flux, the emotion-triggering potential of a given word is variable and can be plotted on a scale from zero emotion to intense emotion, negative or positive. These plots will be different for each person. Further, each word has its own limitations as a trigger. For no one will *hate* stand at zero—except perhaps in the special context of discussing its phonetic values or spelling or other linguistic characteristics. Likewise, *lamp* will probably not go very far up the emotional scale, either towards powerfully negative or powerfully positive except in the rare instance where a particular respondent has had some sort of traumatic experience with a lamp: e.g., was burned, got into trouble for breaking one, etc.

Words can also be scaled according to *semantic load*. For various reasons, words like *love*, *home*, *city*, *run*, etc., carry heavy semantic loads. *Run*, for example, not only shifts its function between noun and verb but denotes such diverse matters as "rapid ambulation on foot," "an induced flaw in the weave of a stocking," "a number of items manufactured without interruption from one batch of raw materials," "a sudden massive buying or selling of corporate shares," "the sudden withdrawal of funds from a bank by large numbers of depositers," "a score in baseball," "a large number of fish of particular species appearing in a localized area," etc. And the word occurs in such compounds and collocations as *run out* (as in "We ran out of gas"), *runout* (an irregular tire tread), *run-in* (as "They had a *run-in* with the law"), *run in* (to arrest someone), *gunrunner* (*i.e.*, one who smuggles guns), *runner up* (an "also ran"), *chicken run* (an area in the farmyard for chickens). On the other hand, words like *antidisestablishmentarianism, molybdenum, taxidermy, titrate, doorway, grist, calculus, qualify,* and *zymurgy* carry light semantic loads. In general, the more commonly used the word, the greater its semantic load (setting aside so notable an exception as *be* in its several forms, as well as most of the structural words).

Many structural words do carry *some* semantic load. Prepositions are clearly and primarily structural, but for some of them at least it is possible to see their connection with the non-language world. *Up*, for example, brings to mind an image of sorts (admittedly, a feeble one), as do the other prepositions with adverbial sense (*down, toward,* etc.). *The, a/an, to* (as infinitive marker), *too, very, why, what,* etc. are virtually devoid of reference except to other linguistic items (*the* precedes, and thus "marks" nouns, that is to say, noun-headed constructions: *the book, the well-bound book,* etc.). But despite the semantic value of some structural words, it is obvious that the difference between referential and structural words is properly one of kind rather than one of degree. To test this point, contrast (1) and (2):

> *The wind is blowing across the moors*
> 1. —— *wind* — *blowing* —— —— *moors*
> 2. *The* —— *is* —— *across the* ——

We can make some kind of sense with referential words alone, even though it be of the "Me Tarzan, you Jane" variety, but this is not true of structural words. One can indeed argue that where some kind of referential sense can be made with structural words, then they are not in that context structural, e.g., in "Up or down?" (1) *up* and *down* are adverbial (hence referential) and (2) the utterance is a question in which part of the structure has been deleted because it is supplied contextually. Incidentally, note that in *The wind was very cold, very* is not an adverb, but rather belongs to a group of structural words called *intensifiers,* which have no direct relationship to the non-language world. (*Rather, somewhat, quite,* etc. function in the same way.) We mention this in order to reserve *adverbial* for the class of referential words that convey the general meanings of *time, place, manner,* and *frequency.* Thus, we do not say *The wind was very.* The comment on the weather suggested by *very* in this context can be made only through a word, namely, *cold. Cold,* on the other hand, can be understood in direct relationship to the non-language world. One can communicate sensibly simply by standing outside and saying, "cold." Not so with "very," unless, of course, "very" is a response to someone else's "cold."

We hasten at this point to mention that relatively few words are learned on the basis of the referential/non-referential opposition. Once beyond acquiring our initial vocabulary, one that does stem directly from our direct observations of things that our elders promptly label for us, we increasingly derive vocabulary from *verbal* (*i.e.*, linguistic) contexts, from being told about (and, later, from reading about) things in terms of words that are used to talk about more things that may not be in our direct experience at all. Thus we may, in our reading, come across the word *astrophysicist*, which is then defined for us *verbally*. We need never actually see a real, live astrophysicist, but we nonetheless have acquired a referential word. Presumably, there is a "thing" out in the non-language world to which the word *astrophysicist* can be appropriately stuck. Indeed, this sense of connection between words and things commonly grows so strong in us that we frequently confuse the two. We fall into believing that the thing becomes the word, so to speak. Hence, if we hold a stereotype that we label with, say, *Polack*, then when we apply the term *Polack* to a real person, we invest that person with whatever our stereotype is and believe that the person *is* the stereotype. The semantic load here precedes our real-world experience and causes us to apply to the real thing, the person in this case, the results of purely verbal experience—an unfortunate use of a valuable mechanism.

Though we have begun our consideration of meaning with those linguistic entities loosely known as words, we do not mean to suggest that we communicate through words as such. The lexicon, as we have said, represents only part of the language. One may memorize an entire dictionary and be wholly incapable of using the language whose dictionary he has memorized. In practical language situations, words find their meanings only in structures of words—more properly, *grammatical structures* that are realized through sequences of words. Thus the meaning of a *sequence* or *sentence* (without at this point attempting a definition of *sentence*) is something both more and less than the possible meanings of the words that comprise it. The linguistic component called *grammar* (structure) channels and interacts with the linguistic component, *word*. Compare:

(1) bill consider Governor's legislature proposed transportation the the tomorrow will

(2) Tomorrow the legislature will consider the Governor's proposed transportation bill.

The first item is an alphabetical list of English words. The list "means" nothing (as a structure) but "alphabetical list of English words." The words mean whatever definitions we can supply or whatever "things" in the non-language world we can take them to be labels for. Even if we could manage to utter the list with the intonation contour that we commonly use for declarative sentences, we would not in fact be speaking English. We would likely prompt no more than a puzzled look in a native listener. If he were patient and we kept repeating the words, he might eventually arrive at the meaning that is immediately apparent from (2), but he would do this only by rearranging the lexical items into a pattern that "makes sense"; that is, a normal English grammatical structure, a sentence either identical with (2) or very similar to it. (Several syntactical maneuvers are available, the simplest being the moving of *tomorrow* to another location, thus: *The legislature will consider the Governor's proposed transportation bill tomorrow.*)

What happens as a result of forming structured sequences (*i.e.*, sentences, in our example) is a new dimension of meaning imposed by the structuring itself—or, more strictly, the relation between the structuring and the lexicon. There are two major components of this meaning: the semantic, what the speaker is trying to communicate, and the grammatical (the structuring that carries the semantic meaning). Without the grammatical structure, the semantic intent could not be realized, or realized only imperfectly: *He have been born since thirty-two years,* which is to say, in English, *He was born thirty-two years ago.* The non-English "sentence" is in fact typical of constructions put together by foreigners who have an insufficient grasp of English structural habits and who therefore try to force English vocabulary into their own quite different patterns.

No *overt* semantic load is carried by an unlabelled grammatical structure: NP + VP (*noun phrase* + *verb phrase*) means precisely NP + VP (or, restated, S, *sentence*). If we move from this highly abstract expression of grammatical structure to something like S + V + O (*subject* + *verb* + *object*), the terminology (at least) implies a certain semantic loading; this grows heavier as we go to *actor* + *action* + *thing-acted-upon*, for we now are talking about a way of understanding the non-language world. When we have filled our patterns with vocabulary, we both realize certain potentials in the structure itself and make explicit our "thought." No one truly knows what a thought is (that is, no one has adequately described and defined thought; we generally accept it as a "given" of existence). Questions of the degree of "completeness" of a "thought" are idle. What the traditional definition of *sentence* is really saying is that a "sentence is a group of words containing a subject and a predicate [NP + VP] and forming an independent structure." There is no point in attempting to use the "complete thought" notion in language study because there is no effective way of dealing with it. One can argue that a whole book is the author's "complete thought" and that anything less (a sentence, say) would be to some degree incomplete.

The sense of semantic completeness we get from an utterance like *The sea is calm tonight,* derives from its structural completeness and the semantic compatibility of its vocabulary. A sentence that is clearly "complete" but at the same time expressing some kind of incompleteness is *He ate a few*, which prompts us to ask, "A few what?" The sentence is still structurally complete and the vocabulary is compatible. (An example of lexical incompatibility: *The elevator cried to eat such a sight.*) But something is missing. *Few*, of course, is the problem. This word, which is commonly a structure word (*a few bananas*) with only weak referential value (technically it is an *indefinite numerator*), has been shifted to a sentence location normally taking a full referential word (*He ate a banana*). In the context of a discourse, there would be no problems in determining meaning (*Did he eat any bananas? He ate a few.*) But in isolation, the sentence fails to communicate, even though it is technically "complete." One obvious lesson to be drawn is that the traditional definition of a sentence can't cope with the language as it is actually used.

We have said that the grammatical meaning of an utterance depends upon the arrangement of lexical items according to certain prescribed patterns; that is, the existing grammatical patterns of the language. But lexical items are particular manifestations of the grammatical entities known traditionally as "parts of speech," which may be thought of as *positional* and *relational functions* within the grammatical pattern. Hence, the simplest of the basic, or kernel, sentence patterns can be symbolized as $N + V_{INTR}$ (Noun + Intransitive verb, where the plus sign includes the notion of agreement). Hence, we have a *noun function* and a *verb function*. The relationship of noun and verb functions is expressed in the present tense by an *inflection*, a sub-lexical meaning unit.

Thus: *bug* + *s* + *crawl* = *bugs crawl* = N $\quad + \quad$ V_{INTR}
$$\text{(agreement)}$$

Modern definitions of the "parts of speech" are based on formal and functional characteristics rather than on semantic characteristics. Nouns do have sentence positions, and they do have certain formal features; e.g., they are marked for plurality. But the traditional definition that says that nouns "name things" is relatively useless because it doesn't work. Any word, as we have said, may be easily construed as the "name" of something. Thus *sing* is the name of a verb. As for the traditional definition of verbs as words that "express action or state of being," what word better "expresses" action than *action*, a noun. And *action* is commonly a noun by virtue of its positional distribution, function, and ability to be marked for plurality; that is, it occurs in slots like *His* _____ *was/were understandable*. It can be a subject or an object; its plain form (*action*) can be modified to *actions* by the addition of an *-s* that means plural. It does not occur as **actioned* or **actioning,** which means that it is not a verb. It may become one some day, but there's little use in speculating about that. Of course, if it does become a verb, then we will

---

* An asterisk (*) in front of a citation means that the cited form is unattested.

have two linguistic entities: *action*, a noun; *action*, a verb. Compare: *run/run*; *walk/walk*, etc.

Part of the meaning of a lexical item, then, is its referential component (if there is one) and part its grammatical character, whether at one level, *noun*, *verb*, etc., or at another level, *subject*, *object*, *predicator*, *modifier*, etc. The referential definition can be communicated simply through the word itself, as is the case when we look a word up in the dictionary. The word's particular utterance meaning, however, is not realized except through the particular utterance. Compare the dictionary definition of *up* with the meaning of *up* in an utterance like *He ran up the road*; then compare *He tore up the road*, where there are two possible meanings depending upon the shape of the intonation contour, in particular the distribution of internal junctures: *he + tore up + the + road/he + tore + up + the + road*. The first means that he ruptured the paving, the second that he drove or ran very fast on the road. The *internal juncture* (+) here represents a brief pause, a signal that is keyed to the intonational structure of the utterance, which in turn is a function of the speaker's intent.

The intonation of a sentence is an element of both its grammar and its non-language meaning. When we bring lexical items together with grammatical structure, we are required by the patterns of the language to intone the resulting utterance in certain ways. We have some intonational latitude, but each language has distinctive intonational patterns that are learned as a part of the language acquisition process, and a native speaker always intones predictably. One of the major problems in learning a foreign language is learning new intonational patterns. At any rate, we can say that, for example, an English declarative sentence has a particular intonation contour, with a number of standard variants, which convey a wealth of largely emotive meanings. For example, *The sun will set at 6:05 this evening* is usually a statement with no emotional overtones, but emotional loading can be accomplished simply by increasing the stress on *will* implying a response to a doubt raised about the accuracy of the statement. These intonational manipulations give us our "tone of voice." They allow us to pack any utterance with a broad range of emotional meanings and thereby to add semantic complexity far beyond that even hinted at by the plain utterance. It would be hard to think of a more innocuous utterance than *The sun will set at 6:05 this evening*, but one would have no difficulty in intoning it in ways that would communicate happiness, sorrow, anger, sarcasm, disdain, etc.*

---

* We are not of course talking of such qualities of voice as absolute pitch, resonance, and timbre. These are unique for each individual, and while they are relevant to *acoustic* analysis, they are not relevant to *linguistic* analysis; that is, they play no formal part in distinguishing meaning. They are, however, the main elements by which we aurally recognize the people we know.

The functions of language discussed in Chapter II are properly a part of the meaning complex of language. By framing an utterance as an imperative ("Answer the phone"), we are, among other things, telling the receiver of the message, "You are in a position that allows me to give you an order." This message may be weakly or strongly felt, depending upon what the directive is concerned with and what the attendant circumstances are. It may be so weakly felt as to be for all practical purposes nonexistent or so strongly felt as to prompt a violent verbal, or even physical, response. In most cases, the recipient of the directive will probably do as we direct; but if he does not, we will know that there is a level of meaning generated by the utterance that is not apparent. Actually, our usual practice of surrounding directive language with request markers ("please," "would you mind?" etc.) betrays some degree of awareness of this more-or-less hidden level of meaning. Thus a common form of the directive is the imperative question, where we mitigate the directive feeling: *Would you open the window, please? Can you hand me that screwdriver? Would you like to put out the cat?*

Though we do in the course of our lives engage in a vast number of "micro-conversations" ("How many?/"A dozen, please"; "Be careful"/ "Okay"; "What's new?"/"Nothin' much," etc.), our most meaningful communications are generally rather longer than this and form colloquies that are comprised of individual discourses. Each colloquy has its characteristic *tessatura*, to borrow a musical term, which is a component of its meaning at the emotional level, and a central *semantic axis*, which forms its meaning at the intellectual level. Within what we might call the colloquium or total conversation, several colloquies might develop, and for each colloquy several discourses.

From sentence to sentence, meaning is carried linguistically by transitional devices like pronouns and connectives, and rhetorical devices like repetition. This linguistic continuity and interrelationship is a manifestation of the discourse logic. The most obvious signals of logic are words and phrases like *if . . . then; on the one hand . . . on the other hand; moreover; however; therefore*, etc. This is not to say that the speaker is being in the strict sense logical, merely that the discourse is being given some kind of inner logic that is meant to knit it together. Thus the listener is able to derive not only a sentence-by-sentence meaning from what the speaker is saying but an overall sense of the relatedness or coherence of the sentences. Discourse meaning, then, derives from a congeries of meanings: lexical, grammatical, intonational, emotive, situational, and logical. Classical, or formal, logic is highly stylized linguistically and very rigorous in its rules of relationship. Nevertheless, in informal linguistic contexts, the same relational rigor can be achieved, though it may not be so obvious. The formal deductive fallacy of the "undistributed middle" is the flaw in the political smear tactic known as "guilt by association." Informally it may come out thus: "Are we going to send a man to the Senate of the United States who supports the get-out-of-the-war line of the commie conspiracy? Do we need another pinko in the Senate?" In formal (syllogistic) logic, the same argument would look like this:

(1)　Candidate Z thinks we should stop the war.
(2)　The communists think we should stop the war.
∴　Candidate Z is a communist.

The middle term of a syllogism is the term that appears in both of the premises. Here it might be cast as "some of those who think we should end the war." In this case, we are saying that (1) Z is one of those who think we should end the war, and (2) the communists are among those who think we should end the war. The problem is that from two such premises we can by the rules of logic draw no valid conclusion because the hinge (middle) term in neither premise is inclusive of *all* people. In our politician's speech there is the inner "logic" of the speaker's intention, but from the standpoint of formal logic there is no argument, just "tilt." Unfortunately, emotive meanings often override logical meanings.

Inductive reasoning, as opposed to the deductive reasoning of the syllogism, is concerned with the rules of evidence. Again, a discourse may have its own internal connections without necessarily being remotely logical with respect to the way in which ideas or data are handled. One may, for example, oversimplify in a perfectly coherent and linguistically well-constructed way.

We have worried this question of natural versus formal logic because, in the first place, they should not be confused one for the other and, in the second place, they are both vital elements in the meaning complex. A speaker or writer who is deliberately violating the rules of evidence can nonetheless come across as sweetly reasonable if he has strung his discourse together with sufficient internal logic to mislead the listener. On the other hand, the speaker who offers sound reasoning in a carelessly built matrix, invites disbelief and rejection. The subtleties, of course, are bewildering. The right proportion of rural homespun might counteract the forceful, tightly ordered presentation, whether logically sound or not; and so on.

We have thus far touched on certain dimensions of meaning apprehended at the levels of word, sentence, and discourse. Our orientation here has been on a micro- to macro-linguistic scale. And we have distinguished between meaning directly related to non-language experience and meaning within the world of language itself; that is, between referential and structural meaning. But we have by no means exhausted the general question of meaning. In succeeding paragraphs we shall explore other dimensions of meaning, but cannot hope to do more than scratch the surface of this incredibly complex subject.

When we speak, we intend to communicate a certain meaning. We shape our expression in a way that we hope will succeed in achieving that communication. If the meaning is simple information, expression is equally simple and probably follows patterns we have used many times before; e.g., *I'll meet you at the theater at 7:00 this evening.* Barring mechanical disruption of the message, perhaps a bad phone connection, our chances of complete success are very good, even predictable. But as the meaning becomes more complex, the expression becomes more complex as well and the possibility of some degree of failure in communication is very real.

Communication requires a sender, receiver, and a channel. Ideally, communication will flow easily between the first two, each playing both roles alternately; but the ideal is not always achieved because, whatever our intended meaning may be, that meaning may be considerably modified by the receiver. As we have said, in simple exchanges of information, problems of meaning are few, though it is not difficult to imagine problems, even in a face-to-face situation. If in response to a request for the time, we answer, "1535 hours," in the military fashion, our non-military communicant may very well be nonplussed. Likewise, if a physician tells us that we have onychocryptosis, we are likely to be far more alarmed than if he tells us we have an ingrown toenail. Our reaction, incidentally, is an interesting one. We have been conditioned to feel that things with ornate names are impressive and that medical problems with ornate names are a negative extension of impressiveness, namely, frightening. Thus, injudicious diction has in each case short-circuited communication. The speaker, in other words, has not been careful to adapt his diction to the receiver, and such thoughtlessness is the cause of many of our failures in communication. One of the meanings of any expression is its *situational* meaning. In broad terms this meaning is the one we notice when diction is inappropriate to context, even though it clearly expresses our literal meaning. The commuter, for example, does not speak of going to the city each day via the "choo-choo train." If he does, he is being deliberately jocular and counting on our noticing the lexical discrepancy. Thus we can say that vocabulary can be identified situationally with such labels as *infantile, slang, taboo, general, formal, pompous,* etc. A pair like *domicile/home* exhibits the contrast *formal/informal* (possibly, *pompous/general*), as does *edifice/building.* Some words can carry several labels. If we say *his vision is dim, dim* is certainly general, even formal; but in *He is dim, dim* is certainly close to being slang. Many, if not most, words require a context before they can be labelled or before we can appreciate the range of possible labels, but many are situation absolutes. Taboo words clearly fit the latter case.

An obvious problem in meaning transference at the lexical level is the one that arises from the speaker's choosing words with either the wrong denotative or connotative meaning. He may have the right situational tone, but he is not saying what he thinks he is saying. Mrs. Malaprop exemplifies denotative error when, for example, she says "shrewd awakening" for "rude awakening." One's calling a structure like Buckingham Palace a "house," however, reveals an insensitivity to connotation; as a rule, *house* connotes nothing very grand (except in proper names like Adare House or qualified terms like "manor house"). The occurrence range of *house* doesn't match that of *palace*, even though both properly denote "residence" or "dwelling." If a person who lives in a palace, invites someone to his "house," he is being either exaggeratedly deprecatory for effect or droll.

If, however, enough people use a particular word with a certain meaning, even though that meaning does not accord with earlier meanings associated with the word, the new meaning must be accepted. Indeed, new meanings often drive out older meanings altogether as is the case, for example, with *deer*, which in Anglo-Saxon times meant "wild animal," as does its modern German cognate, *Tier* (in German, a zoo is a *Tiergarten*, an "animal garden"). Both *silly* (cf., German *selig*, "blessed") and *nice* have gone through many semantic changes to reach their present meanings. At various times, *silly* has meant "blessed," "innocent," and "useless"; *nice* has meant "fine," "sharp," "precise," "persnickety." To argue that the current meanings are "incorrect" would be senseless, as it would be to argue that *disinterested* means only "objective," when most speakers today use the word as a synonym for *uninterested*. If one wishes to exhibit in one's use of vocabulary what has been called "purism," that is one's perfect right; but to insist that one's compatriot's do it is to be both arrogant and uninformed. A word finally means what we mean it to mean; and if we can get others to go along with our meaning, then we are party to a normal linguistic process. The only true purity for English, after all, must be Anglo-Saxon; and what is the final purity for Anglo-Saxon? Perhaps Proto-Low-West-Germanic. At any rate, if one argues that by such deference to the majority we lose good and valuable words, it can be counter-argued that there never is any net loss in language. So long as a bit of reality or experience *needs* linguistic identification, we shall have the means to identify it. If a word is lost, another is gained; and the language is always approximately equal to the tasks demanded of it. If we can no longer use *disinterested* without being misunderstood, then we shall have to use *objective*. It is no very taxing job to fill a dictionary with words we no longer use and whose meanings are no longer what they once were. But what have we lost? *Halieutics* once enjoyed some currency in English, and there must have been those who mourned its passing; but we do very nicely without it, for we can say "angling" or "the art of fishing" instead. Nor in this age does one hear *mactation*, for *killing* says it well. *Loyalty* does admirably for *rihthlāfordhyldo*, as our Anglo-Saxon forebears put it. And if we are put off by those who say *infer* when they, by rigorous standards, mean to say *imply* and thereby "strike another blow" for ignorance, let us remember that many of the words we use today do not mean precisely what they meant to speakers of the past. When we say that we are *enthusiastic*, it is not likely that even the most puristic of us feel that we are "full of the god." Of course, many of us do not use *infer* for *imply*, *flaunt* for *flout*, and so on. These and other choices represent for us our normal way of speaking, and there will be no need to change these habits until we can no longer communicate effectively with them.

In the case of malapropism, we have the result of a "bad ear." The speaker is approximating instead of precisely rendering what he has heard. In most cases the listener can make the necessary adjustments and grasp what the speaker is trying to say. The person who says that he "ran *amuck* of the demonstration" is easily understood to be saying that he ran *afoul* of it; but if we meet such usages as the following, we must conclude that they were produced by non-native speakers of the language or perhaps by native speakers who are being or attempting to be humorous:

> dry water
> pregnant tomcat
> he combed his nose
> she swam the car home
> he shrugged his leg

From a purely structural point of view, the examples are grammatical; but if we take semantic issues into account, the examples are virtually without "real world" sense. Of course, writers play with language to achieve certain effects, and we can be put off by such deviations, at least until we have taken the trouble to draw from them meanings consonant with the context in which they are used. E. E. Cummings is a notable example; in "Spring is like a perhaps hand," *perhaps* is made to do something it doesn't ordinarily do, i.e., act as a noun modifier. But in a non-specialized or non-poetic context, we would have to judge our examples as unacceptable because of their semantic incompatibility. Shoulders, not legs, are for shrugging; water, by definition, is wet, etc. The semantic values of these words could conceivably change in the course of time, but for the present they cannot stand together as they do in the examples. A native speaker is not likely to commit such lexical mayhem except in connection with technical matters for which he has not been lexically trained: A novice at sailing will "murder" the language of sailing until he has, so to speak, learned the *ropes*, most of which are called *lines*, *sheets*, or *braces*. A foreigner, at least until he has become linguistically acculturated, may often make mistakes deriving from mistranslations from his native language: One hears such locutions as "I cannot good English make." *

A particularly vexing problem at the lexical level is our inability on various occasions to "find the right word." It is difficult to say what may cause any particular lapse, but several causes are available: (1) we may simply "go blank"; that is, exhibit a momentary and temporary aphasia; (2) we may not have the word we want in our word store even though we know such a word exists; or (3) we may not actually know what precisely we are trying to say. Whatever the cause, the effect is one of frustration and irritation. It does not, however, represent a major problem in communication. Indeed, often our auditors are sympathetic and anxious to help us find the word we are looking for. When we take our ailing car to the mechanic, for example, our vocabulary is likely to fail us as we try to explain what seems to be wrong with the car. For such occasions we have a few useful, though wholly uninformative, words that fill the blanks: *thing, dingus, whatsis, gizmo, thingamajig, gadget*, etc.; and since the mechanic does manage to make some sense of what we're trying to communicate, we probably won't bother to learn the specialized vocabulary of the mechanic. Generally, our language mechanism is reasonably efficient; and if we can get by without something, we will.

Failures in communication at the sentence level commonly arise from two sources: failures in the antecedent thought process and structural ambiguity. The former is so complex and variable as to preclude brief analysis. Generally, these failures emerge as various types of logical fallacies within the context of the larger discourse. The latter can be more easily examined. We need but glance at the following examples of structural ambiguity to perceive the problem:

1. A Japanese teacher recently joined the faculty. (A Japanese or a teacher of Japanese?)
2. That was a clever kid's fib. (Is the kid clever, the fib clever, or is it a fib like a kid's?)

* A typical confusion for new speakers of French is the distinction between *le gens* and *le peuple*, the former meaning *people* (*persons*), the latter a *people* or *the population* in anthropological and political senses. Using the one term where the French expect the other would serve merely to confirm the French in their belief that the subtleties of French are beyond the English-speaking world. The French, incidentally, use the term *faux amis*—"false friends"—for words like *peuple* that are mistranslated on the basis of their overt resemblance to words in the foreign language. Thus, *actuel* properly translates as "present," not "actual." *Actual* translates into French *réel*. And so on. An example that would cause rather more embarrassment than the innocuous *gens/peuple* contrast is the direct translation of *I am warm* (with reference to the external temperature) to *Je suis chaud*. The correct translation is, of course, *J'ai chaud* ("I have warmth"). The use of *suis* ("am") dramatically changes the intent of the sentence.

3. We have a new program in modern math teaching. (Teaching modern math or modern methods of teaching math?)
4. Big trouser sale! (Big sale or sale of big trousers?)
5. The colors he wanted were Chinese red, purple, and yellow. (Does *Chinese* modify just *red* or all three of the colors?)
6. The apartment pool is open to residents only from 1:00 p.m. to 5:30 p.m. (Residents only or only from . . . ?)
7. The new overpass failed completely to solve the traffic congestion problem. (To avoid "splitting" an infinitive, the writer succeeds in saying something he may not intend. Read the sentence "failed to completely solve. . . .")
8. George told Harry that he was in trouble. (Who? *He* can mean either George or Harry.)

The resources in English for structural ambiguity are manifold and the effective communicator will take the necessary precautions. We must, however, appreciate that the speaker, more commonly the writer, has no sense of ambiguity when he uses any of these types of expressions. He knows which of the two or more possible meanings he intends, and he is probably not even aware of meanings other than his own. In speech, the intonation will in many cases resolve the inherent structural ambiguity, but in writing intonation is absent and there is no way to resolve the ambiguity other than by recasting the sentence.

A third type of failure at this level is simply that of getting tangled up in an ineptly structured sentence. In daily conversation we frequently start a sentence with the intention of going in one direction, but quickly decide to change our direction or intent and so break off and start again. If we fail to break off and merely try to correct the sentence as it comes out, we end by producing an all but unintelligible monstrosity. This problem can also arise in writing but can be corrected before reaching an audience.

At the level of discourse, problems in transference of meaning are legion. Any of the preceding problems will of course arise in the larger context; but because the discourse generally aims at meanings larger and more complex than the meanings of any of its component units, it cannot so easily be examined. If the speaker or writer is trying to convince or persuade, he must include logic in his discourse. His reasoning may, however, be wholly or partially sound or wholly unsound. If unsound to whatever degree, we must consider his intentions as part of the total meaning; that is, has he deliberately chosen to mislead us, or is he simply inept at argumentation? We have already touched on classical deductive argumentation and on the rules of evidence. The reader is urged to examine a book like *Thinking Straight* (see Bibliography) for a detailed treatment of these matters and those we will glance at below. Among the most common faults in reasoning are *begging the question; post hoc ergo propter hoc; oversimplification;* and *jumping to conclusions.* These constitute, we would judge, the majority of distortions of meaning due to weaknesses in logic. When one begs the question, one addresses himself to an issue irrelevant to the discussion. If the issue is whether the People's Republic of China should be admitted to the United Nations, the question beggar talks about the undesirability of the "communist system," or about "godless communism." The *post hoc* fallacy is based upon the assumption that two events that are close temporally or spatially are necessarily related to each other causally, the one event in some way affecting or effecting the other. It establishes false causality; e.g., the rooster may think his crowing causes the sun to rise. When we oversimplify we attempt to explain complexities with simplicities. The 1970 elections illustrate the fallacy quite clearly. The party in power tried to explain America's problems to the voters in terms of giant, ill-defined generalizations like "radical liberalism" and "law and order"; and complex issues were grossly oversimplified. The advertising industry also makes great use of this fallacy: Use this deodorant and achieve social and marital success. The nonsense of it is abundantly clear, yet the fact that advertisers keep plugging away with the same message suggests that they are having at least some degree of success. To jump to a conclusion is to draw a conclusion from insufficient evidence. "One swallow does not a summer make." We are not warranted in concluding that Mr. Nern is wealthy simply because he drives an expensive car.

As we live so deeply immersed in a world of words, we tend to confuse the world of language and the world of non-language. To be sure, we deal with that world of non-language linguistically. Relatively little of our experience of life is truly wordless. Nevertheless, it is useful to appreciate the difference between the two worlds. From the standpoint of communication we should be aware that utterances framed exclusively from the intensional or inner world have a different kind of truth or validity from those framed from extensional experience. Intensionally we may, because we have been propagandized, believe that "Orientals are crafty and untrustworthy." Intensional communications commonly are prejudiced communications. Our extensional experience will prove otherwise if we can set aside our programming for prejudice—not always an easy thing to do. We are conditioned to giving credence to words—particularly if they are in print or uttered by an "authority." *

* The *appeal to authority* is a common device in advertising, usually taking the form of "testimonials" for products by celebrities whose celebrity alone presumably gives them some special authority. For many, parents constitute the ultimate authority. And while we don't wish to quarrel with "parental authority," which has its proper role in the running of the household, we do strenuously dispute the (mis)use of parental authority to establish and engender prejudice in the child.

Communication can be defined as the transference of sense from one person to another. We grasp "sense" by understanding meaning, but we can be fooled into thinking we are dealing in sense when in fact we are dealing in *non*-sense. We can believe we are understanding and can be led to act on the basis of that belief. If we fail to recognize the fallacies in an argument, if we fail to understand the tricks of the advertiser, we will end by playing the fool. Following the 1970 elections, word got out that the Administration was casting about for a new "image" for the incumbent to use in the 1972 elections. This image, which will be generated with language, will attempt to get the voter to "see" something other than what is apparently before him. It will appeal to the intensional world; it will indeed try to program that world. To say that a box of candy is "half full" rather than "half empty" is to play on certain psychological realities. Contrast "half full" with "half a box." Then with "half empty." Each gives us a different feeling toward the reality being discussed. Take the word *liberal* and attach it to *radical*, to which we have been negatively pre-conditioned. Soon the word *liberal* alone takes on in our minds the negative feelings of *radical*. We have created a negative emotional response toward people who are properly called (political) liberals. (One of the national polls reported during the campaign that more people responded favorably to the word *conservative* than to the word *liberal*— perhaps a measure of the success in degrading a word.) To protect ourselves we must learn to look beyond the labels to the discrete persons and things upon which these labels are so freely stuck.

We spend a lot of time talking nonsense. Part of the problem arises from our failure to recognize the difference between questions and non-questions. Children ask many genuine questions but many non-questions as well. "How high is up?" is a child's question. As it is stated, it is unanswerable and thus is not, logically, a question. Such a question may, of course, eventually prompt us to ask genuine questions and will thereby have served a useful purpose. But of itself it is a non-question. More touchy but equally empty questions are of the type, "What is God?" "Where is God?" and the like. Any "answer" one might offer would be as "true" or "untrue" as any other, our notions of truth here being based on whatever orthodoxy we have been conditioned to.

On the question of how high up is, we can properly ask, "Can the universe be measured?" "By what means?" "What is the mean distance between the earth and the sun?" etc. With regard to God, we can ask, "What evidence can be offered for the existence of God?" "What counter-evidence?" "What meaning does the concept of God have for us?" etc. Among the marks of intellectual maturity is one's ability to understand that certain types of questions lend themselves merely to idle speculation and not to new knowledge.

In his condemnation of traditional speculative philosophy, Hans

Reichenbach examines one of the great fallacies of speculation, *pseudo-explanation*. He writes

> The desire to understand the physical world has at all times led to the question of how the world began. The mythologies of all peoples include primitive versions of the origin of the universe. The best known story of creation, a product of the Hebrew imaginative spirit, is given in the Bible and dates about the ninth century B.C. It explains the world as the creation of God. Its explanation is of the naïve type that satisfies a primitive mind, or a childlike mind, proceeding by anthropomorphic analogies: as humans make homes and tools and gardens, God made the world. One of the most general and fundamental questions, that of the genesis of the physical world, is answered by an analogy with experiences of the daily environment. That pictures of this kind do not constitute an explanation, that, if they were true, they would make the problem of an explanation only more difficult to solve, has often been rightly argued. The story of creation is a pseudo-explanation.
>
> And yet—what a suggestive power lives in it! The Jewish people, then still in a primitive stage, gave the world a narrative so vivid as to have fascinated all readers down to our day. Our imagination is held in thrall by the awe-inspiring picture of a god whose spirit moved upon the face of the waters and who set all the world into being by a few commands. Deep innate desires for a powerful father are satisfied by this brilliant antique fiction. The satisfaction of psychological desires, however, is not an explanation. Philosophy has always been impaired by a confusion of logic with poetry, of rational explanation with imagery, of generality with analogy. Many a philosophical system is like the Bible, a masterpiece of poetry, abundant in pictures that stimulate our imagination, but devoid of the power of clarification that issues from scientific explanation.
>
> (*The Rise of Scientific Philosophy*, pp. 8–9.)

To be sure, discussions of the unknown have their emotional and psychological meanings. But substantive intellectual meaning is of a different order, and we must not confuse meanings of soul and psyche with meanings of intellect. We need not derogate one to the presumed benefit of the other; each has its proper range of operation. The problems arise when one is wrongfully substituted for the other. Thus a man may sway voters by playing on the powerful emotions associated with religion and nationality.

We have by no means exhausted this endlessly fascinating subject, but have opened a considerable number of areas for exploration. (Others will be touched on in the projects below.) In brief, we can say that meaning on the communicator's side is his intent, on the receiver's side his understanding. The intent, however, is often conveyed only poorly or not at all, for while language itself has extraordinary potential for transferring meaning, there are, as it were, a number of bugs in the system, not the least of which is human frailty of several kinds. Hence, what is *understood* may bear little or no resemblance to what is *meant*. An appreciation of the possibilities for failure can go a long way to minimizing failure. The study of meaning should, after all, have the end of improving communication.

Implications for Teaching

There is perhaps no dimension of language study more enthralling, or frustrating, than the study of meaning. This affords both opportunity and challenge. The projects that follow will provide inductively a basis for exploring meaning. With suitable modifications the questions can and should be used at every grade level, for as the child matures his techniques for asking and answering questions will mature, and responses to any given question will change, reflecting this growth often dramatically, from year to year.

1. Make a list of contexts in which you would use some form of *to mean* (e.g., *Keep off the grass—this means you; She's a nuisance, but she means well; Woe is me, life has lost all its meaning*, etc.). Try to explain the meaning of *mean* (in any of its forms) in each example. How many different meanings can you isolate?

2. In the exercise above we looked at the diversity of meanings that can be drawn from one root word, namely, *mean*. Now let us try to pin down what meaning itself is. First of all, what is the difference between a word and the "thing" it labels? Is it possible to know the "thing" without having a word for it? Explain. Can you explain what you mean when you say that you "know what you mean" but you "can't explain it"? In *Matters of Style*, a book on writing, Professor J. Mitchell Morse writes

> A person who says, "I know what I mean, but I just can't say it," is wrong. He can't say it because he doesn't know what he means, and he doesn't know what he means because he can't say it. He hasn't worked out his thought. When he works it out—when he composes it as a sentence—then he will know what he means, for it will be clear. Thoughts are not born clear, they are made clear. No clear sentence, no clear thought. We can't have deep or subtle or clear thoughts if we lack the language to construct them, (p. 6).

Do you agree or disagree? In either case, support your point of view convincingly. If you speak or write to someone and he responds in a way that suggests he *misunderstood* you, what actually has happened? What *is* "misunderstanding"? How do you become aware that there has been some kind of misunderstanding of your communication? How can misunderstanding be corrected? Can you set up a chart or table of types of misunderstanding? Include, if possible, methods for overcoming each type. Can you explain what it is to *understand*? How is *meaning* implicated? Make a list of your recent failures in understanding. Try to explain the reasons for each failure. What does each require in order that you achieve understanding?

3. Try to define (for, say, a person seeking *useful* information) a few words like the following: *the, tall, spiral, pain, bacterium, centrifuge, love, anguish, patience, is, excitement, birdbrain, wiseguy, snob, Christmas spirit,* etc. (Don't use a dictionary until you've defined the words as well as you can without it.) Explain how you tackled each problem in definition; *i.e.,* what was your method or "philosophy" of definition? Can all of these words be defined according to the same principles? Explain. How are your definitions similar to and different from those of your dictionary? Compare the definitions of these words in several different dictionaries. Are there differences among the definitions? Discuss. Are your definitions in any way unsatisfactory? How? What about those of the dictionary? Which words seem easier to define than others? Explain. Which seem more difficult? Explain. If words are defined by other words, are we not in danger of losing touch with "reality"? What is the relationship between words and "reality"? What is the difference between defining the word *elephant* and defining the thing *elephant*? Try to define the reality *singing* and the reality *thinking*. Contrast the two definitions according to ease or difficulty, adequacy, etc., and try to account for these differences. Do definitions ever cause you difficulty in communication? Explain the circumstances and the difficulties. Make a dictionary of words and terms that you and your friends regularly use in ways different from the ways your parents and older relatives and acquaintances use them. Try to define each word in a way that will make your meaning for it clear to these "outsiders." Discuss the problems involved in such an undertaking. How do you suppose that dictionary makers (*lexicographers*) arrive at their definitions? New words enter the language every day and until they are defined "formally" (for purposes of dictionary-making), their definitions must be found elsewhere. Do some thinking and some research, if possible, about this and make a report on your findings. Make believe you are trying to define some new words in (1) space science, (2) medical science, (3) international politics, etc., that have started to appear in newspapers and magazines (e.g., *vietnamization*).

4. Our language is filled with *metaphors*. We speak, for example, of the *mouth* of a river, the *eye* of a hurricane, the *bridge* of a nose, a *shot in the arm, the shadow of a doubt, loss of face, hogwash,* and so on. Explain the meaning of these and a dozen or so others you can find in daily conversation. How do the metaphorical meanings relate to the referents they are meant to identify? Of what use in communication are metaphors? Try writing a paragraph or two on any subject that interests you

without using metaphors. Then write the same passage and use as many metaphors as you feel appropriate to the content. Metaphors occur widely in imaginative literature but frequently are of a different kind than the ones listed above. Give some examples of "poetic" metaphors. Try rewriting a poem by substituting explicit language for metaphorical language. What happens? Of what value is the metaphor to poetry (or any kind of elevated writing)?

5. In addition to specific, concrete referents (*denotations*), many words are at the center of a galaxy of meanings (*connotations*). Each user of the words has some (but certainly not all) of these meanings in his personal experience. For example, *ship* for the average landlubber will denote "ocean-going vessel" and connote but a few meanings derived perhaps from reading; but for the sailor, the connotations of *ship* are numerous and intense. Choose a dozen or so fairly common words, give for each its denotation and its connotational field; that is, the connotations you have for it. Then try to assign an emotive value to the word on a scale from zero (no emotion) to ten (intense emotion). Explain the emotion and, using + and −, indicate whether the emotion is positive (pleasant) or negative (unpleasant). Try to account for your reaction to the word. Then try writing two accounts of a recent event using first "positive" vocabulary, then "negative" vocabulary. (Don't confuse "positive" and "negative" with *affirmatives*, e.g, yes, absolutely, etc.; and *negators*, e.g., no, not, etc.) Describe the effect of each account. Try to find examples of this kind of *slanting* and *loaded language* in news reports on TV, newspaper and magazine articles, etc. What does this suggest about the *reliability* of these sources? Contrast the use of language in news articles and editorial columns. Discuss the differences, if there are any. Are such differences as you may find in anything but word choice. Return now to the original list of words and add to the connotational range of each by finding out what other people associate with them. How well does your connotational field match with theirs? Under what circumstances might some degree of mismatch cause problems in communication? Can you exemplify any of these problems from actual personal experience? Discuss.

6. Read a newspaper or news magazine very carefully and try to pick out as many different ways as you can in which the publication is *misleading* the reader. Try rewriting a few passages in a way that seems to present a fairer, more reliable view. Characterize the differences in intent between news reporting and editorializing. Write as reliable a news report as you can of a recent event. Then write an editorial concerning that same event. Describe your procedure in each case.

7. Mingled in whatever sense we manage to convey is a great deal of nonsense. But nonsense is of numerous kinds. Make a compendium of

nonsense that you detect in your listening and reading, attempt to classify or categorize it, and explain wherein the nonsensicality of each example lies. Does nonsense serve any useful purpose? Explain.

8. Aristotle asserted that all realia (things, entities, etc.) contained within them something he called *entelechy* (Gr., *entelekheia*, "complete reality"), which was responsible for each entity's fulfillment of its nature. Thus, a rock was a rock because its entelechy made it a rock. Would you judge this to be a reasonable idea? Discuss the kind of meaning such an idea has. Can one demonstrate the actual existence of the entelechy? How may Aristotle have arrived at such an idea? Do a little research and see if you can discover how some well-known modern scientific theory was arrived at. How can any of these ideas be tested or examined? What part does language seem to play in these ideas and in their examination?

9. If one attaches an *s* to, for example, *book*, the *s*, which by itself has no meaning, takes on the meaning *plural*. Can you explain how this meaning suddenly comes into being? Find some comparable meanings but use examples other than plurality, such as *irritate/irritated/irritating*.

10. Make a list of compounds, such as *nightfall, water spout, water rat, shellfish, shell shock, foot stool, piano stool,* etc., and try to explain how each element of the compound contributes to the meaning of the whole compound. Note, for example, that while both *foot* and *piano* modify *stool*, the relationship between a foot and a stool is a good bit different from the relationship between a piano and a stool. Also note that modifier-noun constructs like *blue bird* (as in *a very blue bird*) should not be taken for compounds (in this case, *bluebird*). Graphic conventions are not necessarily helpful in making this distinction (*woodcock* and *wood duck* are both compounds, even though one is spelled as a single word and one as two words). *Intonation* is the best clue. Say *That is a blue bird* (the bird's color is blue) against *This is a bluebird* (a bird of a certain species). Technically, the contrast is between / ˆ ′ / and / ′ ˋ /; that is, between two sets of *stress* (loudness) *patterns: secondary-primary* and *primary-tertiary*. Say the examples over a few times and you will easily hear the differences in loudness. These patterns can be called (1) modifier / noun superfix (*blûe bírd*) and (2) compound superfix (*blúebìrd*).

11. Both *prefixation* and *suffixation* modify root elements of words in order to create new meanings, hence "new" words. Compare *possible/ impossible; generate/generation; appear/reappear; absolute/absolutely/ absolutism; penetrate/penetration/impenetrable,* etc. What kinds of meanings do prefixes and suffixes convey? Make a collection (in addition to the examples above) of words to which affixes (prefix and/or suffix) have been added. Explain precisely how the root in each case has been modified by affix. Which of these can be made redundant by context. *Impossible*, for example, can be expressed as *not possible; reappear* can be expressed by *appear again*, and so on. Are there any subtle differences in meaning between these two ways of saying the "same thing"? Make a catalogue of commonly occurring affixes. Define the meaning (or meanings) of each and show how each is used. Try creating some new words out of old by adding prefixes or suffixes appropriate to some useful meaning. Thus we might find it handy to have a word like *unsad* (*un*, "not," + *sad*), which doesn't mean quite the same thing as *happy*. (Compare the advertising word *un-cola*.) By way of a footnote to this project on affixes, you might like to try finding out why the "same" affix can occur in several forms; *im*possible, *in*ept, *ir*respective, *ig*noble, etc.

12. Choose several passages from poems, plays, or stories and read each several times aloud with a different intonation each time. Ask someone to listen to your various readings of each and try to characterize both the differences in meaning you were trying to suggest and the differences in intonation you used. Reverse the roles and have someone read to you. What kinds of meaning are possible through intonational changes? Listen to two or three different recorded versions of a play, and choose two or three key passages for close comparison. Write a report in which you explain where the differences lie and what effect dominates each version. Discuss what you learned about meaning in literature from working through this project.

13. Find several translations into English of the same work of literature. These are readily available for a number of European classics: the Greek classical tragedies, the *Iliad* and the *Odyssey*, Goethe's *Faust*, etc. Choose two or three passages for close examination. How does each passage differ from the other? How is each similar to the other? Characterize the "feeling" of each. To what extent does the meaning of each passage seem to be affected by the translation? (Without being able to read the original fluently, you will have to get at this inferentially.) Explain how you interpret the term *meaning* in this context. What does such a comparison of passages tell you about literature in translation? If you can find someone who reads the language of the original work, ask him to give you a more-or-less literal translation of the passages you have chosen for this project. This should be helpful to you in working through the project. If you are studying a foreign language, try your hand at translating a passage or two from a piece of literature. Is translating word for word a satisfactory solution? Explain. Can you develop a "philosophy" of translation? Can you determine what philosophy of translation the translators of the various versions used to arrive at their versions? How does one transfer *meaning* from langauge to language? Does there seem to be any merit in the assertion by Werner Winter that

we may compare the work of a translator with that of an artist who is asked to create an exact replica of a marble statue, but who cannot secure any marble.

("Impossibilities of Translation," in *The Craft and Context of Translation*, p. 93.)

Discuss.

14. Various techniques to "measure" meaning have been contrived. One such technique is to set up a series of scales, the poles of which are adjectival opposites, e.g., good————bad; hard————soft; active ————passive, etc. The scales are divided into intensities (*extremely, very,* etc.) from either end, the midpoint representing neutrality. Thus, *baby, house,* and *love,* for example, would each "live" in its own *semantic space* as specifically delineated by the test scales. Attempt to define the semantic space of a wide range of nouns using this technique. Add other scales if doing so seems to promise more precise and useful measurement. Then try developing scales appropriate to *verbs, adjectives,* and *adverbs.* What practical use might be made of the findings of this experiment? Can you imagine, for example, a new kind of dictionary based on semantic space? Try setting up a few typical entries for such a dictionary. What advantage might this kind of dictionary have over present dictionaries? Once you have worked through this project you should have some sense of the weaknesses and drawbacks of the technique in actually accomplishing its purpose, namely, that of measuring meaning. What are these weaknesses? Can the technique be refined in any way? Can you contrive any other techniques for measuring meaning?

15. In a sentence, the components stand in a formal as well as a semantic relationship to each other. The key semantic relationships arise between the sentence verb and its associated nouns. Thus the semantic relationship between *Harold* and *supper* is quite different in these two sentences:

1. Harold sang for his supper.
2. Harold ate his supper.

Can you describe the nature of the relationship in each sentence and the nature of differences between the two sentences? Now try these:

3. Nellie gave Harold a candy bar.
4. Harold got a candy bar.
5. Harold parked his car.
6. Harold's car is parked.
7. Harold fixed the chair with glue.
8. The chair was glued.
9. Harold felt good.

10. Harold felt the texture of the wood.

And so on. If you examine a sufficiently large and diverse sampling, you should be able to identify all the fundamental semantic relationships in the language. (See Wallace L. Chafe, *Meaning and the Structure of Language* and Geoffrey N. Leech, *Towards a Semantic Description of English.*)

16. Though most dictionaries provide synonyms for various words and though works like Roget's *Thesaurus* are built on the notion of synonymy, it has been said that "there is no true synonymy." Can you work out a method for testing synonymy? Does your experiment with synonymy tend to support the assertion that there is no true synonymy, or does it tend to support the idea of the thesaurus?

17. Many words have "opposites," that is, antonyms. Make a list of words and their presumed opposites. Are the opposites always obvious or unequivocal? (One might take *music* to be the opposite of *noise* as easily as the opposite of *silence*.) What causes the doubt or ambiguity in each case? What words and kinds of words can you find no opposites for? Why don't these have opposites? Can you explain what the concept of "opposite" here means? Is this opposition always reversible? Consider: if *short* is the opposite of *tall*, is *tall* necessarily the opposite of *short*? What about *long* as the opposite of *short*?

18. Many words are, as it were, self-explanatory, or "transparent," like *hiss, lightbulb, eyebrow*. But many such as *dog, cat, walk, talk* are "opaque" or unrevealing of their meaning. Make a list exemplifying each type and explain the differences between the types; that is, how does a self-explanatory word in fact explain itself? What makes the opaque word opaque? Does there seem to be any relationship between the etymological source of the word and its membership in one group or the other? Using an English-German/German-English dictionary, compare a selection of opaque English words with their German equivalents. (For example: *cotton* = German, *die Baumwolle*, literally, "tree wool." *Habit* = *Lebensweise*, lit., "manner of living." *Royal* = *königlich*, lit., "king-like.")

19. When you say that something you have read or heard is "meaningless," what precisely do you intend to convey by that word? (Saying that "meaningless" means "incapable of being understood," or words to that effect, does not really explain anything; rather, you have merely rephrased the original term.) Offer specific examples of communications that you feel are "meaningless" and discuss what would be required to make them "meaningful." While you're at it, explain what *meaningful* means to you.

20. At various times in your life you have probably been involved in a "failure in communication." Try to diagnose a few of these failures. The "generation gap" is presumably such a failure. Diagnose some examples of the generation gap. (These need not be based on your personal experience but may be if you wish.) Can you develop a set of rules or principles that might alleviate or even prevent such failures in communication?

21. At various times in your life, you have suddenly become aware of something or understood something that you were unaware of or failed to understand before. Explain what seems to have happened to make you aware or bring you to understanding.

22. The type of referential meaning that is signalled by words like *house, tree, book,* etc., is relatively easy to discuss and understand. But consider the following words: *heaven, spirit, unicorn, vampire, truth, metaphysical, astral projection, success, belief,* etc. Can these words be defined? How? To what realia do they point? What do these words and other words you can easily add mean to you when you encounter them in reading or conversation?

23. Gestures and facial expressions convey a considerable number of meanings. Attempt to contrive a "gestural dictionary" that will be useful to our visitor from the flying saucer. As a preliminary step, write a report discussing the types of meanings that can be conveyed gesturally, to what extent these meanings are free of language involvement, how we learn these meanings. Then figure out some rational and self-explaining way of presenting your gestural vocabulary to the man from the flying saucer, who is bright and interested but very literal-minded. Have you ever been in a communication situation in which gestural signals were misinterpreted or mis-produced? If so, discuss the nature of the particular problem. You may enjoy reading an account of non-verbal human communication by an anthropologist: Edward T. Hall, *The Silent Language,* 1959. Cross-cultural misinterpretation of gestures has frequently caused very serious problems in communication.

24. When we call someone we don't like a "bad name," what are we doing? Many people will fight because they have been called "bad names." Why? The ancient Greeks called the Furies, which were believed to be frightful beyond description, *Eumenides,* the "well-disposed ones." In a similar vein, many people today speak of *dying* as "passing away." Why? Track down some other examples of euphemism and try to account for each. Make a list of words that sound unpleasant to you and try to account for your feeling in each case.

25. Here are two statements of quite different kinds:

1. *Hamlet* is a marvelous play.

2. $y^2 = \dfrac{x^3}{2a - x}$.

How are they different? Determine as well as you can all of the meanings resident in each. What kind of a language (in terms of meanings) is the "language of mathematics"? What relationship does mathematical language bear to "natural" language? When people use, for example, the term *average* ("He's an average kind of person") do they mean what the statistician means when he speaks of a *numerical average?* Explain the meaning of each and discuss the differences.

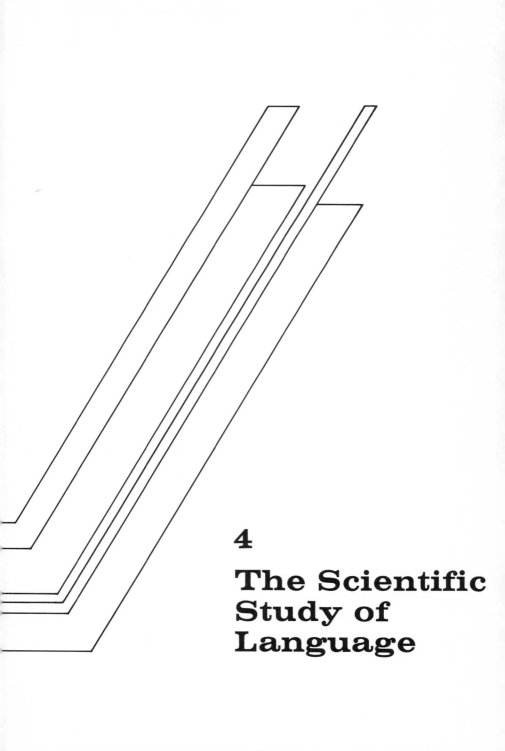

4

The Scientific
Study of
Language

Linguistics, like any other science, builds on the past; and it does so, not only by challenging and refuting traditional doctrines, but also by developing and reformulating them.

(John Lyons, *Introduction to Theoretical Linguistics*, London.)

Although linguistics as a science is relatively new, man's interest in the nature and origin of language dates at least as far back as historical antiquity. The ancient Greek historian Herodotus (484–432 B.C.) tells us that an Egyptian pharaoh, Psammetichos by name, was (with commendable curiosity) concerned to find out which was the most ancient of languages believing, erroneously of course, that the "oldest" language would also be the most "primitive" and the one from which all the other languages would have either evolved or descended. He theorized further that this presumed original, primitive language must be instinctive in man. To prove his theory he devised an experiment to identify such a language. Two infants were put in the care of a shepherd with instructions that they be reared in strict isolation from any human voice. The shepherd was to see to their well-being and to inform the pharaoh of any sounds made by the children that resembled human speech. After two years, they were heard to say something resembling *bekos*. The pharoah's linguistic advisers identified this as the word for *bread* in Phrygian (the language of Phrygia, a province in Asia Minor); and the pharaoh concluded that Phrygian must be the oldest, hence the original "parent," language. This naïve notion—that older languages are more primitive and that primitive languages are contemporary—did not disappear with the ancient Egyptians. Many otherwise well-educated people today mistakenly equate technological primitivism with linguistic primitivsm; and one can hear such people asserting that, for example, the American Indian languages consist of nothing but a few grunts. Let Robert A. Hall, Jr., repudiate this:

> There must have been a stage at which human speech was much less developed than it is at present, but that period was at least hundreds of thousands of years ago, and no traces of it have survived anywhere. All languages spoken at present, even those of American Indian, African, or Australian Bushman tribes, have reached substantially the same stage of development and are equally susceptible to linguistic analysis.
>
> (*Introductory Linguistics*, p. 14.)

The biblical story of the Tower of Babel marks the first recorded attempt to account for the diversity of tongues; at different times, various languages have been credited with being "the first," "the most pure," and so on. Hebrew, by virtue of its biblically attested antiquity as well as its status as the language of sacred scripture, has frequently been honored as the first and parent language. The scholars of seventeenth- and eighteenth-century Europe accorded Latin first place among languages. (A number of English teachers to this very day retail the misinformation that English "comes from" Latin.)

Thus, early approaches to the study of language were often fanciful and influenced by myth, folklore, superstition, and outright ignorance. This legacy of linguistic naïveté continued well past the Middle Ages despite occasional pieces of sound linguistic work done here and there. Generally, instead of examining the available linguistic data objectively, these early students of language preferred to make the facts of language fit a variety of preconceived "principles."

The philosophical foundations of language study were laid down by the Greeks, who, though intensely interested in the nature of language, limited their speculations to Greek as the only language worthy of their attention. Other languages were, after all, barbaric (from the Greek, *barbarismos,* "incorrect speech"). This curious attitude existed despite the fact that the Greeks were great travelers and accomplished speakers of many languages and often served as royal interpreters.

It was the Sophists (fifth century B.C.), those resolute empiricists of antiquity, who, in their zeal to reduce everything to neat measurement, dug the cellarage, so to speak, for later linguistic masonry. Their prime concern in language was to determine what constitutes its "best" use, and they quite naturally turned to the work of the great rhetoricians of the age. Their labors produced what for the Western world is still the basic vocabulary of rhetorical terminology. They likewise made significant observations on certain elements in phonology. But since their purpose was not the study of language *qua* language, their contributions to the linguistics of the day were of small moment. It is not until we come to the *Cratylus* of Plato (427?–347 B.C.) that we find the Greek world knee-deep in great linguistic issues. The *Cratylus* is dominated by the controversy between those who believe that the words of a language are the consequence of what those words designate—which is rather like saying that a *bird* is called a *bird* because it looks like a *bird* —and those who believe that words are merely conventions—which is rather like saying that a bird is called a bird because we agreed to call it something and *bird* was as good a thing to call it as anything. This controversy goes by the name of *physis-nomos* (literally "natural-name") and points to the notion of "natural" naming as against "conventional" naming. The discussion that Plato gives to Socrates in mediating this controversy turns out to be an important step in Greek linguistic-philosophical reasoning. But while the *Cratylus* is primarily concerned with *etymology,** the *Theatetus* and *Sophists* focus on questions of relationships among language, thought, and reality. In the latter dialogue, not to be confused with the philosophical school known as the Sophists, Plato addressed himself to the problems of definition, which is principally a semantic matter. By the technique known as division, definitions are arrived at based on the concept of *genus* and *species;* that is, the general category subsuming a set of particulata. Thus his definition of *fishing* as "the art [the *genus* of the whole definition] of acquiring, by capture, live animals living in fluid, namely fish, by striking with a stroke from below by day." Not the most satisfactory definition of fishing, but significant in its effort at methodological rigor and philosophical consistency. The *Theatetus* introduces the philosophical concepts of *onoma* and *rhēma*, which in their grammatical application came close to our traditional notions of noun and verb, or as they can be translated from Plato, "the name of the doer" (*onoma*) and "the name of that which is done" (*rhēma*). A third term, *logos*, is used by Plato to mean a number of things including what we would call a sentence. Thus, Plato has given us at least the tentative beginnings of a linguistic description, although we must appreciate that his primary focus was semantic and not structural. In the *physis-nomos* controversy, which came to be known as the *Analogist-Anomalist* controversy, Plato's position seems to have been on the side of the *nomos* (Anomalist) position, namely, that there is no "natural" connection between words and things.

What of linguistic matters is merely hinted at or suggested by Plato, Aristotle (384–322 B.C.) explored in detail and enlarged upon. In such works as *On Interpretation, Categories, Rhetoric,* and *Poetics,* Plato's famous pupil not only noted important stylistic differences between speaking and writing but recognized the existence of various levels on which language can be studied. His intensely analytic mind likewise led him to identify sentence types as well as word types and meanings both in isolation and in context. He was a four-square anomalist, holding that the connection between sounds and meanings (*i.e.,* between words and their referents) was wholly arbitrary and conventional within any given language.

It was the Stoics (fourth century B.C. to about A.D. 180) who were most obsessively concerned with language, for it was their philosophical belief that in order to conduct onself with due propriety one must live in harmony with nature and further that knowledge required the conformity of one's ideas with this reality. The implication of this point is

---

* From the Greek words *etymos* "true" or "real," and *logos,* "word." Thus etymology means "finding the true shape and signification of words" and presumably of nature.

that ideas are the image of reality, and since ideas are bodied forth in language, language then is the logical focal point of Stoic philosophy. While they examined many dimensions of language, identifying five "parts of speech," the concept of case, and several characteristics of verbs, their most extensive work was in logic, in particular the syllogism. Yet their work in grammar was robust enough to have influenced the study of language in the Western world for some two thousand years.

It was left for the Alexandrian Dionysius Thrax (second century B.C.) to bring together the bits and pieces of linguistic insight left by his predecessors. His short (about four hundred lines of text) but notable work, translated into Latin by Remmius Palaemon as *Ars Grammatica* (*The Art of Grammar*), was to become the model on which all subsequent works of grammar—not only of Greek and Latin but of most European languages—would be based for the next two millenia. The advent of Imperial Rome did not diminish the status of Greek art and science, and Rome borrowed from the conquered Hellenes in carload lots. Wealthy Romans sent their sons to Greece much as the Russians much later would send theirs to France. Many a Roman household had its Greek tutor-slave into whose tuition the sons would be given, and fashionable Romans affected Greek as the fashionable Russians affected French.* In time, Greek schools sprang up throughout Italy, and Latin learning of grammar and rhetoric kept the Greek tradition alive, perpetuating it through Empire and Church into the Middle Ages and beyond.

In essence, Dionysius Thrax analyzed Greek into eight parts of speech: noun, verb, participle, article, pronoun, preposition, adverb, and conjunction. He defined each class and outlined its uses in the sentence. He further classified all Greek words as to gender, number, case, tense, mood, "kind" (voice), "type" (root or derivative), and "form" (similar to "type"). He discussed syllables and letters (showing some appreciation for the difference between letters and sounds) and offered some instruction in "correct expression" as practiced by respected writers. His definition of grammar is worth quoting here:

> Grammar is the technical knowledge of language generally employed by poets and writers. It has six parts: (1) correct pronunciation, (2) explanation of the principal poetic tropes, (3) preservation and explanation of glosses and mythological examples, (4) the discovery of etymologies, (5) the discovery of analogies, and (6) a critical consideration of the compositions of poets, which is the most noble part of this science.
> (Quoted in F. P. Dinneen, *An Introduction to General Linguistics*, p. 98.)

---

* Plutarch tells us that Caesar's last words were not the Latin *Et tu, Brute* but the Greek *kaì dú, téknon,* "And you, child?"

The didactic spirit of this incredibly influential little work has shaped language study until very recent times and has, alas, often blinded the student of language to the nature of language itself.

Thus, among the contributions of the Greeks to the study of language are (1) the invention of a metalanguage; i.e., a linguistic terminology, a necessary step in any field of rational inquiry; (2) the identification of certain language entities; e.g., nouns, verbs, etc.; and (3) the practice of prescriptive analysis based on written language. They likewise fixed the forms and modes of logic and urged that this was the "correct" and "universal" logic of language, upon which all thought should be based.

As the Romans were sedulous followers of Greek grammatical thinking, it was fortunate for Roman grammarians (and unfortunate for later grammarians) that Latin was in many respects similar to Greek, though was it by no means derived from Greek. Forcing Latin, therefore, into the framework of Greek grammar was not difficult, though some accommodations had to be made. From the standpoint of the developing discipline of grammar study, however, the most important influence of the Greek tradition was the prescriptivism based upon the written language. Indeed, the attitude persists still that written language is somehow "better," more "authoritative" than speech.

Marcus Terentius Varro, a contemporary of Dionysius Thrax, was engaged by the analogy-anomaly controversy and produced a study of Latin, De Lingua Latina, that ran to twenty-five volumes. Though thorough and detailed, the work seemed to have had little or no influence on the grammatical thinking of the age. From our point of view, perhaps Varro's most original observation was the difference he detected between a language in general and that language as it is actually spoken, which appears to be precisely the distinction the modern linguist Ferdinand de Saussure makes between what he calls la langue and la parole. On the other hand, Varro did clearly present an analysis of the parts of speech based primarily upon form rather than meaning vis-à-vis language as it is actually spoken.

With Donatus (fourth century A.D.) and Priscian (sixth century A.D.) the Western grammatical tradition hardened into the mold that was to characterize it well into our own age. The great value of Priscian's grammar is the insight it affords us into the Latin of the age, for the work is the most accurate and most nearly complete description of Latin by a native speaker. Nor can we overlook the profound influence the format and orientation of the grammar has had on grammar study over the years from Priscian's time to ours. It is the direct ancestor of the so-called traditional school grammar—whether for Latin, French, English, or virtually any other European language.

Through historical accident Latin became the language of Church scholarship, which meant in fact all scholarship, and its medium of instruction in medieval times. Yet this was the period in which the several Latin dialects developing in different parts of Europe had deviated sufficiently from the parent Latin to be mutually unintelligible, emerging as what we now call the Romance languages (Italian, French, Spanish, Portuguese, Rumanian, and a few minor tongues). The grammarians of the age, bound to the classical Latin language and the linguistic traditions of the Greeks, insisted on imposing the "rules" of Dionysius Thrax and his successors to these emerging languages and any others with which they dealt. They had some success with the Romance languages, of course, for these did descend directly from Latin. Elsewhere, the results were less happy. The "universal" Greco-Latin grammar soon became a bed of Procrustes; and when the facts of a language did not square with the "rules," the facts were altered accordingly. Since the received grammatical principles were considered a branch of universal logic, which in turn was considered immutable, conflicts between rules and usage were disallowed. The rules prevailed.

English was a language the grammarians labored mightily to "latinize." And they achieved a certain specious success by imposing rules and ignoring difficulties. But English will, after all, not be bound by Latin or Greek grammar. Though English and Latin (and Greek and Russian and Armenian and Sanskrit, etc.) are "cousin" languages by virtue of their mutual descent from *Indo-European*, the postulated parent language of our language family, English belongs to the Germanic branch and Latin to the Italic. The grammatical habits of each of these branches as well as the grammatical habits of the individual languages within these branches are distinctive and are not usefully dealt with in terms of each other. In any case, the cultural preëminence of Latin during a period in the development of Western civilization gives the language no special linguistic authority. It is merely, from a purely linguistic point of view, another language. This was not the thinking that obtained, however, during the "latinizing" period (mainly through the Renaissance and Neo-Classical periods). The continuing dominance of Latin, and to a lesser extent Greek, in the great educational centers resulted in a bias in the vernacular language in favor of latinate constructions, latinate vocabulary, and Greco-Latin rhetorical figures of speech. The so-called "battle of the Purists and the Inkhornists" sprang from these efforts to gild the language, the Purists pleading for a return to the native "purity" of English, the Inkhornists for a "glorification" of English. Sir John Cheke (1514–57), Regius Professor of Greek at Cambridge and tutor to Edward VI, sets forth, with much energy and pedantry, the purist doctrine in a letter to Thomas Hoby, translator of Castiglione's *Courtier*. Here is a brief excerpt (in Cheke's own "reformed" spelling):

I am of this opinion that our own tung shold be written cleane and pure, vnmixt and vnmangled with borowing of other tunges, wherein if we take not heed by tijm, euer borowing and neuer paying, she shall be fain to keep her house as bankrupt. For then doth our tung naturallie and praisablie vtter her meaning, whan she bouroweth no counterfeitness of other tunges to attire her self withall, but vseth plainlie her own. . . .

The works of Sir Thomas Browne and John Lyly exemplify the Ink-hornist position in practice, the King James Bible (1611) the Purist. Fortunately, neither position prevailed and general English struck a reasonably happy balance, though the prescriptive grammarians of the eighteenth century labored to force the inherently Germanic habits of English into Greco-Latin patterns and to give their grammatical statements the force of law by calling upon the "authority" of long-dead writers who wrote in languages that behaved quite differently from English.

But the winds of change were blowing and Europe's linguistic insularity was soon to end (at least among serious scholars, if not among the schoolmasters). Sir William Jones (1746–94), a functionary of the British Raj in India and something of an amateur philologist, interested himself in the languages of India and in Sanskrit in particular, his studies convincing him that Sanskrit

> bears a stronger affinity [to Greek and Latin], both in the roots of the verbs and in the forms of the grammar, than could possibly have been produced by accident; so strong, indeed, that no philologer could examine them all three without believing them to have sprung from some common source, which, perhaps, no longer exists; there is a similar reason, though not quite so forcible, for supposing that both the Gothick and the Celtick, though blended with a very different idiom, had the same origin with the Sanskrit.
>
> (Quoted in H. Pedersen, *The Discovery of Language, Linguistic Science in the Nineteenth Century,* p. 18.)

With Jones's evidence and clear statement of principle, it was not long before new branches of language study emerged. The first was what we now call *comparative linguistics* and concerned itself with comparing various languages to determine and attempt to account for similarities and differences between and among them. It was soon realized that comparisons had to be made with a view to historical dimensions of language and *historical linguistics* (now often called *diachronic linguistics*) evolved. Philologists, as linguists were termed, recognized that a "parent" language had to precede its "offspring." In order to assume a "parent" or "source" language for a progeny consisting of both European and Asiatic languages, it is necessary that the period of time during which the hypothetical language flourished be more remote in time than any of its offspring. Since the "daughter" languages were known to exist well before the Christian era, the hypothetical language was placed in a position of authority formerly granted Greek and Latin. Moreover, the new comparative/historical linguists were interested primarily in the relationships *between* languages, and grammar was important only insofar as it accomplished the purpose of helping to show these relationships. There was no interest in establishing prescriptive rules to be applied to a language that might be older hence more authoritative than the "authority" used in making the rules. The linguistic approach had now shifted from subjective to objective. "New" languages (which is to say, languages previously ignored) were learned, masses of data accumulated, and lifetimes spent poring over data, classifying it, and trying to establish objectively valid rules that would account for the correspondences being found among the now named *Indo-European* (or *Indo-Germanic*) language family. A detailed view of the great comparative/historical linguistic studies of the nineteenth century can be got from Pedersen's *The Discovery of Language*. Of particular interest in the work is the wealth of language samples (with translations) offered by way of illustration.

Careful historical/comparative studies of the sounds (phonetics) of the various languages revealed that changes occurred systematically and that these changes could be related to other languages within the same family. Further, it was found that words, inflections, and even syntax undergo systematic change. By working backwards through written records that illustrated the known changes, linguists could limn patterns of development, patterns that in turn could be projected into a remote period of time for which no written records existed. This provided a sound, though inferential basis for the hypothetical parent language ("Indo-European"). Dialects as well as the major languages were accorded intensive study and it soon became apparent that contemporary dialect differences from area to area, geographical as well as social, provided much valuable insight into the problems of language change. This concentration on language at a given point in time (and without regard to the past) is called synchronic linguistics and the theories and methods that arose from this new way of looking at language were eventually to have profound effects on the classroom study of language.

Although linguistics was already a burgeoning science by the early nineteenth century, the orientation of its academic linguists was predominantly historical. During this period the linguist occupied himself almost exclusively with written materials, despite the fact that the sounds of living languages are most accessible of approach and most readily amenable to scientific analysis. Rather than devising accurate descriptions of the sound systems of modern languages and drawing phonological theories from them, the linguists of this era resorted to statements about the use of "letters" in the "writing" of languages; *i.e.*, they were really talking about reading rules. The concept of field work with spoken languages was known only to missionaries working in remote areas of Africa and Asia, and their connection with academic circles was as yet too tenuous to allow much feedback.

But as linguistics moved into the twentieth century, it advanced quickly beyond the historicism that had dominated it. Indeed, it was to a certain extent the exigencies of the historical/comparative approach that forced linguists to undertake the descriptivism that became the dominant mode of twentieth-century linguistics. It is Ferdinand de Saussure (1857–1913) who is credited with being the father of modern descriptive linguistics, for it was he who clearly delineated the boundaries, nature, and applications of synchronic and diachronic linguistics. He was thus a theoretician and his theories organized a diversity of linguistic material and provided a solid foundation for succeeding developments in the science. We have already touched upon his understanding of the term *language* (Chapter II) and need not cover that ground again here other than to remind the reader of implications of his thinking on this issue in contemporary transformational-generative theory. De Saussure's structural approach to the study of language was a major tributary feeding into the "Prague school" of linguistics, the single most important contribution of which was N. S. Trubetskoy's *Grundzüge der Phonologie* (*Principles of Phonology*), published in 1939. This work sets forth the *phonemic* principle, which provided the first workable basis upon which a modern, comprehensive theory of descriptive linguistics could be based.

In America, the first great pioneer in linguistics was the anthropologist Franz Boas (1858–1942), who, with his students, was to become the nucleus of the "American school" of descriptive linguistics. Prior to Boas, linguistic work on the American Indian languages had followed the traditional path of trying to force the facts of these languages into the Greco-Latin mold. Needless to say, little of linguistic value could be expected from this unfortunate liaison. Boas and his followers, however, broke with European grammatical traditionalism to the extent of an almost total unwillingness to admit semantic considerations in grammatical analysis; and distrusting the text-centered work of the historical linguists, the Boas school concentrated on spoken language and promulgated the dogma that "speech alone is language."

The second major figure in the American school was Edward Sapir (1884–1939), a student of Boas and one well versed in developments in contemporary European linguistics. Indeed, it was Sapir who introduced the phoneme theory of the Prague school to America, and for the next thirty years the primacy of the phoneme was seldom questioned. American descriptive linguists, who were at the same time structural linguists, held that all linguistic analysis had to start at the "bottom" with the sound system and its key unit, the phoneme, and work up from there to the "higher" levels of morphology, syntax, and semantics.

In the 1930's and early 1940's, the Boas-Sapir linguistics was supplanted by the ideas of Leonard Bloomfield (1887–1949), who in general followed Sapir but did break important new ground. His single book-length publication, *Language* (1933), dominated American linguistics until the 1950's and served for that time as a kind of bible for young linguists. He provided conceptual unity for a large segment of the profession despite the fact that there never was a completely uniform body of doctrine. So while many linguists differed with Bloomfield on a variety of specific points, they were nevertheless sufficiently alike in their thinking to be in the broad sense, "Bloomfieldians."

Phonetic science, which had led to the development of the phoneme principle, originated in nineteenth-century physiological studies. By turns, psychologists, engineers, physicists, and linguists involved themselves in the new discipline and made their contributions to it; but the multitude of divergent interests and approaches impeded any very rapid progress. It was not until the adoption of statistical methods by phonologists to obtain inventories of the sound elements of a language that it became possible to compare the qualities of the sound system of a language with the actual linguistic behavior (i.e., the speech) of speakers in various speech situations. All native speakers of a language use a common sound system even though the individual manifestations of it (i.e., individual pronunciation) might vary over a fairly wide range of dialects. This posed a vexing question for phonologists: If each language had a fixed system of sounds and all speakers learned the same system, why were such variations possible and how were they at once completely intelligible to all speakers? (Indeed, a language *had* to have a "fixed" or stable sound system, for if every speaker went his own phonetic way, speech communication would become impossible.) The answer that became structuralist doctrine was that many diverse sounds in actual speech were manifestations of a single "idealized" or "abstract" sound unit that every speaker knew "internally." However, because of such influences as education, environment, and personal physiology, these abstract sound units were manifested idiosyncratically; instead of myriad speech sounds, a limited number of distinctive "bundles" of sounds could be postulated. These "bundles," which in a curious way are both abstract and concrete, were called *phonemes* and provided the theoretical ground upon which linguistics as well as phonology would build.

Simply put, speakers of English literally produce an uncountable number of sounds, but these many sounds are always "understood" to be a mere handful. A dozen different people saying, for example, the word *kink* will for the initial and final sounds of that word produce a large number (in sum) of physically different sounds that we will all accept as being k sounds. Or consider *kin* in contrast with *skin*. The first k is accompanied by a strong aspiration, the second k has virtually none. This demonstrates the actual difference between the sounds. But we speakers of English do not notice this difference and consider each sound to be simply a k. This means that we do not treat aspiration in English as distinctive. That is, aspiration alone will not separate sounds in English into contrasting phonemes. The occurrence or non-occurrence of aspiration, then, makes no significant difference, though there are languages in which it would. Just as we respond to *voicing* of consonants while some languages do not.*

Important to the definition of the phoneme was the principle that the phoneme itself carried no meaning, although the presence or absence of a given phoneme could result in meaning or changes of meaning. (Thus none of the phonemes that comprise *pit*, namely, /p/, /i/, and /t/, "means" anything though all three together "cause" meaning. Likewise, if we add *s* to *pit* we modify the meaning of the word to convey the sense of plurality: *pits*. But we don't think of *s* in isolation as expressing any meaning at all.) It is possible for the human vocal apparatus to produce about seventy-two readily distinguishable consonants and forty-two classes of vowels. No one language, however, makes use of all of them. Ubykhian, a language of the northern Caucasus, uses sixty consonant and three vowel phonemes. Bella-Coola, an American Indian language of the Northwest, is alleged to have no vowels. In English we have about forty-five phonemes including those for *pitch*, *stress*, and *juncture* (see Appendix). There appears to be a phoneme inventory from which each language has in the course of its history made selections. While pronunciation may change quite rapidly (over a time base) and even radically, the underlying phoneme system seems to remain relatively stable. (On the interrelationships between writing systems and speech, see Chapter VIII.)

Having satisfactorily resolved phonological problems (for the time being, at least), linguists turned their attention to the "words" of language, seeking a theoretical unit comparable to the phoneme. They noted that some words could be separated into components, each of which carried a meaning, and that some words were indivisible at this level of meaning. A unit of language that conveyed meaning and that could not be subdivided was called a *morpheme*. There are two general types: *free* (e.g., words like *boy*, *girl*, *like*, *learn*, *the*, etc.) and

---

* A *minimal pair* in English can be made with the single phonetic difference of voicing; that is, with the vocal bands vibrating instead of at rest: *kale/gale*, wherein the initial sound of *gale*—*g*—is merely a *k* with voicing added. In many American Indian languages those two words would be thought of as slightly different pronunciations of the "same" word, until at least the speakers of those languages learned to pay attention in the same way we do to the *voicing-unvoicing feature.*

bound (affixes like *-ish, -ly, dis-, un-, -ing, -ed, -s*, etc.). Free and bound morphemes combine to produce complex morphemes (e.g., *boy-ish, girl-ish, learn-ing, un-learn, like-s*, etc.). Free morphemes can combine to form *compound* morphemes: *rail-road, time-table, type-writer*, etc. Morphology is thus the study of linguistic forms and parallels in structural theory; *phonology*, the study of *sounds* (more precisely, the *sound system*). It was upon these analytical levels that structuralism was built. Grammar, including syntax, was to be described by establishing classes of morphemes and selectional and combinatorial rules. *Boy* and *girl*, for example, belong to the same class, a fact that allows them to substitute for each other, without regard to semantic questions, in virtually all syntactic contexts. Referential classes (nouns, verbs, adjectives, and adverbs) were large and "open," that is, they could be added to at will; *structural* or *functional* classes were relatively small and virtually "closed." Thus whenever we need a new noun we simply create it or borrow it. New articles, prepositions, conjunctions, and the like are apparently not needed, nor do we have any mechanisms (such as compounding) for producing them. The task the structuralists set themselves was to tabulate the circumstances under which the member words of each class (and sub-class) could be "grammatically" used.

Structuralism has been called "the great *emic* hunt." That is, having adopted the phoneme as the base unit for phonological analysis, investigators felt compelled to postulate and search for comparable units on all levels. The literature of structuralism includes, in addition to the phoneme and the morpheme (and their variants, the *allophones* and the *allomorphs*—the allophones being the different actual renderings of any given phoneme, the allomorphs, the same for morphemes) such *emic* units as *sememe* (the meaning of a morpheme), *taxeme* (a grammatical feature), *tagmeme* (the smallest meaningful unit of grammatical form), and *episememe* (the meaning of a tagmeme). The interface of phonology and morphology was called *morphophonemics* and concerned itself with the phonological diversity of, say, the allomorphs of the morpheme for plurality (thus: $bug + pl = bugs$, the plural marker being in this pronounced as a z; but $burp + pl = burps$, the plural marker being pronounced s; and $buzz + pl = buzzes$, the plural marker being pronounced *iz*; and so on).

Bloomfield, like many scientists of his day, was strongly influenced by the psychological theories of J. B. Watson (see *Behavior: An Introduction to Comparative Psychology*, 1914). Motivated by Watson's mechanistic or behavioristic approach to all human activities, including speech acts, Bloomfield attempted to eliminate meaning as a tool of analysis. This is not to say that he denied the place of meaning in language, but that he tried to develop rigorous analytical methods ("discovery procedures") that would produce a description of a language without recourse to meanings that may or may not be in a speaker's mind. The "mind," indeed, was for all practical purposes nonexistent in Bloomfieldian theory. Any attempt on the part of students of language to appeal to "ideas," "understood meanings," and the like, for purposes of linguistic analysis was stigmatized as mentalism. The linguist's proper and scientifically sound role was to gather data, and classify, analyze, and describe that data. This approach has been derisively termed *taxonomic* linguistics, a study that makes exhaustive tabulations and explains nothing. Be that as it may, the science needed both the bracing effect of methodological rigor and the neat assemblages of hard data, and Bloomfield's position is not without merit. He wanted to maintain descriptive consistency and precision. He felt that questions of meaning were not capable of objective verification and should therefore be placed outside the field of linguistics proper. Two independently working linguists could agree to the phonetic description of an utterance, agree to the phonemic structure of that utterance, agree to its occurrence in English (*i.e.*, under what linguistic circumstances it is likely to occur), and could further agree on such matters as its compounds and derivatives. They could agree on all these matters while at the same time not necessarily agreeing on the "meaning" of the utterance. Meaning is, after all, the sum of our experiences with a particular word, and no two human beings have identical experiential backgrounds. Concepts as well as connotations may occupy considerable semantic space within our minds. Bloomfieldian rules, therefore, tend to take the form: "In thus-and-such a linguistic environment, the form of the morpheme is—————." Such a statement avoids saying that the language item itself "changes." A complete description of a language, according to Bloomfield, would .

> list every form whose function is not determined either by structure or by a marker; it will include, accordingly, a *lexicon*, or list of morphemes, which indicates the form-class of each morpheme, as well as lists of all complex forms whose function is in any way irregular (*Language*, p. 264.)

What, then, did these developments in the study of language mean for the teaching of English? Looking back to eighteenth-century England, we find lexicographers and encyclopedists dabbling in grammar as a sideline and mixing into their grammatical formulations often as much whimsy as observable fact. The most influential of these "grammarians" were authoritarian and primarily concerned with "propriety" in language, often citing the King James Bible as the proper model for speech. Only when the alleged "proper" patterns were overwhelmingly contradicted by general usage did the prescriptivists defer to actual speech. Those few grammarians who favored local speech as the basis for authority or who moved toward scientific attitudes in language study were not looked upon with favor. Indeed, during the first half of the century there was a movement afoot to establish an English equivalent of the French Academy whose primary purpose it would be to "officially" regulate the language, to "fix and ascertain" English, as people like Jonathan Swift put it. But even so four-square an authoritarian as Samuel Johnson rejected such an idea as being inimical to the traditions of English freedom and impossible of accomplishment in any case.

At the beginning of the nineteenth century, textbook writers under pressure from the schools for practical grammar books turned more and more to the study of syntax. Rules for the "parsing" of sentences were developed that depended upon intensive syntactic analysis, analysis that was not always beyond reproach. As sentence parsing caught on, various systems of diagramming were devised as aids to the student. These various systems eventually fell together into the still widely used Reed-Kellogg system:

Subject	Verb	Direct Object

The school grammars based on this "sentence analysis" were unhappy blends of prescriptivism and necessity. Definitions of the parts of speech were based partly on "meaning" ("a noun is the *name* of a person, place, thing, etc.) and partly on function ("an adjective *modifies* a noun"). The aim of diagramming proved to be that of simply labelling sentence parts. For all but a very few students, grammar study under this approach was a crashing bore. For none of them did it accomplish those ends claimed for it; and to the present day, the term "grammarian" summons up for most Americans the archetypal dry-as-dust academician, just as "grammar" summons up remembrance of scolding schoolmarms presiding over untold hours of unproductive tedium.

While the schoolbook grammarians of England and America were busy contriving techniques for teaching grammar rules, Continental scholars like Otto Jespersen, Hendrik Poutsma, and Etsko Kruisinga were at work on detailed reference grammars of English, academically sophisticated and in touch with the advances in linguistic thinking that came with nineteenth-century historical/comparative studies. Unfortunately, these scholarly works had virtually no impact on the schoolbook tradition, which continues, with a few exceptions, to the present day to be innocent of linguistic science.

It can be said of "traditional grammar" by way of summary that its underlying philosophy was the ancient notion of *universality;** i.e.,* that particular languages are individual manifestations of something common

---

* Contemporary linguistic thinking has returned to the question of universals in language, but from the solid foundation of scientific linguistics and anthropology.

to all mankind; but these manifestations were thought of as fixed. Consequently, early grammarians were doctrinally unequipped to deal with the dynamic nature of living language. Furthermore, they believed that written language, especially as exemplified by the "best" authors, was more significant and important than speech. The dominance of the Analogist view of language stamped language study until very recent times with a bias in favor of meaning against form, a fact that militated against the development of sound descriptive techniques. The *deductive* bias in Western thought, springing from the dominance of the classical syllogism in formal education, urged a reliance on established principles—in the case of grammar, a reliance on what the Greeks, as interpreted by the Romans, had concluded about language. It does seem remarkable that alongside the great advances in science and mathematics that were made from the Renaissance onward, language study should have fared so poorly. Noam Chomsky's "rehabilitation" of the Port-Royal *Grammar* of 1660 suggests that there were a few bright spots in pre-nineteenth-century linguistic thought. His efforts on the part of the Port-Royal grammarians, however, is not unchallenged. See, for example, Hans Aarsleff, "The History of Linguistics and Professor Chomsky," *Language*, Vol. 46, September 1970, pp. 570–585.

With the development of structural linguistics in the United States, it became apparent to some professors of English that traditional school grammar was in need of serious rethinking. In 1952, Charles Carpenter Fries published *The Structure of English*, which rejected (1) the traditional parts of speech and (2) the authority of written language. His *corpus* was a collection of recordings made of telephone conversations. He resolved his data into four major *form classes* and fifteen groups of *function words*. The form classes were roughly equivalent to the nouns, verbs, adjectives, adverbs of tradition; but since they were determined strictly according to form and position and not at all according to meaning, he identified them by number (1,2,3,4) and recommended discarding the traditional terms. His primary method for defining categories was the syntactic *frame:*

The————————is/are good.

(This frame defines words of Form Class 1.) Supplementary observations regarding formal marking of plurality, possession, tense, etc., the occurrence of stress patterns, the existence of derivational paradigms (like that of the pronouns), and so on, served to refine his description of the language. The four form classes are open-ended. The function word groups are defined by listing member words and noting their typical occurrences. Fries' attention is on pattern and distribution rather than on specific words and their meanings, and he does give some attention to *immediate constituent* analysis (see the following chapter).

Working from the theoretical position established by Bloomfield, Fries set the style of American structuralism as it was applied to the teaching of English grammar. Paul Roberts' very popular *Patterns of English* is Fries methodized for high school students—though even this work, which is superannuated by a long way, has had small impact on grammar teaching in the schools, and it has frequently been misused to serve as a "rule" book to be memorized.

Linguistic science did not, of course, end with structuralism. Indeed, "classical" structuralism has passed its heyday, to be displaced or superceded by *transformationalism*, or *transformational-generative grammar*, the groundwork of which was laid by a former Bloomfieldian, Noam Chomsky, who is properly considered one of the major linguistic theorists of all time. The landmark works in this new direction are *Syntactic Structures* (1957) and *Aspects of the Theory of Syntax* (1965). The former, which owes not a little to Chomsky's work with Zellig Harris (whose own book, *Structural Linguistics* [1951] is an attempt to provide a unified statement of structuralist theory and practice) is fundamentally structural, but the "new orthodoxy" (as Chomsky's critics term it) is implicit. The latter represents a revision of certain basic principles in Chomskyian thought and breaks almost wholly with structuralism. *Syntactic Structures*, incomplete as it was, triggered a flood of scholarly work and in a relatively short time transformationalism dominated linguistic thinking. Since the three chapters that follow examine in detail linguistic theory and practice, it will be sufficient to point out here that Chomskyian linguistics rejects both the anti-mentalistic dogma of the structuralists and their insistence on rigorous, "objective" discovery procedures. Considerations of meaning are brought into linguistics proper, and conclusions about language operations may be arrived at by any means (including intuition and guesswork), their soundness determined not by the type of discovery procedures used but by whether they "work." Language now will be studied as *process* rather than *state*. Set-piece analysis, in which respect the structuralists were not very different from the traditionalists, gives way to process description.

Implications for Teaching

We see little point in dealing with the historical backgrounds of linguistics on an informational basis. At an appropriate time, however, the teacher should be able to put the study of language into its historical perspective, reminding the student that those insights and discoveries that we take for granted in any field do have their antecedents, that modern advances are, after all, possible only because those who came before asked questions and tried to find answers. In keeping with the educational philosophy of this book, the student should be directed toward raising questions about language rather than merely squirreling away names, dates, and so on, in the history of linguistics. The projects that follow derive in various ways from the materials of this chapter and at the same time are designed to put the student into the role of language researcher. The projects should be considered open ended and productive of many more questions and projects. Ideally, the teacher will work along with student rather than expecting pre-determined answers.

1. Traditional school grammar books commonly offer the following definitions:

a. A *noun* is a word which names a person, place, or thing.

b. A *verb* is a word which expresses action or state of being.

What is the basis of these definitions? To what extent do they usefully define *noun* and *verb*? How do they differ from the traditional definitions of *adjective* and *adverb*?

c. An *adjective* modifies a noun.

d. An *adverb* modifies a verb, an adjective or another adverb.

Choose a paragraph or two from something you are reading and try to classify the nouns, verbs, adjectives, and adverbs strictly according to the traditional definitions. (Consider a sentence like *The action was over in an hour.* Is *action* a "thing"? Does *was* express "action" or "state of being"? Explain.) Describe the problems you encountered. Try to work out a rational and consistent way to identify nouns, verbs, etc.

2. What rationale seems to underlie the term *parts of speech?* Are all of these "parts of speech" in fact comparable? (Compare, for example, the noun with the preposition or conjunction.) As you actually use your language in daily conversation or in writing letters, and so on, what role do the "parts of speech" play in your thinking? Do you construct sentences thinking as you do so that here you are "naming" something and there you are "expressing action" or "state of being"? Before you ever knew that nouns, verbs, and so on, existed, you both spoke and understood your language very well; that is, you knew what to do with the entities that you later learned were nouns, verbs, etc. with very little difficulty and with great precision. (Strike up a conversation with an average four-year-old to test this assertion.) Can you offer any explanation of how you managed to perform as you did? Is "imitation" a sufficient explanation?

3. Since nouns are indeed different from verbs, we can grant the validity of "parts of speech." However, since the traditional definitions seem to tell us very little of use about the "parts," perhaps other bases

of classification can be discovered. Return to the paragraphs you used above and see if you can distinguish nouns, verbs, etc. in some clear and reasonably unequivocal way. Think about form, think about function, think about position.

4. The question of how language first came into being has long fascinated mankind, and yet nobody has thus far come up with a satisfactory explanation. Why do you think this is so? What tentative suggestions regarding the origin of language can you offer? What evidence prompts these suggestions? How can theories of language origin be tested or proved? Closely related to the question of origin is that of the presumed form and character of the "first" language. (The issue of whether there was a single "parent" language or several simultaneous parent languages has not been resolved, nor does it seem likely to be so. Why is the issue probably insoluble?) Among the several theories regarding the primordial language(s) is the "bow-wow" theory, which would derive language from human attempts to imitate the sounds of nature (mainly animal sounds). The "evidence" for this theory is the stock of *onomatopoeic* or *echoic* words that can be found in all extant languages (*bow wow, oink, tinkle, boom, quack*, etc.). Other than the fact that these words are merely stylizations of sound (dogs don't really say "bow wow"; cf. the Japanese echoism for the "same" sound: *wan wan*), why does the "bow wow" theory seem inadequate to account for the nature of a language? Can you suggest any lines of inquiry that might shed some light on the question of the form and character of a first language? What blind alleys might you expect to run into in dealing with this problem?

5. It has been said that a language is a complex, multi-levelled, interlocking set of *contrasts*. Can you find any evidence that would seem to support this notion?

6. Some language theorists today are attempting to formulate a set of *language universals*; that is, a core of linguistic materials both grammatical and semantic that seems to be common to all languages. How might one pursue this goal? After all, each language is on the surface unique. If one seems to have got hold of a linguistic universal (*i.e.*, a characteristic of language that is universal), how might one test the validity of his discovery? As an example, one obvious universal of language is the fact of *phonation:* All natural languages are primarily rendered *phonetically;* that is, with what are known as speech sounds. (Graphic renderings are taken to be displacements of or substitutions for speech.)

7. With a good desk dictionary in hand (e.g., *The American Heritage*) track down the source of every word in each of five paragraphs of

prose. Each paragraph should come from a different source; e.g., one from a current popular magazine, one from a story by Hemingway, one from a textbook of some sort, etc. Describe the character of each paragraph with respect to the "vocabulary profile" you have discovered. Try modifying the "feel" of any of these paragraphs by substituting for a significant number of key words, synonyms with a different origin. For example, pull out words of French origin and substitute words of native English origin. You must, of course, maintain the original overall meaning of the passage. Analyze a few paragraphs of your own writing to determine its vocabulary profile and then try changing it by substitution as above. What effects arise from, say, words of Latin and Greek origin predominating over words of native (Anglo-Saxon; that is, Old English) origin? What types of words are most likely in any piece of writing in English to be of native origin? What seem to be the main subject areas of words from Latin and Greek? French? Italian? Other? Compare the vocabulary profiles of the King James version of the Bible with the Douay-Rheims. Use parallel passages and describe both the differences and the effects of the differences.

8. Track down about twenty common, everyday words (e.g., *hand, foot, mother, father, cow, one, two, three,* etc.) in German, Dutch, Danish, Swedish, and Icelandic. Describe what you have found and discuss the implications. Do the same for Latin, French, Spanish, Italian, and Portuguese. Are there any similarities between the Germanic and the Romance groups? Among the tools of comparative linguistics is a formulation known as Grimm's Law, after the German philologist Jakob Grimm (1785–1863). Find out what you can about this "law"— a better word here would be "correspondences"—and write a brief report on it, including examples of the "law's" operation. Do not use the examples that you find in the source of information about the law, but try to work out your own—just as Jakob Grimm had to!

9. Nineteenth-century historical and comparative linguistics focused mainly on tracing "genealogical" relationships among languages. Thus, it was demonstrated, for example, that English, Greek, Sanskrit, and Russian were "genetically" related to each other. This approach to languages represents one possible method of language classification. Can you think of other ways in which languages can be classified? What does the "genealogical" classification reveal that other systems do not? What do other systems reveal that the genealogical system does not?

10. Look up a few common words like *run* in the *Oxford English Dictionary.* What does this dictionary tell you about these words? For the same words, make your own "anthology" of sample contexts. Start with early sources, perhaps Malory's *Morte d'Arthur,* and bring your exam-

ples up to date according to the system used by the OED. Do the meanings in your contexts seem to accord with those in the OED? If there are differences, explain them. Try using the context method for defining the meaning and usage of a few recently coined words that don't appear in the OED (e.g., *transistor, wiretap, kibitzer, hot rod, hippie, blast off, moonshot,* etc.). Have you noted any changes in the meaning of any familiar words during your lifetime? Which words? See if you can bring the OED up to date on these words. Consider, for example, *cool.* Check the OED against the word's general use among young people.

11. From a rigorously structuralist point of view, these sentences are precisely the same:

1. The boy moved.
2. The rock moved.

Both, that is, are (or seem to be) sentences of the type:

(D) $N + V_{INTR}$
(Determiner + Noun + Intransitive Verb)

But any native speaker of English senses that despite their surface similarity, these sentences are really quite different from one another. These differences can be easily seen if we think of the sentences as similar *surface* manifestations of two different underlying or *deep* structures. Can you work out these differences? Can you find other examples of this general type of linguistic phenomenon? (Consider, for example, *water vapor* in contrast to *water rat.* Here we have compounds that are structured precisely alike, but it is clear that the structuralist statement that these are simply examples of compounds formed by combining two nouns: $N + N$, is inadequate. *Water vapor* is vapor made of water; a *water rat* is *not* a rat made of water. Carry on from here.) On the basis of this project can you suggest why a purely structuralist approach to linguistic inquiry is inadequate?

12. Try to schematize the correspondence between conventional English spelling and English sounds. For example, what sound values can the letter *s* represent in English. By some diligent dictionary research you should be able to account for many of the apparent inconsistencies in English spelling. (Hint: check the *etymologies.*) Try it with a selection of words exhibiting these inconsistencies. Now try to develop a wholly consistent system of spelling. What does this entail? What are its advantages? Disadvantages? Write a paragraph or two in your new spelling system. Try it out on a few readers for "readability."

12a. Each language has its own *phonotactical* habits; that is, it allows certain sounds to occur with certain sounds and forbids certain sounds to occur with certain sounds. In English, for example, we can end a monosyllable with /l/ followed by /t/, but we cannot begin a monosyllable that way:

melt
*lt . . .

Nor is it possible in English to produce a sound sequence like krzyczeć, though in Polish it is perfectly normal. (The Polish word means "cry.") Try to work out the phonotactics of your dialect of English. Base your observations on the monosyllabic word. As a first step, however, you will have to determine the "canonical forms" of the English monosyllable, e.g., V * (*I* [diphthong, in this case], first person pronoun), VC (*in*), CV (*day*), CVC (*book*), etc. Remember *not* to confuse conventional spelling with pronunciation. On the basis of what you learn about English phonotactics, can you account for some of the difficulties one has in learning to accurately pronounce a foreign language? Are there any normal sound sequences in English that cause you any difficulty? If so what are they? Can you account for the difficulty? What normal English sound sequences do very young children seem to have particular difficulty with? Can you account for this? What is the maximum number of consonants that can cluster on either side of a vowel in English? What consonants seem to enter most readily into clusters? Try to account for this relative combinatorial ease. What consonants tend to be "loners"? Try to account for this "consonantal exclusivity." In these explorations of English consonant clustering, be sure to include observations on those clusters that arise as the result of joining the end of a word to the beginning of the following word in an utterance, e.g., He *pushed straight* ahead (/štstr/). Again, it is the pronunciation that counts here, not the spelling.

12b. *Phonological conditioning* is the term given to the effect (or apparent effect) of certain sounds on other sounds in the same environment. Thus the sound used to indicate plurality is not always the same. Consider:

stick	sticks	/s/
bug	bugs	/z/
prize	prizes	/ɨz/

(Note that in the case of *prize*, the final *e* is only a spelling convention; it does not occur in the pronunciation: /prayz/.) What is happening here? Are these merely random occurrences? How in fact does the prin-

---

* V in this context means vowel, C, consonant. These generalized phonological notations are applicable to all languages, though the acceptable C-V patterns will differ from language to language. Thus Japanese allows CV, but not CCV, etc.

ciple of phonological conditioning seem to be operating here? Can you find other examples of phonological conditioning? Collect examples like those above and any others that you find. Try to develop an explanation that will enlighten our visitor from outer space.

12c. Like sounds, morphemes have their rules of order (*morphotactics*). Thus we can say *walking* but not *ingwalk, *interdepartmental* not **almentdepartinter*. And *lighthouse* means something quite different from *houselight*. Can you find any order in this potential chaos? Try to derive some morphotactical rules for the enlightenment of our alien friend.

The following questions deal explicitly with aspects of the history of the English language and represent problems of the sort that occupied philologists of the nineteenth century. (Not that every detail of the history of the English or any other language has been revealed nor that linguists are today uninterested in these matters!) We have found that explorations of this sort have a great deal of appeal for the student.

13. Following are modern English and modern German versions of The Lord's Prayer. Examine them closely. Can you offer any evidence from the two versions to support the conclusion that English and German have a common ancestor? (*N.B.* Understand that English doesn't "come from" German. Rather, English and German come from the same source.)

> Our Father Who art in heaven, hallowed be Thy name. Thy kingdom come; Thy will be done on earth as it is in heaven. Give us this day our daily bread, and forgive us our debts as we forgive our debtors. And lead us not into temptation, but deliver us from evil; for Thine is the kingdom, and the power, and the glory forever. Amen.

> Unser Vater in dem Himmel, Dein Name werde geheiligt. Dein Reich komme. Dein Wille geschehe auf Erden wie in Himmel. Unser täglich Brot gib uns heute. Und vergib uns unsere Schulden, wie wir unseren Schuldigern vergeben. Und führe uns nicht in Versuchung, sondern erlöse uns von dem Übel. Denn dein ist das Reich und die Kraft und die Herrlichkeit in Ewigkeit. Amen.

14. Examine the following lines describing the famous Wife of Bath in the General Prologue to *Canterbury Tales* by Geoffrey Chaucer (1340–1400). How does the English of this passage differ from the English you speak? Try working out (1) a literal (word-for-word) translation and (2) a readable, intelligible translation. Discuss the problems. What is lost by the translation? Does translation *within* a language differ from translation from one language to another? If so, how?

> Bold was hir face and fair and reed of hewe.
> She was a worthy womman al hir live:
> Housbondes at chirche dore she hadde five,

Withouten other compaignye in youthe—
But hereof needeth nought to speke as nouthe.*   5   *now*
And thries hadde she been at Jerusalem;
She hadde passed many a straunge* streem;   *strange*
At Rome she hadde been, and at Boloigne,*   *sites of shrines*
In Galice at Saint Jame, and at Coloigne:
She coude* muchel of wandring by the waye.   10   *knew*
Gat-toothed * was she, soothly for to saye.   *gap-toothed*

The pronunciation of Middle English was quite different from that of modern English. How do we know what it sounded like? Most (though not all) of the final e's were pronounced (roughly with the same sound normally given the final a in *sofa*). For a long time, however, this fact was not known. Are there any clues in the lines of poetry that might lead you to conclude that these e's should be pronounced? In line 5 above, there is an unpronounced final e. Which one is it, and why do you feel that it should not be pronounced? Try reading a complete tale from *Canterbury Tales* in Middle English. Use a translation to help you over the difficult parts. Do you think that it is better to read the original or the translation? Discuss. What do you find most difficult about reading the original? [Teacher: A recording of Chaucer done in Middle English should be played and discussed.]

15. Listen to the record *A Thousand Years of English Pronunciation.* Discuss the nature of the changes of English pronunciation from Old English (Anglo-Saxon) to the present. You will have to listen carefully and play the record over several times. Are there any elements of Old English that seem distinctively "English" (*i.e.*, the language, not the political entity known as *England*) to you? What are they? Here are some Old English words. Can you figure out what modern English words derive from them?

æppel, any kind of fruit   *lār*, learning, science
behealdan, to look at   *mōdignes*, pride
cnotta, a fastening   *nīwe*, recent
dysig, foolish   *ofercuman*, conquer
eornistlīce, truly   *rihtlic*, proper
fyrmest, first, best   *sellan*, to give
godspel, glad tidings   *synn*, mischief
godsibb, a sponsor   *tigel*, clay pot
heald, custody   *ūteweard*, external
hūsbonda, householder   *wyrm*, snake

Describe the changes that have taken place. Can you find any other modern words that descend directly from Old English. What kinds of words do they tend to be? Collect some modern English words of

French, Italian, and Spanish origin. What kinds of things are these words mainly concerned with? Can you account for the differences between the borrowed words and the native words?

16. British English and American English are mutually intelligible, though each is distinctive. The most obvious difference between these two general dialects of English (remember that each has its own considerable number of local dialects) is in pronunciation. Can you accurately explain wherein these differences lie? If you wanted to play the part of a Britisher on the stage, what changes would you make in your pronunciation to give the impression of being British? Compare what you would do with some actual samples of British English. (Use a recording like the Richard Burton *Hamlet*.) How does your "stage Britisher" differ from the real thing? Another difference between British and American English stems from the vocabulary. The British say "lorry" for "truck" and "lift" for "elevator." What other lexical differences can you find? How can you account for them? Localize your dialect study now and try to gather as many examples of American dialect characteristics as you can that distinctively differ from your own "hometown" dialect. Dialects can be thought of as incipient languages. Indeed, the great diversity of languages in our own Indo-European family arose from dialects of the parent language. How can you account for the dissimilation of a single language into a group of distinctive dialects? Does it seem likely that the various dialects of American English will ever develop into independent languages? Why or why not? Does it seem likely that British and American English will dissimilate into mutually unintelligible languages? Though English and Dutch are historically closely related languages, they are now mutually unintelligible. How can you account for this?

17. *Meander, mausoleum,* and *tantalize* are examples of *onomasia;* that is, words from proper names. (*Meander,* a Greek river; *Mausōlos,* an ancient king; *Tantalus,* a mythical character). What contemporary sources can you find for this word-making process? In each case explain what dimension of meaning the proper name adds to the word (*e.g.,* King Mausōlos caused an elaborate tomb to be built for himself; hence, a *mausoleum* is an elaborate tomb).

18. We have in English a number of words that imitate, in a highly conventionalized way, various sounds: *rumble, bubble, burp,* etc. English, however, is not overly rich in *echoism* (or *onomatopoeia*); Japanese, for example is far richer. What are some sounds for which we have no conventional echoisms? Try to devise appropriate words for these sounds. Explain how you arrived at each conventionalization of sound.

(Suppose, for example, you had invented the word *gurgle* for the sound that it represents for us. Why *gurgle?* In Japanese, *bota-bota* and *tara-tara* are conventionalizations for the same sound.)

19. In Shakespeare's time, the second person pronoun (modern you) consisted of the following forms:

thee, thy, thine, thou
you, your, yours
ye (plural)

These forms were not used indiscriminately. Through a close reading of a play by Shakespeare, see if you can determine their proper uses.

20. Shakespeare causes the modern reader a number of linguistic difficulties. List and characterize the problems you had in reading the play for the preceding exercise. If you were attempting to interest someone in reading Shakespeare, what kind of linguistic preparation would you think it wise to give him. What, if any, of the linguistic archaisms of Shakespeare do you find appealing? Explain.

5
Constituent Analysis & Phrase-Structure Grammar

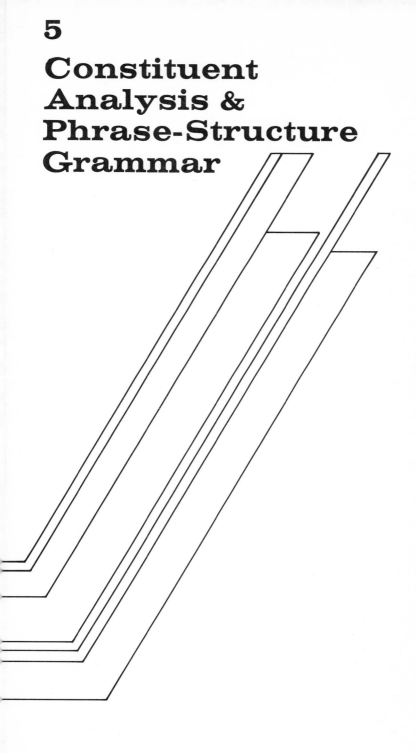

The description of the syntax of a language must include two major components: a classification of the words and other elements, and a statement of their relations.

(H. A. Gleason, *Linguistics and English Grammar*, New York.)

All languages are predicational. This means that we speak in sentences not in words, though words "realize" sentences. Schematically, sentences are anterior to words; that is, we combine words as we do because we have "pre-existent" rules available that predict or require certain arrangements and forbid other arrangements. It can be argued that the first words of a young child are in fact reduced predications, not merely "names," and even prior to overt verbalization the child can be heard *intoning* according to the normal intonational patterns of the language. One major function of intonation is to define or reinforce predications.

If we think of a sentence as a series of locations, each of which can accept only certain kinds of words, we will be faced with the problem of organizing our lexicon *typologically*. We will, in fact, end with a classification rather like the traditional parts of speech, though our classificatory principles will, or should, be rather more rigorous than those that obtained prior to the modern period of linguistic science. And while the traditional terms may carry with them some of the misconceptions of the past, they are useful because they are familiar. We see no great advantage in, say, the Fries expedient of using numbers and letters to represent what he terms the form and function classes. So we shall content ourselves with *noun, verb, adjective, preposition,* etc. Nor is there any great need to "define" these terms. Every native speaker of any language knows on a purely functional level what the meaning units (*i.e., morphemes,* which comprise both words and the various affixes) are. Definition by exemplification is usually adequate. (Nouns are words like. . . .)

While we may imagine a sentence as a series of word locations, it is only that ultimately, not immediately. Before we get down to the individual words, we respond to *sets* of words, which are unitary structures within the overall sentence structure. These substructures are "layered" or hierarchically ordered, and where the ordering has been faulty, communication falters. For example, *He put on a white shirt and tie* is ambiguous because, in the absence of intonational or contextual

clues, we don't know which of the following arrangements is intended:
(1) [white [shirt and tie]]
(2) [white shirt] [and] [tie]

Almost all native speakers of English will intuitively divide any given sentence into identical substructures. This implies, of course, that, consciously or not), we all follow the same patterns in producing and in structurally interpreting sentences. Consider

1. *Hyenas laugh throughout the night.*

Our "instinct" for the English sentence, the result, of course, of our "programming" during the early years, prompts that we first "cut" the sentence into

Hyenas + laugh throughout the night.

These two units—"subject" and "complete predicate"—are called the *immediate constituents* of the sentence. In turn, we would cut *laugh throughout the night* into

laugh + throughout the night.

The obvious reason for this cut is that neither *laugh throughout* nor *laugh throughout the* is felt to be a constructional unit; that is to say, a constituent. The third step "down" will yield

throughout + the night.

And finally, we will split *the night* into its immediate constituents (the + night), which are also its ultimate constituents. The immediate constituents of the sentence, then, are a *noun phrase* and a *predicate phrase* (NP + PredP). The immediate constituents of the predicate phrase are a verb (V) and a prepositional phrase (PP), and so on. Several graphic devices are available for schematizing sentence structure, though the *tree diagram* is currently the most fashionable because of its intensive use by most contemporary theoreticians; it does reveal structure more explicitly than the other devices.

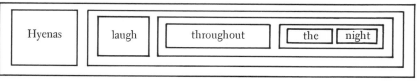

(CHINESE BOX)

[[Hyenas] [[laugh] [[throughout] [[the] [night]]]]]

(BRACKETING)

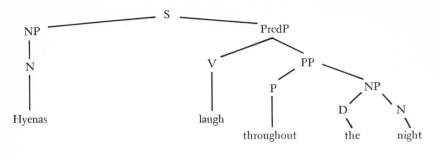

(TREE DIAGRAM)

Consider the following sentences:

1.   Hyenas]   [laugh throughout the night.
2.   Hungry hyenas]   [laugh throughout the night.
3.   Several hungry hyenas]   [were laughing throughout the night.
4. A number of hungry hyenas]   [prowled around the camp last night.
5. The fact that a number of]   [made me nervous.
   hungry hyenas prowled
   around the camp last
   night

Despite the fact that there is structural diversity among the left-hand IC's (immediate constituents) and among the right-hand IC's, all the left-hand IC's serve the same sentence function and all the right-hand IC's serve the same sentence function; namely, that of (respectively) *sentence noun phrase* (= "subject") and *sentence verb phrase* (= "predicate"). At the sentence level, then, we have two slots, each of which can accept a variety of fillers.

In structural grammar, the sentence is called a *predication structure*; but a predication structure can serve as a unit *within* a predication structure. In (5) above, the subject side of the sentence is itself a predication structure, a "noun clause." A *modification structure* is a *headed* construction, consisting of a *headword* and one or more modifiers: *Hungry hyenas, several hungry hyenas,* etc. Here, *hyenas* is the headword, *hungry* and *several* the modifiers. Note that in a headed construction, the whole construction performs the same function as its headword. Thus *several hungry hyenas* is functionally a noun and can fill noun slots just as easily as the single noun, *hyenas. Laugh throughout the night* is a verb-headed modification structure with a prepositional phrase acting as an adverb (a verb modifier). Prepositional phrases are *subordination structures*, the noun phrase (*the night*) subordinated to the preposition (*throughout*). Transitive verbs (e.g., *give, send, throw*, etc.) combine with nominal elements to form *complementation structures* (N + *threw the ball: threw* [verb] + *the ball* [complement]; N + *gave the dog a bone: gave* + *the dog a bone*, etc.) The fifth (and final) of the basic structural units of the English sentence (according to structuralist theory) is the *coordination structure*, any two grammatically equivalent units linked with a coordinating conjunction: *town and country, she sang and she danced*, etc.

With these five structures (*viz.*, predication, modification, subordination, complementation, and subordination), all the sentences of the language can presumably be built. They do not represent a structural hierarchy. Rather, they can occur at various sentence "levels" and perform various functions. Thus a compound sentence is, overall, a coordination structure. Each half of the coordination is a predication structure, and each half of each predication structure may be a modification structure. And so on:

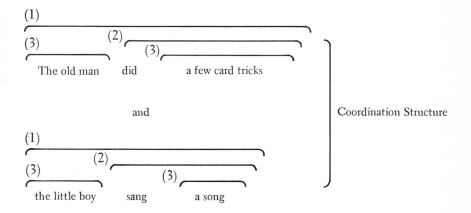

(1) Predication Structure
(2) Complementation Structure
(3) Modification Structure

The term *immediate constituent* was introduced by Bloomfield (*Language*, pp. 160 ff.), but he did not pursue the concept much further than to point out that IC cutting was a "proper" type of sentence analysis. Subsequent developments in IC analytical theory showed that sentences are not only *linear*, because of the time-based nature of physical speech, but *hierarchical* or *layered* (the sentence "levels" of the preceding paragraph), a structural schema that can be diagrammed as a pyramid:

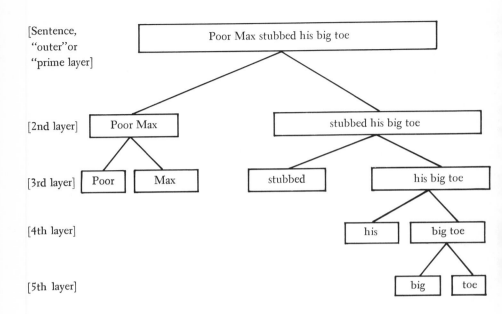

More abstractly:

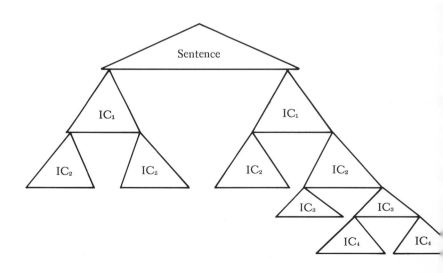

A compilation of all possible "pyramids" and their potential layer-by-layer expansions, constitute in IC (*i.e.*, structuralist) theory the grammar of the language. Every grammatical sentence would be described as a particular pyramid with particular, labeled constituents. This general compilation is called a *constituency* or *phrase structure* grammar (PSG).

Evidence has been presented by both phoneticians and psychologists that the labeled bracketing of immediate constituents does represent the collated surface structure of sentences as uttered and perceived physically. That is, we do actually perceive sentences on the basis of a phrasal structure or organization of the sentence. However, this kind of analysis is still essentially a taxonomic process and does not attempt to get at the deeper, more abstract structural properties of the sentence—which are in turn associated with underlying semantic structures.

Knowledge of a language implies the ability to make a connection between the semantic interpretation and the actual speech signal at a much deeper level than that of "sequenced words." This knowledge is "boundless," in that it extends over an infinity of such connections and is rarely repetitive (with the exception of clichés or stylized social greetings, which for their part usually lack the sort of structure we expect in sentences). It is an underlying semantic proposition (or system of propositions) of a *logical* nature in the mind, organized via language into a *deep structure* of abstract categories—as opposed to "words." It is this deeper structure that then provides the frame for both the semantic *and* the structural integrity of the sentence. This integrity does not derive, therefore, from the mere association or relationship of parts accomplished under immediate constituent analysis. This is not to say that the deep structure will not also have labeled bracketing, but only that such will differ from that of the surface structure of the same sentence.

With the eclipse of structuralism by generative and transformational grammars, box diagramming has given way to tree (phrase marker) diagramming and virtually all new grammar books (either introductory or advanced) are heavily laden with tree diagrams. Despite the fact that these diagrams can be forbidding to both student and teacher, they have unquestioned value in graphically revealing certain basic features of structure. In our subsequent development of them, therefore, they should never be "taught" simply for themselves, but for the insight into grammatical problems which they provide.

We are able now, at this point in the analysis of phrase structures, to formalize it at the more abstract level, using abstract categories, and expressing the rules more rigorously. We can use the symbolic notation already developed (N, V, etc.) and add one new symbol, →, the *rewrite arrow*. (Hence the often-used term, rewrite rules.) Thus,

S → NP + PredP   A *sentence* may be rewritten as (or consists of) a noun phrase and a predicate phrase. (The + sign is often omitted.)

PredP → AUX + VP   A *predicate phrase* may be rewritten as auxiliary and verb phrase.

AUX → (T) (M)   *Auxiliary* may be rewritten as tense and mode. (The parentheses indicate optionality of choice.)

NP → (DET) N   A *noun phrase* may be rewritten as a noun, optionally preceded by a determiner (article, demonstrative, etc.).

VP → V (NP)   A *verb phrase* may be rewritten as a verb, optionally followed by a noun phrase.

And so on. This is, of course, nothing like a complete analysis of the abstract categories of S, NP, and VP, and does not treat the remaining symbols, but is only a very limited and circumscribed presentation for the sake of example. A body of such rules, fully worked out for a language, would constitute the phrase structure rules for that language. It would generate (state explicitly) the *underlying phrase markers*, the abstract structures at a deep level, that will provide a complete description of the grammatical relations among the parts of the sentence. The various grammatical functions of a noun, for example, subject, object, indirect object, etc., can then be determined on the basis of position within the phrase marker. When the branching tree diagram that represents the abstract phrase marker is labeled and associated with equally abstract representations of lexical items, (which are words at the surface level) it provides the deep structure level output sentence underlying an actual speech utterance. These deep structures will carry both the logic and the actual proposition as originated in the mind. The distinction is important to keep in mind, because various physiological and psychological processes may interfere with and disturb the production of sentences in speech. Linguistic ineptness, memory limitations, outside interruptions—all these and many other factors can combine to drastically change the final speech act from the proposition as originally conceived.

Applying our simplified phrase structure rules successively, *one at a time*, we can expand S (our symbol for the initial abstract category of sentence) as follows:

Initial Symbol			S				
Rule 1	NP			PredP			
Rule 2	NP	AUX			VP		
Rule 3	NP	T			VP		
Rule 5	NP	T	V			NP	
Rule 4	DET	N	T	V		DET	N

By connecting the various symbols as they are successively rewritten (expanded) we arrive at the phrase marker for a typical English sentence:

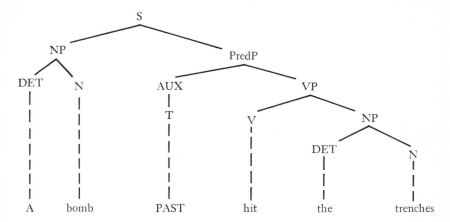

The tree diagram or phrase marker provides a simple and "natural" demonstration of both the hierarchical levels and the abstract deep structure of the sentence. It is not the actual sentence itself, of course, but the structure that underlies the sentence. It should be remembered, moreover, that, like all other schemata, it is only a model, a theory, a working hypothesis. To the extent that this (or any) model adequately explains realia or helps to solve problems, it suffices until a better model is contrived.

A speaker's grammar is considered to be a formalized representation of his linguistic competence. It is possible that the grammar might also be an actual component of the psychological processes involved in understanding sentences, although the way in which the two would be related is not at all clear. It is not even clear that complexity in one would parallel complexity in the other. The multiple strategies of our mental processes of speaking and understanding are probably sufficiently complex in their organization as to make the connection between grammar and performance rather indirect. But because so many grammars either are based upon phrase structure grammar, or can be explained in terms of it, many linguists feel there is a reasonable probability that such a system may, in fact, reflect at least partially whatever does actually underlie human speech.

Implications for Teaching

Grammar (of any kind) should not be taught as a separate "subject," and it should not be taught as data. This means that the student will be exploring grammar, not memorizing rules and definitions. It also means that grammar explorations can arise from the study of a writer's style or the nature of poetry or the linguistic manipulations of advertising copy.

The body of this chapter is brief, for we feel that the student who is using this book as well as the student who will some day be taught by him can learn better by working through problems in grammar than by trying to directly absorb a mass of technical information. In the past, because of the artificiality of the memorize-and-regurgitate approach to the traditional, and still very prevalent, grammar lesson, grammar teaching has been the bane of English courses. The student is not challenged, but defied to work.

The exercises that follow touch on most of the important theoretical issues of constituent and phrase-structure grammar. These exercises should be wrestled with before going on to transformationalism (Chapter VI), and they should be expanded by examining "real" sentences; that is, sentences from various works of literature as well as from current newspapers, magazines, and so on.

1. Make a list of *nouns* (words like *boat, car, rice, flower, beerbottle, nostril, mayor,* etc.), *verbs* (words like *crawl, stagger, scratch, think,* etc.), and *adjectives* (words like *silly, nauseating, ecstatic, dull, gigantic,* etc.) and try to develop a set of *frame sentences* that can be used to identify each of these word classes (and their sub-divisions). Then collect new lists of nouns, verbs, and adjectives and test them in your frames. Do the frames work consistently? What problems (if any) did you run into? Were you able to solve these problems? How? Can you develop a set of adverb frames? Does the adverb present any special problems? Do not include words like *very, rather, somewhat,* etc., in your adverb list. These belong to the general class of *structure words.* Why? (Compare the *type* of meaning conveyed by *rapidly* in *he spoke rapidly* with the *type* of meaning conveyed by *very* in *he spoke very rapidly.*) Can you develop frames that will unambiguously mark words like *the, to, by, with, three, never, who, what, why, which, that, if,* etc.? What problems arise in trying to work out these frames? In a modification structure like *all ten highly polished bright red crash helmets* is there an *order of attribution* or are the modifying words strung out more or less at random? Gather a number of modification structures (with noun headwords) from your reading and try to develop a "formula" for attribution. This will in effect be a multi-slotted frame, thus:
_/____/____/____/____/____/____N. Not all slots will always be filled, and there may be more allowable slots than shown above. What is the *theoretical* limit of pre-noun modification? What is the *practical* limit? Discuss.

2. Three of the four form classes provide base forms for functional shifts by addition of derivational affixes—nouns, verbs, and adjectives; but few derivational shifts come from the adverb class, and most of the words we call adverbs are derived from adjectives (*quickly—quick, intensely—intense, regularly—regular.*) Adverbs containing a noun base (*away, aboard, ashore*, etc.) usually represent a syncopation of a prepositional phrase (*on way, on board, on shore*). . . .

(Baxter Hathaway, A *Transformational Syntax*, p. 58.)

Make a collection of nouns, verbs, adjectives, and adverbs that reveal the mutual convertibility claimed for them by Hathaway. Here is an example to get you started: *romantic* (adjective, occasionally a noun), *romanticist* (noun), *romanticize* (verb), *romantically* (adverb). Expand Hathaway's list of adjective-derived adverbs. Make a list of suffixes that are commonly used to mark nouns, to mark verbs, to mark adjectives, to mark adverbs. (*E.g.*, *-ness* is a noun-marking or deriving suffix: *happy—happiness.*) Test your derived nouns, verbs, etc., in the frames that you developed in the preceding exercise. Any problems of fit? Discuss. Write a short paper summarizing your discoveries in respect to the "parts of speech."

3. Any language is a congeries of systems (e.g., *phonological*, *morphological*, *syntactic*, etc.). Syntactically, modern English is preeminently *analytic*; that is, meaning depends upon *word order*. Old English was preeminently *synthetic*; that is, meaning depended upon *inflections* ("case endings," and the like). To what extent does modern English still depend on a set of inflections? What kinds of "endings" can we affix to nouns? Verbs? Adjectives? Adverbs? What kinds of meanings do these endings convey? Consider the following equivalent pairs:

the bark of the tree   the tree's bark
the taste of the coffee   the coffee's taste
the howling of the wind   the wind's howling

Explain how each of the phrases (in each pair) is related to the other. The constructions in *of* are called *syntactic genitives*; those in *'s* are *inflected genitives*. Gather some additional examples of commutable genitives (like those above) from your reading. Can you determine why the writer in each case chose the one pattern in preference to the other. Rewrite some passages substituting syntactic genitives for inflected genitives and vice versa. Now make a collection of constructions in *of* that are *not* commutable to inflected genitives (e.g., *a time of war*). Can these constructions be commuted to acceptable equivalents (e.g., *wartime*)? Try rewriting a passage by making such "translations" of this kind as you can. Discuss the effects of your changes. Try to account for the writer's decision to choose the structures he did rather than the possible equivalents.

4. The contrast afforded by differences in *stress* (loudness) allows us. to distinguish meaning thus:

Noun	Verb		
CONtrast	conTRAST	a blue BIRD	(a blue-colored bird)
PERmit	perMIT	a BLUEbird	(a species of bird)
SUSpect	susPECT	a cold SORE	(a sore that is cold)
		a COLD sore	(a type of sore)

and so on. Can you find any other examples? Are shifts in stress ever accompanied by any other changes in pronunciation? If so, what are they? A sentence, when spoken, usually consists intonationally of one *nuclear* (primary or highest) stress and an assortment of lesser stress points—as well, of course, as other intonational features. Make up some sentences like *the little blue bird that you called a bluebird is really a member of an altogether different species.* Say the sentences aloud in a natural, conversational style and try to locate the nuclear stress of each sentence and the other stress points. How do you contrast, for example, *blue bird* and *bluebird* in the context of the sentence above? (A tape recorder will be of considerable help in this project.) Tune in on the intonational component of speech and try to figure how it is used and what kinds of meaning it signals. Does anyone really speak in a monotone? Try speaking in a monotone the next time you are having a rap session. Discuss the results of the experiment.

5. Sentences are composed of *syntactic structures*. At the most abstract level, we can say that any sentence is a *noun phrase* plus a *predicate phrase* (S = NP + PredP). This statement can be thought of as the prime grammatical rule. At lower, more concrete levels, NP and PredP are seen to represent a variety of syntactic structures (which is to say, *constituents*). In the sentence *some students are raiding the refrigerator*, the immediate constituents, that is, the NP and PredP, are *some students* and *are raiding the refrigerator.* Why not *some students are* and *raiding the refrigerator*? The *phrase marker* (or *phrase-structure diagram*) below schematizes the relationships among the syntactic structures of the sentence. What can you learn from such a diagram? At what *node* (point) are *students* and *are* brought into direct relationship? What does the diagram reveal about the relationship of the two NP's? The abbreviations in the diagram are as follows:

NP, noun phrase
PredP, predicate phrase
VP, verb phrase
DET, determiner (article, etc.)
N, noun

V, verb
AUX, auxiliary

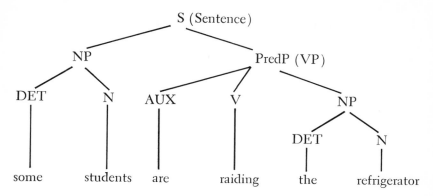

Pick out a few sentences of varying length from something you are reading and try to diagram them. As you work out the diagrams think about the way the sentence is layered and which level node controls what structures. Find some ambiguous sentences and show how phrase markers can resolve the ambiguity. Here is a sentence to get you started: *They are flying saucers.* The ambiguity here springs from not knowing whether *flying* is meant to be a verb or an adjective. The type of nodal arrangement you diagram will resolve the ambiguity one way or the other, thus:

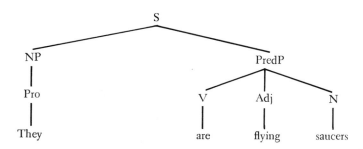

Or

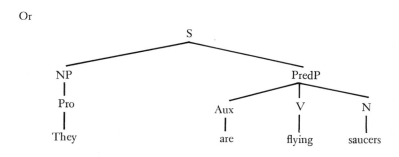

Now try these: *The son of the Pharaoh's daughter is the daughter of the Pharaoh's son. Visiting relatives can be miserable. Teaching machines can be fun.* Do you find anything unusual about the last sentence? Find some other examples of this type of ambiguity.

6. Just as there are but a few syntactic structures so these few structures can occur in but a few basic sentence patterns. Beyond these basic patterns there are only variations achieved mainly by expansions of several kinds. Here are the four basic patterns:

    I. Noun+ Verb
       Hyenas laugh
   II. Noun + Copula + Adjective (or Noun)
      Linda is lovely
      Linda is leader
  III. Noun + Verb + Noun
      Harry hates cigarettes
  IV. Noun + Verb + Noun + Noun
      Sherman owes Herman money

Each pattern has four (possibly more) variations. Can you work them out? (A simple example to get you started: Pattern I, N + V, can appear as Determiner + N + V. *Most hyenas laugh.*) Set your variations up as formulas and realize the formulas with a number of different lexical choices (e.g., *A leaf fell, several dogs barked,* etc.). Try to find examples of each pattern and its variations in your reading (preferably magazines, newspapers, etc., not "grammar books" and the like). Can these sentence types be combined into larger sentences? How? Do it. Try to find some examples of combined patterns in your reading.

7. English verbs are either simple (*sing, sings, talk, talked,* etc.) or syntactic (*was singing, could have been talking,* etc.); main (*sing,* etc.) or auxiliary (*could, might,* etc.). Try to develop a reasonable way of revealing all the complexities of the English verb system to our imaginary visitor from the flying saucer. It will perhaps be easiest and most efficient if you start with a single verb, say, *walk.* As you get along, you should make a collection of all the different verb patterns you can find (e.g., *is walking, had walked, should have been walking,* etc.) using both your original verb and others. You will note, for example, that you can say *He walks,* but that it sounds odd to say *He puts.* (As the purpose of this exercise is not that of identification, don't be afraid to ask that verbs be pointed out for you if you are uncertain about identifying them.)

8. Though the verb *be* is sometimes used to convey the meaning *exist,* it frequently is purely formal and therefore conveys no referential meaning. In which of the following sentences is *be* used to mean *exist* and in which is it a purely formal signal of predication?

1. There *are* numerous farms in this area.
2. He had *been* in Asia for several years.
3. He *is* certainly a hungry little beast.
4. The ocean *is* a beautiful shade of green.
5. Prices these days *are* far too high.

Find some other examples of each use of *be*. The verb *have* exhibits an analogous difference between referential and structural meaning. Consider:

1. What *has* he?
2. What *has* he got?
3. They *have* to register next week.
4. Desmond is *having* a new house built.
5. Iris *had* a good time last night.
6. The Sturdleys *had* twins.
7. Tillie *has had* a Rolls Royce for years.
8. *Has* George's book been published yet?

Which of these uses of the verb *have* are referential and which are structural? For those that are referential, try to explain the meaning.

9. Predications (sentences) occur as independent units or as parts of other sentences. A *compound* sentence is two sentences joined (*conjoined* is the technical term) by a coordinating conjunction:

Jack fell down the hill *and* Jill came tumbling after.

Diagrammatically:

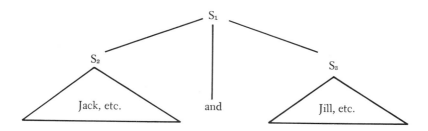

But there are other kind of combinations. One of the most common is that of *embedding*. In *Tillie knew Melmoth was cheating*, the object of the sentence is *Melmoth was cheating*, which is itself a sentence. Diagrammatically:

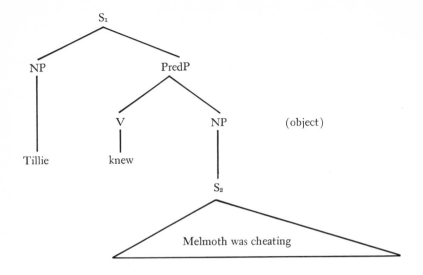

Embeddings can, of course, occur in other sentence positions. Is there any *theoretical* limit to the number of embeddings a sentence may have? Consider the poem "The House that Jack Built." Is there a *practical* limit? What determines the practical limit? Embedding, incidentally, is said to be *recursive*; that is, each embedded sentence can contain its own embeddings. Gather from your reading several examples of sentences containing one or more embeddings. Identify the embeddings and try to explain their function. Use tree diagrams if they are helpful. Do some writers make greater use of embedding than others? Closely examine a few paragraphs from the work of two writers with distinctively different styles. Does one writer make significantly greater use of embedding than the other? Try writing two paragraphs on any subject that interests you, one with few or no embeddings and the other with as many embeddings as you can comfortably work in. Is there a difference in tone between the two? Try to characterize the difference.

10. Certain modificational elements within a sentence can be moved around in the sentence to change emphasis, rhythm, style, thus:

(1) He left the city the *following morning*.
(2) He left the city on the *morning following*.
(3) *On the following morning* he left the city.
(4) He, *on the morning following*, left the city.

And so on. Gather from your reading a variety of sentences in which modificational elements can be moved. Subject each sentence to as many of these moves as possible. Explain what you did and what resulted in terms of emphasis shift and stylistic variation. Read a few paragraphs from each of two or three writers and try to establish some "norms" and "deviations" for the placement of modificational elements. Try to develop a "stylistic profile" of each writer with respect to his predominant pattern of modifier placement. How significant and useful does this type of syntactical maneuvering seem to be?

11. *Conjunctions* are words like *and, but, yet, as, though, consequently, however, although . . . yet,* and so on. Gather from your reading a sizable sampling of sentences in which one or more conjunctions occur, and attempt to explain how conjunctions are used and what they are used for. (*E.g., as, such as, as . . . as,* and *as . . . so* are used to signal comparison: *Tweedledee was AS silly AS Tweedledum.*) Your examples should include as many *different* conjunctions as possible. Try working out a phrase structure diagram for the sentence above (*Tweedledee,* etc. Clue: Try starting with *Tweedledee was silly to an extent equal to the extent Tweedledum was silly.*). Try diagramming sentences that use *either . . . or, insofar as,* and *nevertheless.* What (if any) problems did you encounter in trying to work out the diagrams? Do some writers seem to rely more heavily on conjunctions than others? Compare two or three writers with respect to their degree of "conjunctivization." Do some writers seem to lean more heavily on certain conjunctions than do other writers? Do a study that will answer the question one way or the other. Now write a paragraph or so in two versions, one with a "normal" (for you) complement of conjunctions, the other with few or no conjunctions. Discuss your findings. (Does, for example, the second version differ much in tone from the first? What problems did you run into in trying to get rid of conjunctions?

12. The grammatical system of English allows for various kinds of *substitution,* arrived at by various processes. Here are examples of some of the types of substitution (but not all):

1. The Walrus sings grand opera better than the *carpenter* (sings grand opera). *Carpenter* substitutes for the predicate, *sings grand opera,* which is deleted.
2. Melmoth drank as much slivovitz as Tillie *did. Did* (*i.e.,* the verb *do*) substitutes for the preceding predicate.
3. He *gave money to* and *fought with* the I.R.A. (Compare: He *gave money to the I.R.A.* and *fought with the I.R.A.*)

Your job is to gather more examples like those preceding and as many other kinds of substitutions as you can find. Rewrite all your examples in their "full" form (as in example (3) above). Try this for a paragraph or two in which substitution occurs. What does the revision do to the tone or "feel" of the original? Do some writers seem to make greater use of substitution than others? Compare two or more writers and report your findings.

13. Try to work out a set of "rules" governing the use of reflexives (*I was determined not to get myself into a bind like this again*). Derive your rules from evidence gathered from actual language usage (include examples from both writing and speech—magazines and casual conversations). Use your rules to predict usage. Are your "predictions" reasonably accurate? If not, you will have to modify your rules accordingly.

14. Try to work out a set of rules governing the use of *tag questions* (e.g., *She works hard, doesn't she? It isn't raining, is it?*) First find as many different kinds of tag questions as you can (from both written and spoken sources). Then categorize them (the examples above represent two types) and formulate your rules for their acceptable use (the prospective user of all of the rules you work out in these exercises is the man from the flying saucer).

15. Try to work out a set of rules for the use of the article (*a/an, the*). Colorless though these little words may be, they offer some interesting problems to both the speaker of the language and the linguist attempting to understand their uses and functions. Gather your evidence as usual (see preceding exercises). You may find it helpful to revise a few randomly chosen samples of writing by adding, substituting, or deleting articles and noting differences in meaning that obtain as well as unacceptable usages (e.g., **A thundering shots rang out*). What are some of the problems that both the speaker and the linguist (*i.e.,* the student of language phenomena such as yourself) face in using and studying the article? Japanese uses no articles. Try explaining the uses of the articles to a Japanese learning English.

16. Consider:
1. He gave *up*.
2. He walked *up* the hill.
The use of *up* in each of these sentences is different. How? Try to find some other examples (both with *up* and with other similar words like *in, out, to, on,* etc.) Can you work out a set of rules or a statement of principle regarding these usages? Diagramming may help you understand the relationships involved (or at least to reveal those relationships to our interested visitor from the cosmos).

17. There is a use of the verb in English called the *subjunctive* (e.g., *If I were you, I'd mind my own business; be he beggar or king . . .*). Do a survey (from both written and spoken sources) to determine the extent to which the subjunctive is in actual use, and categorize its uses (*i.e.,* show what its purposes seem to be). Don't, however, try to find out about its uses by asking people why they are using it. You will in all likelihood gather a lot of misinformation that way! Try to determine meaning and intent from *context*.

18. Consider:
1. The pilot is *sleepy*/the *sleepy* pilot
2. The *main* event/_____
3. A book yellow with age/_____

In example (1), the adjective (*sleepy*) can be either *attributive* (in front of the noun) or *predicative* (following the copula, *is*). But the attributive adjective in (2), *main*, cannot occur predicatively; that is, **The event was main* is not an attested usage in English. Try to find some examples of both kinds of adjectives and to develop a set of rules with respect to their use attributively and predicatively. Can you account for the non-predicative use of adjectives like *main*?

19. Gather as many different kinds of *questions* as you can and classify them according to (1) grammatical structure, (2) normal intonation (*N.B.*, most questions probably *don't* require that the voice rise at the end), and (3) type of answer desired (informational, yes/no, or whatever). Are all utterances that are structured like questions intended to solicit a question response? If not, what is their intention?

20. Given such syntactic units as modification structures, complementation structures, etc., can you work out a set of rules for their combination into sentences? Your rules should be so stated as to prevent unacceptable arrangements (e.g., **The boy the boy threw the ball the ball*). Can you likewise work out a set of rules for combining lexical items; i.e., words, *within* the various syntactic units (as, for example, D + Adj + N, *a sick cow*, but not **cow a sick*)? Try to express your final rules either "algebraically" or diagrammatically. Of what value, incidentally, is such an abstract statement? Does it have any significant advantages over a narrative or anecdotal statement?

6
Transformationalism

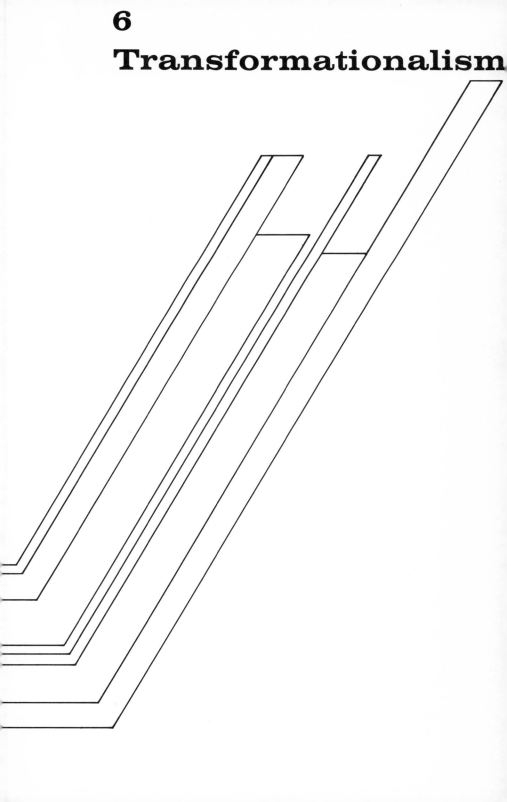

The limitations of traditional and structuralist grammars should be clearly appreciated. Although such grammars may contain full and explicit lists of exceptions and irregularities, they provide only examples and hints concerning the regular and productive syntactic processes.

(Noam Chomsky, *Aspects of the Theory of Syntax*, Cambridge, Mass.)

Any native speaker of English will probably agree that the following sentences are in some semantic sense the "same."
1. Melmoth gave Tillie a potted petunia.
2. Melmoth gave Tillie a petunia that was potted.
3. Melmoth gave Tillie a petunia which was potted.
4. Melmoth gave a potted petunia to Tillie.
5. It was Tillie Melmoth gave a potted petunia to.
6. It was a potted petunia Tillie was given by Melmoth.
7. Tillie was given a potted petunia by Melmoth.
8. A potted petunia was given to Tillie by Melmoth.
9. To Tillie, Melmoth gave a potted petunia.
(And so on). How do we know that they are all really the same? Indeed, in some of the sentences one of the "objects" becomes the "subject" and the "subject" becomes an "object." Word order is markedly different between, say, (4) and (5), and (7) and (8), etc. The structural grammarian would not concern himself with this intuitively obvious relationship among the sentences but rather with the shape of each sentence as a fixed bit of syntax. He would assign a structural description to each and place each sentence with others of the same shape, his concern being primarily classificatory. But we know intuitively that the nine sentences (and several more that could easily be produced) belong to the same "family" with respect to their meaning. The *transformational* grammarian postulates a common source for groups of sentences like these on the assumption that the semantic identity predicts an underlying structural identity. Thus the source of the superficially diverse sentences lies "below the level" of the sentences as actually spoken. This insight into the nature of complex sentences—that they are somehow composed of simpler, more elementary sentences, and that these do not necessarily appear unchanged on the "higher" level, but may undergo various permutations and deformations—has provided the motif for transformational grammar. Grammar is now seen to be operational rather than stative (*process* rather than *object* oriented), the operations being largely concerned with transforming deep structures (from an abstract

and deep semantic level) into surface structures (at the phonological or speech level). In brief, the meaning in the mind is transformed into the expression on the lips.

In moving beyond structuralism, the transformationalist has not really rejected it, for structural descriptions of both deep and surface structures are an important part of transformational methodology. What the transformationalist has done—which the structuralist wanted no part of—is to attempt to understand both linguistic *competence* and linguistic *performance* and, further, to attempt to unify them into a single theory of language with its concomitant, a unified theory of grammar. Competence (which approximates de Saussure's *la langue*) is a deep grammar phenomenon, performance (de Saussure's *la parole*) the surface manifestation of speech. Competence is what *may* be said; performance is what *has* been said.

Underlying transformational (and all other) theories is the fundamental assumption that there exists for all languages a set of sound-meaning relationships, which is to say that a sound or sequence of sounds can arbitrarily be assigned a meaning and that a change in meaning will require a change of sounds (and, conversely, that a change of sound will impose a change of meaning). This more-or-less stabilized relationship between the sounds of a language and their culturally assigned meanings is a necessary precondition to language and communication as we know it.

A grammar, in one way, is a set of rules to express the correspondence of these sound-meaning pairings, and much of the controversy in linguistics has arisen over how best to state this relationship. On the one hand there is the "sound spectrum," the physically oriented analysis of speech, phonetics and acoustics, which has been reasonably well developed. On the other hand, there is meaning, semantics, which has barely been touched. Syntax stands, as it were, between the two. (Syntax and semantics are the most active and controversy-ridden areas of current linguistic research.) Syntax tells the speaker which structural arrangements are grammatical; phonology tells the speaker how any linguistic entity is to be pronounced; and semantics tells what the meaning of any structured string is.

To arrive at the "nature" of syntax, therefore, it must be determined (1) what kinds of structures sentences have and (2) how the structures are put together to form sentences. Somehow, the syntactic component of our language production apparatus, together with its lexical subcomponent, produces well-formed sentences that are additionally assigned both a phonetic shape and a meaning. The transformationalist consequently does not consider the grammar as a single block of rules but rather as a series of components whose integration and interaction provide the complexity and diversity of language.

In the preceding chapter we discussed the hierarchical structure of the sentence and the graphic device—the phrase marker—used to visualize the model. According to this approach, some of the rules of the grammar must be the sort of rules that construct hierarchies, or trees. Then, the syntactic structure of a sentence will be best viewed as a sequence of trees; i.e., a *deep structure* tree and a *surface structure* tree. (See diagram on p. 125.) The deep structure trees (abstract in concept) would be produced within the *base* of the grammar, by the operation of phrase structure (rewrite) rules upon abstract categories such as noun, noun phrase, verb, etc. The resultant tree—the *underlying* phrase marker— would have as its terminal or ultimate constituents abstract categories into which lexical items (words) are inserted from the lexical component according to its corresponding rules (lexical insertion rules). (The lexical component is itself complex, having to deal with phonological, syntactic, and semantic information connected with each word.)

Given a syntactic component that in some way produces trees with lexical items (words) attached to it, these structures must then pass through or be operated upon by a semantic component to provide a semantic reading or interpretation. This reading will derive from the lexical meaning of the words, plus the meaning attached to the particular internal structure of the tree. These same structures must at the same time provide a *reasonable* base from which the semantic component can make interpretations. If the base structure is unduly complicated or non-structurally ambiguous, the semantic component will be faced with unnecessarily complex activities or the making of arbitrary selections. This would greatly reduce the efficiency of human language and make communication uncertain. For example, *The cop shot the man with a gun* is ambiguous because two possible syntactic structures may feed into the semantic component. The fact that two syntactic structures exist simplifies the semantic component's job, as the deep structure component of the syntax will send only *one* of these possible structures to the semantic component for interpretation. The resolution of the possible ambiguity will take place within the syntactic component at the deep structure level. Were this not the case, the semantic component would have to choose between two interpretations, equally valid and without any structural clue for guidance. Choice would have to be either arbitrary or random. In some way, the semantic component would then have to introduce additional meaning in order to differentiate semantic readings. This runs counter to the transformational theory that meaning is determined within the syntactic component and is only "read" or "interpreted" by the semantic component. The hypothesis is, therefore, that the syntactic component provides the base or *input* for semantics and takes care of ambiguities through structural arrangements schematized by branching tree diagrams. In short, there is an intimate relationship between syntax and semantics. Deep structure, thus, has two defining characteristics: (1) it is the point just before which grammatical transformations are made, and (2) it is the point of semantic interpretation (*i.e.*, semantic interpretation is *wholly* determined by the deep structure).* Diagrammatically the interrelationship of syntax to language would appear as follows.

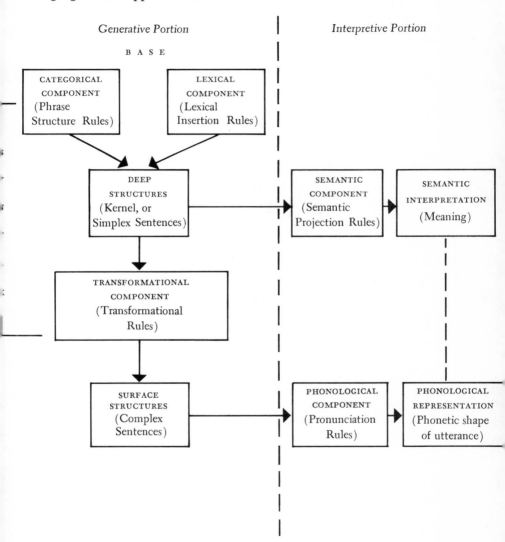

As a theory of language, transformationalism assumes the existence of two general linguistic levels: *deep* (abstract underlying structures derived from a base of phrase structure and lexical components to pro-

* See also the discussion on page 141.

duce meaningful "kernel" sentences) and *surface* (derived structures—the actual sentences we speak, transformed grammatically and rendered into sound). It further assumes that

> Knowledge of a language involves the ability to assign deep and surface structures to an infinite range of sentences, to relate these structures appropriately, and to assign a semantic interpretation and a phonetic interpretation to the paired deep and surface structures.
>
> (Chomsky, *Language and Mind*, p. 26.)

As a generative theory of grammar, it attempts to provide an explicit schematization (phrase-structure rules, transformational rules, etc.) of this theory of language, both for language in general and for specific languages.

When we refer to the set of sentences at the beginning of this chapter, intuition tells us that the underlying structure is *Melmoth gave a petunia to Tillie.* (Only incidentally does the petunia happen to be potted.) Assuming this as a "base," our grammatical problem is how to account for the wealth of "surface" forms; *i.e.,* how to state explicitly the rules or mechanisms for getting from the one deep structure to the many surface structures—all without significantly changing the meaning.

The mechanism postulated is the T-rule, the transform, a rule of tremendous grammatical "power" that will create additional complexity in the sentence structure. Because of this power, T-rules obviously cannot be applied randomly or indiscriminately to any and all deep structures. Transformations are purposeful; *i.e.,* they seek to achieve certain linguistic goals of expression. As with other sets of rules in language, there appears to be a small, finite set of T-rules, capable of projection into an infinity of instances.

In order to determine *when* a transformational rule may be applied, we need to know its *domain; i.e.,* the classes or types of sentences that the grammar admits as susceptible to a particular rule. To formulate or to discover a T-rule, therefore, our first necessary ingredient is an accurate structural description (SD)* of the type or class of sentences to which the rule can be applied with grammatically acceptable consequences.

Using the underlying *Melmoth gave a petunia to Tillie,* we find that this sentence consists of the elements *Noun—Verb—Noun Phrase₁* *—to—Noun Phrase₂,* in that order. At the moment, the exact nature of the first noun is relatively immaterial to the structural description (assuming the sentence to be grammatical in the first place); that is, any person or persons, institutions, etc., or combination of these, could

---

* In some of the literature, this is referred to as the *structural index* (SI). This abbreviation is easily confused with that for *semantic interpretation,* and we prefer, therefore, to use SD.

fill the noun slot occupied by the word *Melmoth*. This particular element is, then, a variable in our phrase marker and, as such, can be represented by the traditional algebraic symbol for an unknown, X. Our structural description can now read:

SD: X—V—NP₁—to—NP₂

The corresponding tree diagram is:

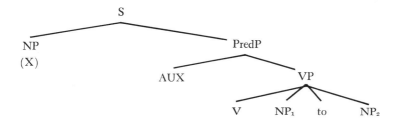

The SD at this point is simply stating that all sentences answering this particular description may undergo a transformation that will, as a consequence, bring about a specific structural change (SC). A typical transformation would be one resulting in the sentence *Melmoth gave Tillie a petunia*, which shows a structural change to: X—V—NP₂—NP₁. In the execution of this change, several *elementary* transformational processes have taken place: (1) The morpheme *to* has been deleted, and (2) NP₁ and NP₂ have switched positions.

Thus, at this point we have stated that there is a rule—let us call it the Indirect Object Movement Rule, or T_I.O.—that can be applied to a specific class of sentences (for which we have a structural description) and that brings about a specific change in the structure of such sentences. We have a finite rule capable of generating a very large, if not infinite, number of sentences. However, it will not take long to come up with a number of sentences that, although fitting the structural description set forth in our rule, become *ungrammatical* upon undergoing the specified structural change. The following, for example, become unacceptable when transformed:

Melmoth delivered a petunia to Tillie.
*Melmoth delivered Tillie a petunia.
Melmoth gave them to Tillie.
*Melmoth gave Tillie them.
Melmoth handed over a petunia to Tillie.
*Melmoth handed over Tillie a petunia.
Melmoth threw his petunia to the floor.
*Melmoth threw the floor his petunia.
Melmoth took the petunia to task.
*Melmoth took task the petunia.

Melmoth drove the petunia to New York.

*Melmoth drove New York the petunia.

Melmoth gave a petunia to a girl who had finally given up her job and consented to marry him as soon as he got his next promotion.

?Melmoth gave a girl who had finally given up her job and consented to marry him as soon as he got his next promotion a petunia.

At this point it becomes necessary to examine the sentences that are exceptions to the rule, and attempt to determine if there is any way to *systematically* account for the non-conforming sentences. If so, the exceptions can then be codified as a set of *restrictions* on the original T-rule.

There are then three necessary ingredients for a complete and adequate statement of a T-rule. That is, any transformational rule can be formulated as consisting of:

1. a structural description — SD
2. a structural change   — SC
3. a set of restrictions or constraints on elements of the SD or on the operation of the rule.

The Passive Rule (T_{PASS}) is an especially interesting transformation in English. It too has a noun phrase switch, in which the underlying logical subject of the deep structure becomes the grammatical direct object of the surface structure. A movement from the initial noun phrase position in English is very disruptive to meaning, since in the normal simple active affirmative declarative sentence this position is reserved for the subject (both grammatical and logical). In the passivized form, the dislocated subject noun phrase is preceded by an insertion, *by*, which serves to mark the logical subject and typical agent of the sentence action. Other inserted material in the passive are a form of *be* and the past participle ending *-en* (or its equivalent) that attach to the verb.

Melmoth gave a petunia to Tillie.

SD: NP_1—V—NP_2—to NP_3
SC: NP_2 be + -en—V—to NP_3—by NP_1

A petunia be PAST give + – en to Tillie by Melmoth

was   given

Though many of the details of transformational-generative grammar have yet to be worked out, and though there is not agreement among all grammarians that T-G grammar is the core theory, it does dominate the grammatical scene today. We have, therefore, included an Appendix that offers by way of both explanatory material and diagrams, an outline of some of the major transformational operations as they are currently understood. This material is meant to be a guide, not a program for teaching. For more detailed information on the subject, the Bibliography lists a number of references, annotated to indicate the technical level upon which they are written.

Implications for Teaching

Various graded textbook series currently on the market incorporate transformational materials as their bow to modernity. Unfortunately, these materials have been plugged in, in modular fashion, to the place formerly occupied by "traditional grammar"; and nothing else has changed. That is, where the student was doing Reed-Kellogg diagrams before, he is doing tree diagrams now; where he was learning one set of labels before, he is learning another set of labels now; where grammar was isolated busy work before, it is still isolated busy work; and where the student was bored to exasperation before, he is being bored to exasperation still. Rules, definitions, memory work, and busy work comprise the real "message" of conventional grammar study, whether it come from the old-fashioned, grim grammar book or the slick, new language arts model. Unless the study of grammar is "organic" (a part of the larger study of language in all its diversity and applications) and exploratory (*i.e.*, examined via the inquiry-discovery method) it might just as well be abandoned altogether. Over the years it fell out that grammar study became the prime, often only, focus of language study because of the mistaken notion that grammar study would "help" the student to other things (e.g., "think more clearly," "write better," etc.). It has long since been demonstrated that the claims made for traditional, normative grammar "study" are only claims. None of the "benefits" did ever actually accrue to the student. Indeed, the tedium and intimidation that was generated in the grammar class served if anything to impede progress in the practical and effective use of language.

What we urge, therefore, is that grammatical explorations be rooted in larger questions of language and be done on an open-ended, open-minded basis. As we have said elsewhere, the teacher is guide, questioner, challenger, resource person, etc., but not the dispenser of "right" answers. The projects that follow touch on a number of ideas currently being explored, questioned, and modified within the profession of linguistics itself. To wrestle with, test, and prove or disprove these ideas will best serve the cause of grammar and, more fundamentally, the cause of education.

1. In theory, transformations do not affect meaning, for meaning is established in the deep structure. But it can be argued that in order to collate phonology (especially intonation) with syntax, the transformational process includes some kind of semantic manipulation. An obvious example is the use of an intonation contour suggesting, for example, anger, which may not be signalled by the syntax at all. Consider the number of ways any simple sentence can be intoned to change meaning radically. Provide and comment upon several examples of the insertion of intonational meaning. Can you find any examples of other kinds of (apparent) transformational changes in meaning? Is it possible to modify transformational theory to allow for phonological insertions in the deep structure? This is a difficult question and is best "answered" by group discussion. All answers must be considered tentative and open to revision or rejection, but not before they are thoroughly examined and tested. In scientific theorizing, the question of the "cost" of setting up a theory one way or another must be taken into account. What may at first glance seem to be an easy expedient, may in the long run cause various difficulties, excessive complications, and confusions. This notion of what you give for what you get in scientific theorizing is itself an interesting one for exploration. This is an obvious point at which several intellectual disciplines can be brought together in an educationally productive way.

2. Sentence (2) below is a transform of sentence (1). Explain what the transformational process here consists in.

1. Melmoth didn't fly the plane because he was afraid to fly it.
2. Melmoth didn't fly the plane because he was afraid.

The term for this type of transformation is *deletion*. Can you find any other examples of sentences that seem to have been produced by this process. Try "reconstructing" the immediate source sentences. [(1) above is the immediate source of (2).] Keep in mind that only those elements of a source can be deleted that will not result in a loss of meaning; i.e., the meaning of deleted elements must be in some way recoverable. In the example above, the meaning of the deleted element is implicit in the part of the original sentence that remains.

3. Sentence (2) below is the result (output) of a *permutation transformation*.

1. Melmoth gave Tillie a potted petunia.
2. Tillie was given a potted petunia by Melmoth.

Explain what was done to (1) in order to get (2). Actually, (1) is itself the result of a permutation transformation. Can you figure out why? What, then, is the source sentence? (Don't overcomplicate the problem!) Find some other kinds of permutation transformations. (Remember that *permutation* means *rearrangement*.) Note, incidentally, that as a result of permuting (1) to produce (2), which is a *passive* (hence, this is called the *passive transformation*, T$_{\text{PASS}}$), it was necessary to add something. This addition of elements in order to complete the transformation is called *insertion*.

4. Transformations that require both a deletion and an addition are called *substitution* transformations. Sentence (1) below is the output of a substitution transformation. Can you determine what was substituted for what?

(1) Snively admired himself in the mirror.

Deep structure (2) is the source, via substitution, for what sentence?

(2) The wheel [the wheel squeaks the loudest] gets the oil.

This particular type of substitution transformation (2) is called *relativization*, T$_{\text{REL}}$. Try to find (or create) some other examples of relativization as well as of other types of substitution transformations. Try to find some sentences from your reading that could be relativized and explain how it could be done.

5. Can you characterize the deviances in each of the following?

1. She sang an exciting.
2. Melmoth gave Tillie.
3. Vase crashed on the pavement.
4. Finley a present for Lillian.
5. Norval has more sense than.

(Don't just add words, but explain in particular what is wrong in each case and in general what is wrong with all five.)

6. Can you characterize the deviances in each of the following?

1. Max sliced evaporation into chunks.
2. I didn't know what to say so I shrugged my ear.
3. Melmoth ate what Tillie had danced.
4. Sherman drank his tractor with an icepick.
5. The postman scraped his air and snored the mail.

What principle of deviance seems to be at work here?

7. The following set of diagrams represents the transformation of an active voice sentence into a passive voice sentence as well as the I.O. Movement, *i.e.*, it represents the passive transformation for a particular set of sentences. Diagram (2) is a necessary intermediate step (the *Indirect Object Movement Rule*). Can you figure out why? What would happen if we tried simply to eliminate this step? What would happen if we applied this transformation after the step shown in diagram (3)?

1.
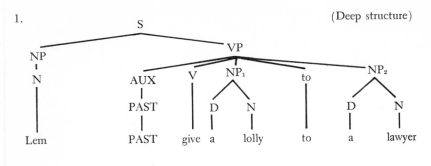
(Deep structure)

2.
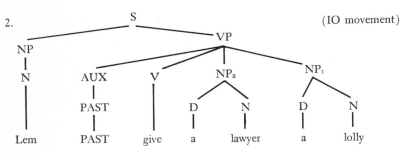
(IO movement)

3.
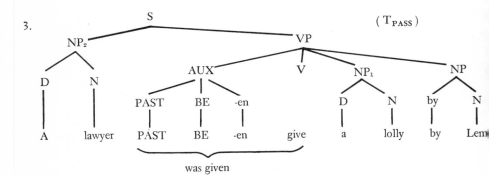
(T_PASS)

8. Questions are the result of transformation. Try to return the following questions to their presumed deep structure form:

1. Were they troubled?
2. Are they being troubled?
3. Have the guests arrived?
4. Can Cranford win the race tomorrow?
5. Would you care to bet on it?
6. Did the train arrive late?
7. Do good guys always finish last?
8. Does Melmoth have a headache?

9. What caused Tillie to faint?
10. Where have all the flowers gone?
11. Who has change of a dollar?
12. How do you plan to recoup your losses?
13. When will we know the truth?
14. To what lengths do you intend to go?
15. At what time is he expected?

Questions (9) and following cannot be "detransformed" so easily as the others. Why? Can you find any other types of questions from those exemplified here? Try to categorize the question types and develop rules for their production transformationally. What type of answer does each type of question ask for? Can the "same" question be asked in more than one way? Demonstrate how. How are these two versions of the "same" question related to each other? Can you develop rules for mutual transformation; that is, for changing the one into the other and back again?

9. Most negations are transformation. (We say *most*, for a sentence like *No children are coming* seems to be a base or kernel sentence.) Gather a variety of sentences and attempt to produce a negative version of each. Describe the nature of the negation transformation for each example. Categorize the various types of negation transformations. Can you find any sentences from which can be produced two (or more) acceptable negations? (Remember, the base meaning must be the same for each version.) Describe the transformational process for each version. How do the two (or more) negations from the same source stand in relation to each other? Can you develop a set of rules (1) for producing each kind of negation transformation, (2) for returning each to its source, (3) for permuting one of two (or more) equivalent versions to the other?

10. Show how *negative questions* are produced and how to return them to their sources. In performing the dual transformation of *negation* and *question*, which of the two transformations precedes the other, or does it make no difference?

11. Though many attributive phrases (*a weary traveler, the hyperactive child, a gorgeous garland,* etc.) are transforms of simple copula sentences (*a traveler is weary, the child is hyperactive, a garland is gorgeous,* etc.), many are not, though they are transforms of something. (E.g., *a/winning game,* as in *He played a winning game,* cannot reasonably be derived from **a game is winning.* What might it be reasonably derived from?) Find a variety of examples from your reading and try to return them to their presumed sources. What problems did you run into and how did you resolve them?

12. Many structuralists classified *it* and *there* sentences ("expletive sentences") among the basic sentence patterns. Can you figure out a good transformational reason why these should *not* be considered "basic"? Here are a couple of examples to get you started:
1. There were several rather obnoxious people at the meeting today.
2. It hardly seems right that they have been allowed to cause so much trouble.
3. It's an ill wind that blows no good.
4. There isn't much to be thankful for these days.

If the *it* and *there* sentences are in fact transformations, can you work out an appropriate set of rules for producing them?

13. In sentences like *I want it clearly understood that we will fight to the finish*, what role does *it* seem to play? Can such a sentence be rearranged to delete the *it*? Does the *it* seem to be the result of some kind of transformation? If so, describe the transformational process whereby the *it* was inserted. Try to find some other examples from your reading of this type of sentence. Does such a construction serve some useful purpose? Discuss. Try rewriting sentences of this type in a passage of prose. What effect does the rewrite have on the passage? (Don't overlook examples like *It was a great moment in my life when I won the rutabaga-eating contest* (and its rearrangement: *When I won the ruta-baga-eating contest, it . . .*).

14. *Participial modifiers* are transforms of predications, thus: from *As I looked up, I saw the hawk dive* we can derive, *Looking up, I saw the hawk dive*. Gather some sentences containing participial modifiers and try to return each participial phrase to its source. (Present participles are words like *looking, walking, talking* used as *adjectives* not as the verbs from which they come; past participles are words like *tired, awakened*, etc., used likewise as adjectives: *Walking across the street, I . . . ; Tired beyond endurance, he . . .* , etc.) Try rewriting a paragraph or two from something you are reading, (1) to transform as many non-participial constructions as you can to participial constructions and (2) to turn the process around and turn all the participial constructions you can find back to predicative constructions. In each case, the passage should be rhetorically acceptable. How is the tone of the passage affected in each case?

15. A common type of reduced predication is the *absolute*. Here are two examples:
1. <u>His thoughts elsewhere</u>, he failed to hear the question.
2. The good old family car was finished, <u>its radiator belching steam</u> <u>and its oil running out all over the street</u>.

Show how the absolutes underlined in the above examples are in fact reduced predications. Try to find a variety of other examples of the absolute. Show how each was derived from a predication, and explain how each (and those above) is related to the main part of the sentence. Try the usual type of rewriting project and discuss the results.

16. Many constructions that use *with* are transforms. Consider:
1. *With my head held high*, I marched into the boss's office. (I held my head high.)
2. Two bankrobbers *with guns* held the police at bay. (Two bankrobbers *had* guns.)

Find a number of different kinds of *with* constructions and determine what role *with* is playing in each. For all cases that seem to be transforms, try to return the constructions to their presumed sources. Do the usual rewriting project and comment on the results.

17. Consider the following pairs:
1. Melmoth sang a song.
   Melmoth's singing of a song. . . .
2. Tillie replied pleasantly.
   Tillie's pleasant reply. . . .
3. Time passes.
   The passing of time. . . .
4. The end is in sight.
   With the end being in sight. . . .
5. He intended to win the match.
   His intention to win the match. . . .

How is the second member of each pair related to the first? In each case, the second member of the pair has undergone a *nominalization* transformation. In each case, attempt to describe the transformational process. Can you develop a general rule or set of rules for nominalization? Find some examples (in your reading) of nominalizations. Try to return the nominalizations to their presumed sources. Try to nominalize a randomly chosen group of sentences. What has to be done to complete the now incomplete sentences? (See above: "What can take the place of the ellipsis marks? Can these nominalizations, or any nominalizations, be used in other than subject positions? Demonstrate.)

18. In theory, any sentence can be derived from the abstract formula, NP + VP. It is clear, however, that lacking any further restrictions, we could produce utterances like *Melmoth ate a bowl of sweet red electricity.* (And many other "sentences" that are semantically unacceptable in present-day English.) Intuitively, we know that people can't eat electricity. But while grammarians rely on linguistic intuition as much as anyone else, they do attempt to find some rational basis for it. One explanation offered for the type of semantic incompatibility we illustrated above is the postulated system of *feature matrices* into which all words can be placed. Thus for each word there is a set of features that attaches to it (or is predicted by it—the mechanism is not clear). The features for Melmoth, then, will be

+Noun

+proper

+concrete
(−abstract)

+animate
(−inanimate)

+human
(−non-human).

These features allow it to combine as *agent* ("doer") with a verb like *eat*. Electricity, on the other hand, has these features:

+Noun

+abstract (?)

+common

+inanimate
(−animate)

+non-human   [implied by
(−human)   preceding feature]

+/− ?

These features prevent *electricity* from combining as *patient* ("receiver") with a verb like *eat*. Can you explain why this is so? The semantic feature theory is appealing and does seem to account for certain linguistic facts. It does, however, also have some weaknesses and "holes." What do they seem to be? Probe more deeply into the concept of *features* than has been done here. What kinds of features might be assigned to verbs, adjectives, etc.? Try creating a feature matrix for an entire sentence. What do the features reveal about the relationship of items within the sentence? Explain what value there would be (if any) in including a feature matrix for every word in the dictionary. Try writing a short dictionary of, say, current slang terms in use among your friends in which each entry contains a feature matrix. Do any problems arise in assigning features? Discuss. Explain to our flying saucer man how he can use the information provided by the feature matrices.

19. Though it is not difficult to see how a sentence like (1) can be derived transformationally from (1a) and (1b), it is less easy to find the presumed deep structure sources for (2). How might (2) be derived? (This is clearly *not* a right/wrong answer situation!)
1. Tillie sang *a delicate song.*
    (1a) Tillie sang a song.
    (1b) The song is delicate.
2. Tillie sang *a hundred songs* that night.

Gather a collection of sentences that seem to offer no possibility for "de-transformation." (Don't, of course, include kernels, *i.e.,* basic patterns, for all that can be done to them is to return them to their phrasal components: *Tillie sang a song* resolves itself into *Tillie* and *sang a song* [*sang + a song*; *a + song*], neither of which is a sentence.) Discuss the difficulty in each case. Share your ideas with others, and perhaps you will find that at least some of the sentences can be shown to be derivations. You might, in fact, make an original contribution to grammar study, one of the anticipated delights of working in an "open" field.

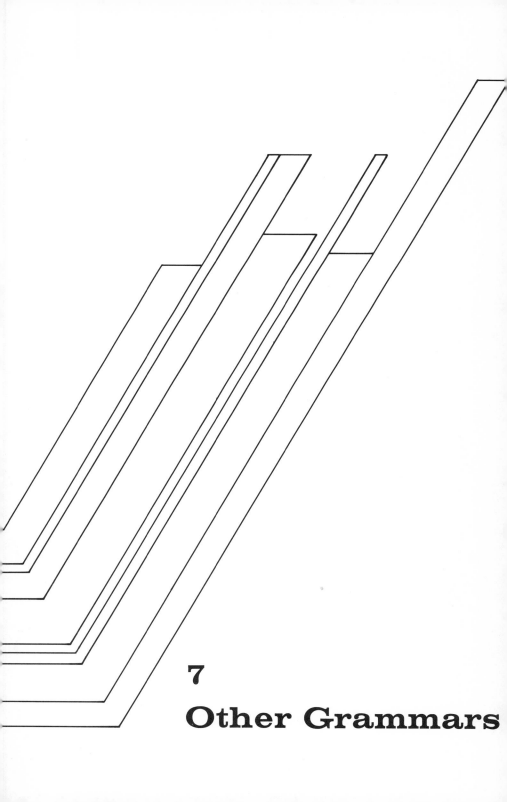

7

Other Grammars

Linguistics as a whole is, as scholars well recognize, in a state of great ferment today. Numerous new approaches are being tried, extended, and applied in various fashions. The focus of different analysts often varies in diverse respects; nevertheless, the central facts of language remain the same regardless of the particular analyst's viewpoint. Sometimes, terminological innovations obscure the essential unity of linguistics, and investigators talk at cross-purposes when they are in essential agreement, although perhaps at the moment they may be examining different aspects of the same complex phenomena.

(Louis G. Heller & James Macris, "Perspectives in Functionalism," *Word*, Vol. 23, Nos. 1–2–3, April–August–December 1967.)

In recent years linguists have proposed several types of transformational-generative grammars. For all versions, the task of the grammar is to pair meanings with phonological representations. The assumption is that there is a surface structure connected syntactically with meanings. At issue is the organization of rules that connect meaning to surface structures.

"Standard" (*i.e.*, Chomsky's version as of 1965 in *Aspects of the Theory of Syntax*) theory posits a sub-surface or deep structure level with these characteristics:

1. It is the *input* to the transformational component.
2. It provides the basis for semantic interpretation.
3. It is the level where lexical (word) insertion takes place (with certain minor exceptions).
4. It is the level at which selectional restrictions are imposed (restrictions, for example, based on the incompatibility of features).

These characteristics developed historically, almost accidentally, during the development of generative theory. In arguing for a more abstract, underlying structure, without meanings, Chomsky conceived the notion of deep structure, together with an *independent* syntactic component (the *autonomous syntax* hypothesis). This concept is, however, only a hypothesis; and it has been called into question by a number of linguists, among them Ross, McCawley, and Lakoff, whose theory of *generative semantics* rejects deep structure in favor of a formulation like this one

Meanings

Surface Structure

where lexical items can be inserted at any point. The generative semantics view is that language is a *code* and that the rules that produce pairings of meanings and surface structures don't have an intermediate level. There are merely syntactic rules with meaning providing the basic input to everything; *i.e.*, the theory coaims a homogeneity of semantics and syntax in which the base component must generate semantic representations directly. It is also considered possible that there is no abstract surface structure; *i.e.*, phonological rules would precede the surface structure and provide the phonological representation directly. Generative semantics thus assumes (1) that there is a semantic interpretation of a sentence, (2) that lexical insertion may be made wherever wanted, and (3) that the set of primitive predicates and indices that determine and define semantic noun phrases will construct a reading directly, without the need for any semantic "projection rules." The sentence *Melmoth murdered Montrose* is presumably generated from the underlying semantic structure *Melmoth caused it to come about that Montrose died.* The problem is how to generate the underlying structure. To do this, elaborate tree structures with higher performative verbs will be necessary. These will have to be *collapsed* by transforms to be replaced by lexical equivalents. If the deep structure is made abstract enough, it will eventually coincide (or virtually so) with the semantic component. It follows, therefore, that standard theory and generative semantics can be inter-translated, except where lexical insertion takes place.

In its basic theoretical motivation, generative semantics wishes to reduce the number and type of non-terminal node labels. In examining the labeled node categories of the standard theory, they found only S, NP and V to be above suspicion. Their present (1971) view of sentence structure is one that is verb oriented:

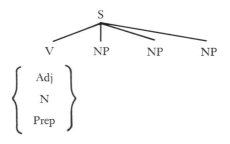

where the "verb" constituent may possess "features" that would make it correspond to the traditional concept of noun, adjective, etc. (See Lakoff, *Irregularity in Syntax*, 1970.) This structure is very similar to that of logicians (especially logical positivists) where *predicates* (verbs) relate the *arguments* (NP's) in a *proposition* (sentence).

The structure of the constituents under an S are then given by simple phrase structure-like statements that amount to being constraints on what is a tree. The NP's may (1) function as indices in a referential system, NP → $\{x_1 \ldots x_n\}$; (2) may be a proposition, NP → S; or (3) may be relative-like in nature, NP → NP S.

The semantic part of the theory assumes a lexicon that is structured in terms of *semantic primitives*. For example,

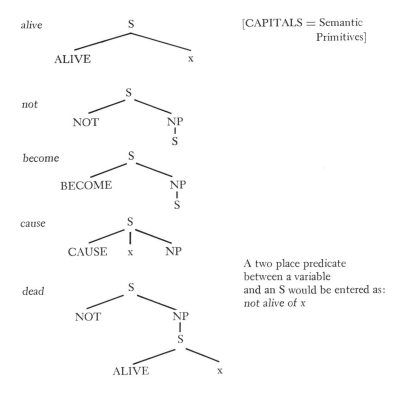

[CAPITALS = Semantic Primitives]

A two place predicate between a variable and an S would be entered as: *not alive of x*

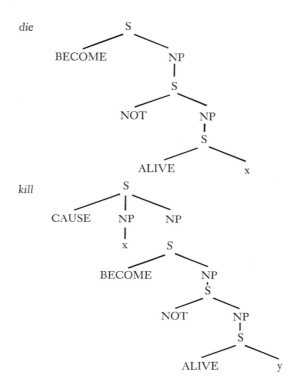

To say *Max killed Harry*, one must construct *kill* as above, and specify x as Max, and y as Harry.

To actually do lexical insertion, there needs to be *predicate raising* (of the verb, or predicate), which collapses the elaborate tree structures, cyclically, from the bottom up, collecting the semantic elements together in the process. The semantic interpretation involves first having a "list" of semantic primitives as shown (which some consider to be the "innate" structures of language). Then, the child learns the way in which the primitives combine in his culture, to form the lexicon, together with the *derivational constraints* that are necessary to ensure the output of well-formed sentences. The derivational constraints constitute the "grammar," and are comparable to the transformational rules of the standard theory. In generative semantics, the predicate in the highest S will have a special relationship to the rest of the structures and will necessarily be illocutionary, constituting the speech act and distinguishing between statement, promise, command, etc.

Chomsky's "standard theory" has evolved since the publication of *Aspects of the Theory of Syntax* (1965), in which he held that deep structure is *alone* responsible for meaning. Chomsky and his fellow theorists now recognize several intermediate levels of semantic interpretation. His *lexicalist* hypothesis and *interpretive semantics* theory assumes that the semantic component operates not only on the deep structure but on the surface structure as well. In the most recent presentation of his position (1971), which he now calls the *extended standard theory* (EST), Chomsky states that perceptual strategies interact with competence (grammar) to account for discrepancies between acceptability and grammaticality and that presuppositions (which must be true) are determined by surface structure. Therefore, meaning is determined by a pairing of deep structure and surface structure, where deep structure controls one aspect of meaning—such as thematic relations or case relations—and others are determined in part (and maybe *in toto*) by the surface structure. Thus the theory handles *topic, comment, focus, presupposition, scope, pronoun and co-referentiality*, etc., better than standard theory. For example:

1. Did Melmoth give a daisy to Tillie?

If this sentence exhibits normal intonation and stress, there are three possible *foci*, which can produce these answers to the question:

    i. No, to Nellie.

    ii. No, he went bowling. (*I.e.*, he did something else.)

    iii. No, he didn't.

Sentence (1) is a surface structure. Since phonology works only on surface structure, one depends on that to know where the *intonation center* is. Only then can we determine *focus* and only then can we correctly choose (i), (ii), or (iii).

Chomsky's earlier and fragmentary *Syntactic Structures* (1957) assumed that the traditional parts of speech were deep structure categories, for which he listed appropriate lexical inventories. Although modified in *Aspects*, the nature of the lexicon continued to be a subject of controversy—particularly regarding whether and how certain items were to be derived from others. Within the theoretical framework of *Aspects*, this was handled by many linguists as transformational. Chomsky has reconsidered his position and now feels that the base must be able to handle directly those items formerly considered related through transformations. He does not wholly exclude the transformational process, but augments the capacity of the base to handle abstract lexical forms that possess the potential to appear variously as noun, verb, etc., in the surface structure.

The *case grammar* theory of Charles Fillmore stood originally somewhere between standard theory and generative semantics, and has recently moved more in the latter's direction. Fillmore contends that grammatical relations should be more abstract than in standard theory; i.e., that the notion of "subject" and "object" are *not* relevant for semantic interpretation. In *Melmoth likes mushrooms*, for example, Melmoth is the deep structure subject, *mushrooms* the deep structure object. But in the examples that follow, Melmoth may or may not be the "logical" underlying subject, despite surface structural similarity.

Melmoth chews tobacco.
Melmoth flatters people.
Melmoth compliments Tillie.
Melmoth fell into the pond.
Melmoth sank into the lake.
Melmoth vanished.
Melmoth died.
Melmoth built an igloo.
Melmoth went crazy.
Melmoth preoccupies Tillie.

In standard theory, the NP to the left would be the subject. Yet the underlying relationships within each sentence vary greatly from sentence to sentence. Fillmore proposes not to abandon the idea of grammatical subject and object, but to take a more abstract view of grammatical relations. *Case*, thus, equals grammatical relation with a constant semantic effect. Consider:

1. Sean is cooking the dinner.
2. The dinner is cooking.
3. Scan is cooking. (Ambiguous.)

In (1) and (2), *cooking* and *dinner* stand in the same relationship despite the change in word order and surface subject. And, of course, *Sean* and *cooking* in (1) and (3) stand in the same relationship to each other.

Fillmore believes that a relatively small inventory of cases (in many ways not unlike the traditional cases of Latin, etc.) will enable one to describe *all* grammatical relations for *all* languages, and that the case relations will remain the same throughout a series of related sentences (such as that given above).

In the examples above, standard theory would have to assume that there were two verbs *cook*, with the same morphological form but with different semantic and contextual properties.

$cook_1$—taking an *animate* subject
allowing an object
$cook_2$—taking an *inanimate* subject
not allowing an object

In such cases, the standard theory deep structures do not tell us very much about the grammatical relationships.

```
          S                                        S
      ╱       ╲                                 ╱    ╲
   NP          VP                            NP        VP
    │       ╱      ╲                          │         │
    │      V         NP                       │         V
    │      │         │                        │         │
  Sean   cook₁     dinner                   dinner    cook₂
```

In each tree structure, the configuration of $\overset{S}{\underset{NP}{\diagup}}$ is the same, although the relationship of NP to S is obviously different in each example. Fillmore would view the structure as

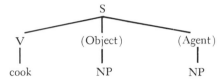

```
                 S
           ╱     │     ╲
          V   (Object)  (Agent)
          │      │         │
        cook    NP        NP
```

In any grammatical sentence, *at least* one case relationship is required. In the example given, the *object* construct is *dinner*; the *agent* construct is *Sean*. If one is left out of the sentence, the remaining NP becomes the superficial subject. The main difference lies in which case relation is chosen or selected in the derivation. Thus,

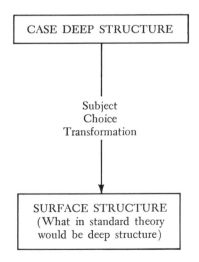

Therefore, it does away with the apparatus of several sets of selectional restrictions on *cook* in the standard theory.

Fillmore's theory is parallel to the standard theory in many respects, except that the deep structure looks quite different, and, instead of branching structure showing NP to the left of VP, there is a V followed by *case constituents*.

Fillmore's initial (1968) model for sentence structure in case grammar was based on the rules

S → Modality (M) + Proposition (P)
M → (tense) (mood) (negation) (aspect) etc.
P → verb (V) + Cases (C)
C → case marker (K) + NP

Application of these rules resulted in the following tree structure:

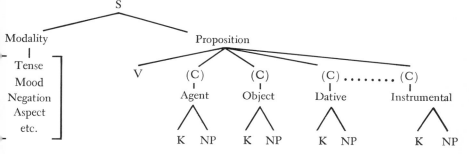

Each case constituent consisted of some case marker (K) and an NP. In English, the K is usually manifested as a preposition. In Fillmore's presentation, the "dative" relationship (case) is usually associated with *to*; the agent with *by*; locative with *in, at, near*; and the instrumental is marked by *with*.

The relation between deep and surface structure is especially noteworthy, as, for example, in the instrumental, whose deep structure case marker, *with*, shows up on the surface. However, the case marker can often be *deleted* on the surface, especially if the case constituent becomes a subject.

The key opened the door. (Deletion of *with*)
John gave Mary a book. (Dative movement, deletion of *to*)

Prepositions as case markers are not inevitable or specific. Some verbs require prepositions, and although English uses prepositions as case markers, not all languages do. Some use postpositions, others use inflections. This makes no difference in case theory; either can be a case marker. Only the manifestations will vary. Fillmore considers the *nominative* and *accusative* to be neutralizations at the surface level of deep structure cases. In his system, English, Latin, and Japanese case structure is identical; the grammatical surface structures are only notational variants.

More recently (1970) Fillmore greatly simplified his sentence structure and moved closer to generative semantics by eliminating the modality constituent (M) and the case marker (K), thus analyzing the sentence at a deep structure level as consisting of verb followed by a series of NP's, each of which is directly dominated by a case. The new case grammar rules are:

$$S \rightarrow V + C_1 + C_2 + \dots C_n$$
$$C_1 \rightarrow NP, \text{ etc.}$$

The deep structure has now moved closer to a semantic representation. What were formally treated as part of the modality constituent are now directly adjoined to the verb, and case markings are correspondingly adjoined to their respective NP's by prepositional selection rules.

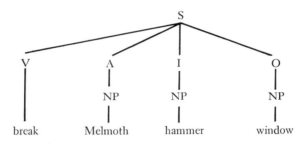

The verbal element is basic, or central, in the analysis, but the remaining elements are unordered, *i.e.*, there is no linear sequencing of the cases.

Fillmore's revised listing of cases as of 1970 is as follows:

A	Agentive	instigator of action, animate
E	Experiencer	affected by action, animate
I	Instrumental	force of object causing action or state
O	Objective	most neutral case semantically
S	Source	origin or starting point
G	Goal	object or end point
L	Locative	spatial location or orientation
T	Time	temporal orientation
C	Comitative	accompaniment role, animate
B	Benefactive	benefactive role, animate

The first six are the most necessary for any type of verbal classification; the rest supplement the descriptive detail relating to the verb.

Given the deep structure assumed by Fillmore, with no such thing as a "subject" or "object," there must be a class of rules to provide a *subject choice; i.e.*, the movement of some constituent into subject position in the surface structure, out of its original unordered position. Although this could be considered as two rules—choice plus movement—Fillmore appears to consider them as one process. There is also apparently some sort of hierarchy in the process of subject choice and this is given as A–E–I–O–S–G. If the deep structure has more than one case, the agentive case will normally be selected as the subject. In the absence of an agent, choice will devolve on the other cases, as listed above. There is likewise an object selection hierarchy, given as E–O–G.

Although this hierarchy prevails in the normal selections of subject and object, provision is made for the overriding of normal process, and, in the passive, the objective case moves to initial position becoming subject, and the agent, if present, becomes the surface object, "marked" with *by*. In some instances, where the agent is unspecified or obscure, again the object case NP may be selected as subject but the instrumental case NP becomes the surface object, as in *This door* (Obj.) *opens with this key* (Instr., implies an agent).

In case grammar, the verbs *have* and *be* do not have any substantial semantic content. Therefore, there is no need for their presence in the deep structure and they should be inserted syntactically. Insertion of *have* or *be* takes place whenever there is an "empty" or "zero" verb element in the underlying structure. The rule for *have* would probably look something like the following:

1. A zero verb, followed by O = *have*

or,

2. Insertion of *be*; then *be* + *with* = *have*

e.g., *John has a book*

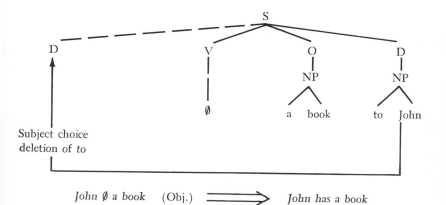

John ∅ a book (Obj.) $\implies$ *John has a book*

Case grammar allows for derived sentences (embedded complements, since the objective constituent can be manifested either as O or as O)

NP   S

as in, for example, *John wants to leave.*

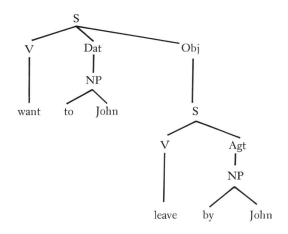

want to John [ₛ leave by John]ₛ

⟹   *John wants to leave*

Fillmore posits that (1) complement clauses are all dominated by an objective node, and (2) in a single proposition (a simple sentence) a given case constituent can occur only once.

A characteristic of case grammar is that it can abstract part of the meaning of a verb and express it as a case relation. Contextual restrictions are regulated by a case *frame*, detailing the allowable co-occurrences. This composite representation of the frame has remained the same in Fillmore's new model. For example, the verb *break* would be shown as

break + [———(A) (I) O]

This tells us that the verb can appear in collocations containing the agentive and instrumental cases optionally, and the objective case obligatorily.

Fillmore wants to be able to get from his deep structure to a surface structure not only through selection rules, but also with a series of transformational rules. His proposed list is not yet complete, but lies in the direction of developing syntactic structures out of his "semantic" base, rather than assigning a semantic interpretation to already existing syntactic structures, à la Chomsky. Among the advantages that case grammar seems to have are

1. lexical simplification,
2. semantic simplification,

3. verb simplification, and
4. ability to account for unexpected prepositions.

Abstract syntax is a version of generative grammar that lies somewhere between standard theory and generative semantics, as does case grammar, but in a different direction. Opting for syntactic structures rather than semantic ones, the theory of abstract syntax presumes a tree structure similar to the syntactic trees of standard theory and a recursive system based on *complementation*. Abstract verbs (such as *causative, performative, inchoative,* etc.) are conceived for this system of analysis and are invested with semantic and syntactic but not phonological properties. In standard theory, a sentence like *Drusilla broke her dentures* is diagrammed quite simply:

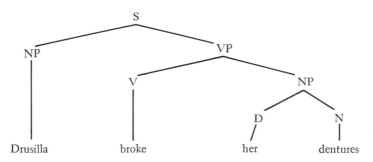

But in Abstract Syntax it would look like this:

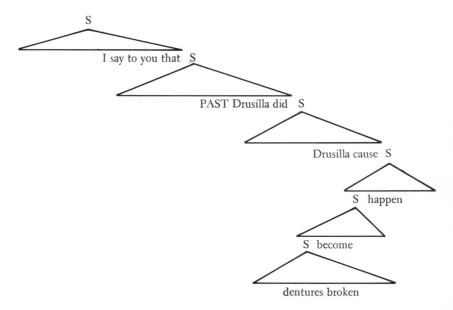

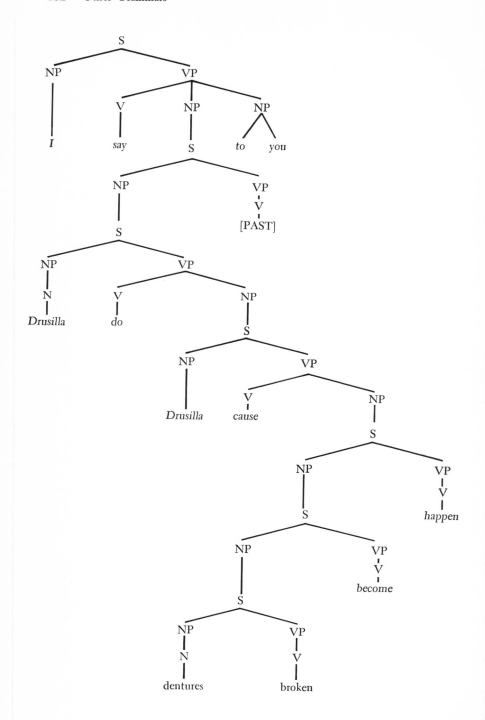

In this abstract syntactic structure, an abstract *performative* verb occurs as the dominant underlying verb. It generally will be deleted by a rule in the process that brings the sentence to the surface. The second part of the tree, the complement, captures the semantics of the sentence, with *become* as an abstract *inchoative* verb. Transformation then creates a sort of "plugging-in" process whereby features are additively incorporated into abstract verbs and carried along into the final surface structure, thus:

$$
\text{break} \\
\begin{bmatrix}
+ \text{ cause} \\
+ \text{ become} \\
+ \text{ broken}
\end{bmatrix}
$$

Drusilla broke her dentures, therefore, carries the features underlying *break.* The abstract verbs (and *do*) do not occur with *all* sentences. The individual sentence will determine their presence or absence in the presumed underlying structure.

By the mid-1950's, the Bloomfieldian tradition had developed significant divergencies. Chomsky's transformational-generative grammar soon emerged as a separate "orthodoxy" in open revolt against Bloomfieldianism, whereas *tagmemics*, under Kenneth Pike, evolved within the older tradition and still bore the Bloomfield impress despite its movement into process grammar and its new name, *grammemics.*

The relevant Bloomfield position is that language has *phonemes*, which are (1) minimal, (2) meaningless, and (3) things out of which *morphemes* are built. The morpheme is meaningful but not its components (*i.e.*, phonemes). Bloomfieldians also maintain that there are minimal, meaningless bits of arrangement (*i.e.*, grammar or order) called *taxemes.* This is to say, for example, that there is no meaning to the fact that r comes before u in *run*, but if such ordering were not possible, language wouldn't work. A combination of taxemes is a *tagmeme*, a bit of grammar or order that means something. For example, English has a tagmeme indicating that something is the subject of a verb. This tagmeme consists of the following sorts of taxemes:

1. *Order*—subject comes first (in "normal" sentences)
2. *Agreement*—if subject is singular, the verb (if present tense) must be marked.
3. And so on. . . .

This complex of features marks something that is meaningful; *viz.*, the idea of the subject of the sentence. This is a Bloomfieldian tagmeme. There are, according to Bloomfield, four types of taxemes involved in the production of tagmemes: order, modulation, phonetic change, and selection.

The question arises as to what the relationship between phoneme and morpheme is. Bloomfield had said that morphemes "consist of" phonemes. This was the beginning of the schism, and it was variously stated that morphemes are "realized by phonemes," "represented by phonemes," "manifested by phonemes," etc. There was no agreed upon terminology, and the precise meaning of the different terms was never made clear. The only agreement seemed to be that of rejecting Bloomfield's "consists of." Orthodox Bloomfieldians worked according to the principle that one starts with phonemes and proceeds in an orderly sequence to morpheme, thence to word, phrase, clause, sentence. If one says, however, that morphemes *do not* "consist of" phonemes, it is the same as saying that the relationship between morpheme and phoneme is not the same as between morpheme and word. Yet words do "consist of" morphemes (e.g., *bookkeepers = book + keep + er + s*). Close analysis reveals that the phoneme-morpheme relationship is a different one. When phonemes are first put together, one gets *phoneme clusters,* which form *syllables:* $s + t + r = str;$ $i + p = ip;$ $str + ip =$ the next level, *i.e.,* the phonological word, *strip* (which in this case is a single syllable comprised of several phoneme clusters). Words can be said *phonologically* to consist of syllables in turn made up of phonemes, but *morphologically* to consist of morphemes:

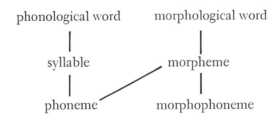

Thus, the difference is between a *single* hierarchy and a *parallel* hierarchy, which tries to account for instances when criteria won't match. The tagmemic movement developed out of such a scheme; Pike actually set up three hierarchies—grammatical, phonological, and lexical. Tagmemics wants to deal with the morpheme as a *form/meaning composite.* Further, tagmemicists believe that every linguistic entity must be labeled both by *function* and by *form.*

Slots in behavior patterns (language being a behavior) are seen as *functional,* and an action must be appropriate to that functional slot that it fills. For each kind of slot there is a *class* of segments appropriate to that slot and that can be observed filling it. This occurrence itself "defines" a class. The tagmeme is a *slot-class correlative,* a concept that assumes a correlation between function on the one hand and class-form on the other. The tagmeme of *order*, the positional slot in a particular frame, can be dealt with at the same time as the tagmeme of *selection*, the filler class for each positional slot. Thus, the tagmemicist's representation of a sentence is:

Subject [S] + Predicate [P] + Object [O]
(filled by)   (filled by)   (filled by)
Noun [N]   Verb [V]   Noun [N]

Or linearly: S:N + P:V + O:N.

The implications of this theory go beyond language to a unified theory of structure for *all* types of human behavior. Pike feels that linguistic and non-linguistic behavior are concomitant and interdependent and have, therefore, analogous structures; that actions speak equally with words if not, as it were, louder. All human behavior, according to Pike, is trimodally structured within his three categories: (1) the *feature* mode, (2) the *manifestation* mode, and (3) the *distribution* mode.

The feature mode is *contrastive*, composed, that is, of simultaneously occurring identificational-contrastive components; e.g., the acoustic features that distinguish phonemes from one another or the distinction in semantic meaning between two words. The *manifestation mode* is composed of non-simultaneously occurring components; e.g., the occurrence of /s/ as the plural marker following *hat* as opposed to the /z/ following *bug*. The total distribution throughout a language of any linguistic unit is the concern of the *distribution mode*. This distribution is both actual, local occurrence as well as total distribution. Not only do the -emic units, the phonemes and morphemes, have their own distributions; but the tagmeme itself, the slot-class correlative, has its characteristic ("permitted") distribution within the hierarchical structure of the language. The tagmeme can be defined with respect to feature, manifestation, and distribution in much the same way as the phoneme and morpheme.

A linear string of tagmemes is called a *syntagmeme* and is obliged to contain at least one tagmeme and may contain others. The construction, which is open-ended, can act as a filler for a higher tagmemic slot. There is no theoretical limit to this "layering." The emphasis in tagmemic analysis is thus upon *units* rather than *relationships*. A particular tagmeme can function only on one level; it is only as part of a *construction* that it appears in another tagmeme at a higher level. Each tagmeme, of course, has its own tri-modal features.

Following the publication of *Syntactic Structures*, which introduced the apparatus of transforms into grammatical theory, tagmemics recognized that certain constructions are related by process to each other and that these relationships can be expressed transformationally. The idea was elaborated on by Longacre (1964), and Pike has predicted that the transformational-generative and tagmemic schools would ultimately coincide. Development of a rigorous treatment is apparently in the making, as tagmemicists are in ample evidence at advanced study programs in transformational-generative grammar. At the practical level, tagmemics has proved extraordinarily useful in foreign language learning, while transformationalism has yet to prove itself in that particular area of language study.

Of increasing interest to theoreticians is a model of grammar called *stratificationalism*, which has its roots in part at least, in the work of Louis Hjelmslev (*Prolegomena to a Theory of Language*, 1961). H. A. Gleason and Sydney M. Lamb are currently the leading stratificational theorists, though more and more linguists are being attracted to this not-quite-new theory, sometimes called *stratum grammar*.

A stratificational model of grammar assumes that there are in language three or more strata, each of which has its own *inventory* of elements and its own *tactics* (rules) relating the elements to each other. How many strata (and stratal systems) there are remains to be determined. Gleason holds that there are at least three, Lamb that there are at least four (and in English, six). To some extent, Lamb's postulated six for English are notational variations of Gleason's three. Both agree, however, that, since sound and meaning are by their natures different, they will each have their own structural system and relationships. Gleason sees language as organized according to the schema on the opposite page.

Thus, in stratificationalism, language is best represented by a multidimensional network, rather than as tree structures alone, for although the phonetic projection of a language is linear, the semology is not. Words and sounds must follow each other sequentially, experiences can occur at the same time. *Sememes* (units of semantic structure) are not only different from morphemes; they do *not* have a one-to-one relationship with them. If all units did match from level to level on a one-to-one basis, the tagmemic approach with its form-meaning composite (equal parts of meaning and form) would be the correct one. However, in stratificational structure, the joining of elements from different strata is done in several stages, employing not only the tactics of each strata, but interface *realizational* rules as well. These interface rules state in what fashion the structures of one level will be realized in the different structures of the other level. To go from semology ("meaning") to

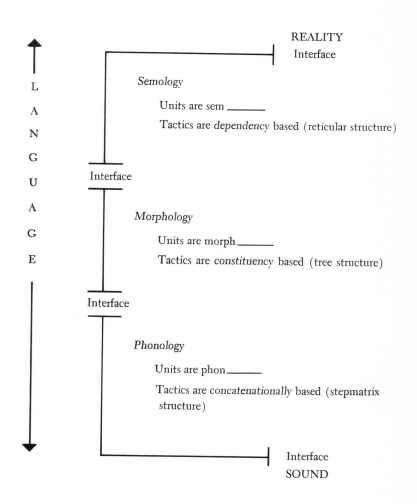

REALITY
Interface

Semology

Units are sem _____

Tactics are dependency based (reticular structure)

Interface

Morphology

Units are morph _____

Tactics are constituency based (tree structure)

Interface

Phonology

Units are phon _____

Tactics are concatenationally based (stepmatrix structure)

Interface
SOUND

L
A
N
G
U
A
G
E

morphology, for example, a network (reticular) structure is first employed to provide full meaning. This structure (still on the semological level) is not then discarded or metamorphosed but is rather connected to the next level (morphological) through a realization rule. A tree structure is, as a result, *added* to the existing network; it grows on it, so to speak. More concretely, by using the semo-lexic realizational rules, a certain lexeme (or tree feature) *realizes* on the morphological level, a certain portion of network from the semological level. The lexotactic rules will then impose elementary order that will eventually lead to the dominant linear ordering of the phonemic structure, but the semo-lexic rules have a part in the assignments. Another example is the use of lexo-morphic realization rules to guide the choices that come up in a set of morphotactic rules. The topology of the morphemic stratum is largely linear, but the transition from morpheme to morpheme can occur in more than one way.

The realizational rules map one type of representation onto another and by affecting generative power are, in effect, comparable to Chomsky's T-rules. The main difference is that realizational rules can be easily applied in both directions—encoding and recoding of language—an aspect that has given transformational grammar a certain amount of trouble in handling.

In stratificational grammar each stratum "consists of" its particular elements. (In all of the relationships between elements and strata, *directionality* is reversible. This represents a significant and basic theoretical difference between stratificationalism and transformationalism.) These elements form various *classes* and *sub-classes*; and the nature of the classes is still not completely known, especially on the semological level. The semology of stratificationalism has a special relationship to reality, which is after all the substance of content. For the user to set up a description of the observed "substance," reality must be "recorded" as sets of discrete data. Now reality may sometimes be shaded into itself (e.g., color distinctions), but the language of description is necessarily delimited and specific. In any case, among the classes that stratificationalists have postulated are *action* and *entity* along with a conjunctional relationship termed *connector*. Two sub-classes of action can be provided. The action *say*, for example, may or may not have a *beneficiary*, or it may or may not have a goal. In the latter case it is always a *quotation*; i.e., another structure of the same kind. A sub-class of entity may be a *participant* and be connected with the action; i.e., play a *role* such as *agent* or *goal*. (The terminology is suggestive of case grammar.) Tactic rules would state, for example, that a particular *action* requires an agent but allows no goal (the condition of *intransitivity*). From the discourse point of view, sub-classes of entities are considered either *old* or *new*.

Finally sub-classes of the connector can be *immediate, simultaneous,* or *lapsed.* All of this is, of course, only a fragment of the semological inventory. Action and entity are in reality large, open sets.

This particular approach is especially useful in discourse analysis, and for constructions extending beyond the sentence, such as anaphora. An interesting example of its application to a narrative in Kâte, a language of New Guinea, is provided by Professor Gleason for his classes as follows (translated literally into English):

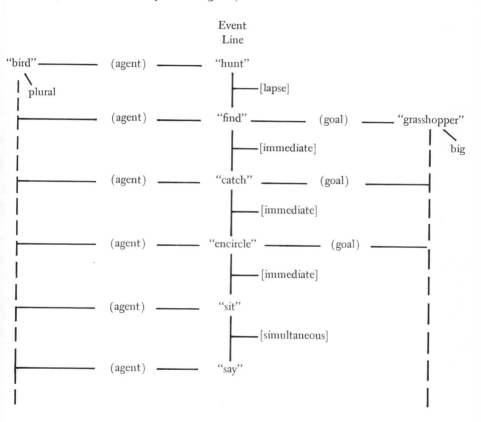

The first action of this narrative is *hunt,* the second is *find,* the next *catch,* and so forth. All are connected by the event line that provides the semantic continuity. The story says they (the birds) went hunting, and there was a long time before anything happened (lapse). After finding something, the next event happened immediately. Following this was another "immediate" event, then came *sit* followed by *say,* which was simultaneous—meaning that the latter action started before the former was finished. There are entities, participants such as bird (+ plural), involved. There is a connection between the participant and the action, and this forms another kind of unit, the *role*. The two roles illustrated here are agent and goal. There are obviously tactic rules in the language, because the action *hunt* requires an agent but allows no goal. The action *find* requires both an agent and a goal. *Say*, as we noted before, may or may not have a beneficiary; if it has a goal, that goal would be a quotation and of course, another structure of the same kind. This narrative is, then, an example of part of a semological structure, involving several kinds of sememes.

In an open-end diagram such as the above, there is vertical or linear ordering on the event line, but no ordering horizontally. The narrative progresses from beginning to end, linearly; but semologically there is no ordered arrangement of the participants around the action.

In stratificationalism, semological structures are open-ended in a special way; *i.e.*, they grow by sequential *accretion*. One can always add another action. The same participant may be involved, or a new one. Accretion, therefore, is a *dependency* structure made by adjoining. Both horizontal and vertical (linear) ordering are allowable. But while a narrative progresses linearly from beginning to end, there is no comparable ordered arrangement of semological elements.*

In the grammar, however, it seems necessary to have fairly rigorous order in the structure. For all intents and purposes, there is an upper limit of grammar, and if there is any overlying structure it is *rhetorical* rather than grammatical. Beyond the upper limit of grammar, grammatical constraints are weak. Below that limit, there are semological constraints; but as one goes to lower and lower ranks, these semological constraints become fewer and weaker.

RANK SCHEMA

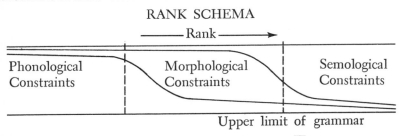

Upper limit of grammar

This schema parallels the phonemic sequencing in language and the

---

* Speech, of course, is *linear*, one element following another on a time base. This kind of ordering is introduced at the point of expression (sound), though in ordinary speech there is a *free associational* dimension. The speaker does not prepare his conversation segment by segment, macrosegment by macrosegment, etc., a fact that is clearly revealed in our meanderings, hesitations, and discontinuities. Formal composition (planned speaking or writing) requires some kind of superordinate structure, where ordinarily none would exist, to correct these free associational tendencies.

articulatory overlapping of linearity in production that results in assimilation of sounds in actual speech (e.g., the assimilated pronunciation of *tourists* as *touris'*, in transcription, /túrɪst/ → /túrɪs/, where the following final /ts/ is assimilated to the preceding /s/). The *phonons* (unordered sets) of stratificationalism (comparable to the *distinctive features* of current phonological theory) also overlap considerably and may not occur simultaneously even though their phonetic effect is, so to speak, instantaneous. (This is to say, for example, that the voicing of a consonant may literally precede its articulation but that both speaker and hearer respond as though these and the other distinctive sound features for that consonant occur at the same instant.)

In transformational-generative grammar a set of tactics produces an output of tree structures, which is the input to a set of transformational rules whose output is again a (different) set of tree structures. To these are applied the phonological rules that produce the phonetic representation (sound) of the utterance. The effect of the transformation rules is to alter the tree structure; *i.e.*, to make continual small changes on the tree. T-rules are a special kind of mutational rule in that they can modify and remodify, *ad infinitum*.

In stratificationalism, the semological output is a reticulum, the morphological output a tree, and one cannot be the output of the other. Nor can either develop from the other by modification. One must assume that in the operation of one of these tactics, the output of the other affects the tactics in some way or another. How this is done is answered by the *realizational rule*. Wherever a tactic rule gives a choice, the rest of the previous structure of the utterance (and the narrative) is looked over and considered for which choice would give the semologically desired output. It is not context-free because the choices are not free. But it is not context-sensitive in the usual sense because one can look outside the clause being built. It is not transformational because the "history" of the structure has not been sought. It is something else, for the speaker looks *outside* to a different structure.

Lamb (*Outline of Stratificational Grammar*, 1966) presents in a graphic schema three fundamental dichotomies that can be permuted to provide eight types of linguistic structuring. These dichotomies he calls AND:OR, UPWARD:DOWNWARD, and ORDERED:UNORDERED. In his model of speech production, he postulates *impulses* moving along lines in either direction, joining with other impulses at various junctures (equivalent to transformational nodes) and even waiting until other connections are activated. The nature of this "gating" has drawn considerable fire from transformationalists.

It is difficult to present a structural analysis based on Lamb's work without first introducing the somewhat unusual notational system employed. However, a diagram for a simple sentence, *A man saw the boy*, is shown below (with glosses for the symbols) followed by a narrative explanation.

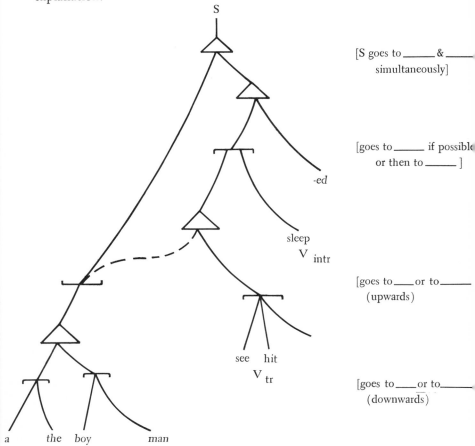

[S goes to _____ & _____ simultaneously]

[goes to _____ if possible or then to _____]

[goes to _____ or to _____ (upwards)]

[goes to _____ or to _____ (downwards)]

Considering the sentence-generating impulse as moving upward along the paths, a noun (*man*) and an article (*a*) are selected from their respective inventories. The juncture (⊼) indicates an unordered or-node, limiting selection to one element below it. At the next juncture (△) a simultaneous *and*-node, the two elements are joined, forming an NP. Meanwhile, a verb (*see*) has been selected, which eventually combines with the tense element *-ed* (realized later as *saw*). A second impulse has generated another NP from the first inventories (*the boy*) that has moved up and was sent along the alternate route (dotted line) to become part of the VP as it forms. The upwards or-node (⅄) ensures that both NP's do not move upward on the same path to conflict ultimately as subject NP's. NP and VP eventually are joined at a higher level *and*-node to complete the sentence.

Lamb's model, however, tries to do more than present a grammatical theory; it tries to account for the actual process of encoding and decoding speech. It is unique, for example, in its efforts to explain (within a theoretical framework) what happens in *translation*. Given any two languages, the stratal schema can be approximated thus:

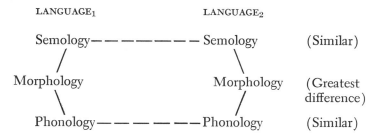

Bilingual individuals may bring the semology and phonology close together. Incidentally, semologies for scientific material are largely similar if not virtually identical, for *belles-lettres* often merging, but for colloquial speech generally divergent.

Language imposes certain constraints, which one increasingly feels as he works through the various strata. Located at the core of language, grammar is remotest and, consequently, able to be most arbitrary and abstract. People are far more conscious of what goes on in semology and phonology than in grammar. Grammar is thus in this view an abstract device for linking semology and phonology. It can indeed be hypothesized that a great deal of grammar is automatic, options being made in the semological stratum. Many different semologies can therefore be made available to one morphological construction, creating thereby *polysemy* (multiple meaning) as well as surface ambiguities.

Implications for Teaching

"The science of language analysis profits from the existence of conflicting theories; each can learn from the other" (Walter A. Cook, *Introduction to Tagmemic Analysis*, p. 11). Indeed, the intellectual health of the science is attested to by the theoretical ferment evidenced by the survey presented in this chapter. (Nor have we exhausted the possibilities, for there are other theories under development: *parametric analysis* and *metafunctional analysis*, to name but two.) It would be a mistake for a teacher to try to explore these theories in any great detail (though particular students may get "hooked" sufficiently by the idea of linguistic analysis to want to do some digging on their own). And such exploring as is done should be done through projects and not "informationally" (as we are tiresomely fond of insisting). Once the theoretical principle has been noted (*discovered*, if at all possible), the explorations should begin.

It is not really clear yet just how much these various theories are in mutual disagreement. As time goes on, it will probably be discovered that many of the "same" things are being talked about with different terminology or shown through different graphic schemata. But whatever the case, grammar study among the professionals will look a good deal different from what it does today. Undoubtedly, certain "hard core" principles will remain. (The *atom* of physics is still with us, but what a changed atom it is from its earlier days in physical theory!) But beyond some very broad linguistic principles, it is impossible to say what precisely will remain. In language study as in all study worth undertaking, the spirit of inquiry is the student's governing principle (whether he be school pupil or scientist).

We are aware that the materials in this chapter are neither easily read nor easily grasped. In the abstract realms of linguistic theorizing, it was ever thus. We hope, however, that the projects that follow will help to pin down at least some of the ideas.

1. Given the fundamental linguistic elements of meaning and sound, can you contrive a grammatical model that will bring them together to produce language? The avowed aim of at least one of the current theories of grammar is to develop rules that will generate all and only the acceptable sentences of any given language. Does this seem like a reasonable aim? What problems might grammarians expect to encounter in developing such a program?

2. Meaning is realized through various linguistic entities and processes (e.g., lexicon and syntax). Is there some point, however, prior to which meaning is somehow separate from these linguistic entities and processes? This is a question that sorely vexes linguists. What arguments might you offer on either side of the issue (*i.e.*, there *is* such a point *vs.* there *isn't*)? Are there any means whereby hypotheses on this issue can be tested? Are there any means of gathering data to use in such considerations? Are linguists, then, reduced to pure speculation? If so, can there be any demonstrable validity to any of these speculations?

3. Since the potential number of sentences in any language is infinite (that is, we can always add one to the "last" one), how is the grammarian to proceed if he is intent upon developing an adequate grammar? He cannot, of course, undertake to describe every possible sentence. This is to say that at some point he will have to decide that he has done

enough describing and that he must now engage in another kind of linguistic activity. How does he know when he has reached that point? And what must he do next? Try to develop a model for solving this kind of problem. Does your model have applicability beyond language problems? Discuss. One of the great uses of mathematics is in this type of model building. (In language study there is a discipline called *mathematical linguistics.*) Try to determine how mathematics can thus serve the cause of practical problem solving. And try to figure out some possible applications of mathematics to grammatical and other linguistic problems.

4. Suppose that someone succeeds in writing a grammar which correctly enumerates the sentences of a language and assigns them the right structural descriptions. Such a grammar would *ipso facto* correctly represent the substance of a fluent speaker's knowledge of this language. But it would not necessarily represent the form of this knowledge in the sense of actually corresponding to the system of rules which is internalized by the speaker and constitutes part of what enables him to produce and understand arbitrary utterances in the language. (Paul Kiparsky, "Linguistic Universals and Linguistic Change," in *Universals in Linguistic Theory,* ed., E. Bach & R. T. Harms, p. 171.)

Why? Discuss. (This discussion might fruitfully be carried on in a panel or symposium format.)

5. Consider

1. Melmoth harvested potatoes.
2. Melmoth harvested potatoes with a mechanical harvester.
* 3. Melmoth and a mechanical harvester harvested potatoes.

Why is (3) unacceptable? (Clue: Do *Melmoth* and *potato harvester* stand in the same relationship *vis-à-vis* the action [*harvesting potatoes*]?) Here are a few more sentences to ponder:

4. The bulldozer crushed the garbage can with *its* blade.
* 5. The bulldozer crushed the garbage can with *a* blade.
6. My son cut his finger with a knife.
7. My son cut his finger with *his* knife.
8. A knife cut my son's finger.
9. His sermon inspired us.
10. We were inspired by his sermon.
11. The pilot landed the plane with care.
12. The plane was landed with care.
* 13. The plane landed with care.
* 14. Care landed the plane.
15. Melmoth exterminated the earwigs with insecticide.
16. Insecticide exterminated the earwigs.

17. The earwigs were exterminated.
* 18. The earwigs exterminated. But:
19. The earwigs died.
20. *Tillie has* a feathered boa.
21. This is *Tillie's* feathered boa.
22. I had a marvelous time yesterday.
* 23. A marvelous time was had yesterday. But:
24. Marvelous times were had in ages past.

In trying to account for the behavior of these sentences and non-sentences, you may find it helpful to apply the *case* concept. Thus *insecticide* in (15) is considered to be in the *instrumental* case (often signaled by *with*). Melmoth is *agentive* (the one who "does") and *earwigs* is *patient* (the recipient). In *He is at home,* home is *locative* (note the maintenance of case in *Home is where he is*).

6. Traditionally, the *sentence* has been defined as "a group of words containing a subject and a predicate and expressing a complete thought." After subjecting this definition to the most intense possible scrutiny, comment on its usefulness and applicability. Now try your hand at defining the term *sentence.* How will you begin? What problems arise? Can concepts like "complete thought" be of any use here? Explain. Explain also what a "complete thought" *is.*

7. One of the problems in grammatical model construction is that of *lexicalization;* that is, the insertion of words into their proper places. For example, in example (18) of exercise 5 (above), *exterminated* is not allowed to occur in the frame, *The earwigs* (*exterminated). Why not? How does the theoretician determine this? What kinds of rules might the theoretician devise to properly lexicalize a grammar? What roles do *meaning* and *form* play? That is, how implicated are purely *semantic* matters in lexicalization? Purely *formal* matters? Or are the concepts *pure* meaning and *pure* form unacceptable? Explain.

8. The following *parametric* (*i.e.,* parameter based) *matrix* identifies three *major sentence types* and three *clause types* that together form nine sentence types.

SENTENCE CLAUSE	Statement	Question	Command
Intransitive	Sol went.	Did Sol go?	Go, Sol!
Transitive	Sol ate it.	Did Sol eat it?	Eat it, Sol!
Equational	Sol is good.	Is Sol good?	Be good, Sol!

Of what use is such a matrix? Can you set up other relevant matrices? What will they reveal? Can you generate from the matrix above all the types of sentences with which you are familiar? If not, which ones can you not? How can they be accounted for? Can you identify some other useful parameters of language? Why are they useful? What can the study of language do with them?

9. Various sentence elements have different degrees of *movability*. Assign what might be clumsily called a *movability coefficient* to the various elements you can identify. (Consider in your pursuit of movability *clause level*, *phrase level*, *word level*, and *morpheme level*.) At each level of analysis, which elements are most movable? Least? Is there any practical use in understanding the principle of movability in language? Does it have any implications for style? Discuss.

10. Given the meaning (semology) of the sentence, *Tillie loves flowers*, can you explain how the sentence itself is produced; that is, how it *realizes* its intended meaning or how its meaning makes, as it were, the sentence? The structural (*i.e.,* schematic) analog of meaning in *stratificational grammar* is a *reticulum* or network (of meaning). At the level of syntax, it is a *structural tree*. Where the meaning level and the syntax level meet is an *interface*. The question is how the network and the tree are brought together to produce the syntax appropriate to the meaning. Can you "visualize" the interface realm and describe what goes on there? Is such a view of language and its operations of any value? Explain. (While you're at it, take a crack at the interface between *syntax* and *sound*, whereby the now meaningful syntax is brought into actual speech.)

8
Speech and Writing

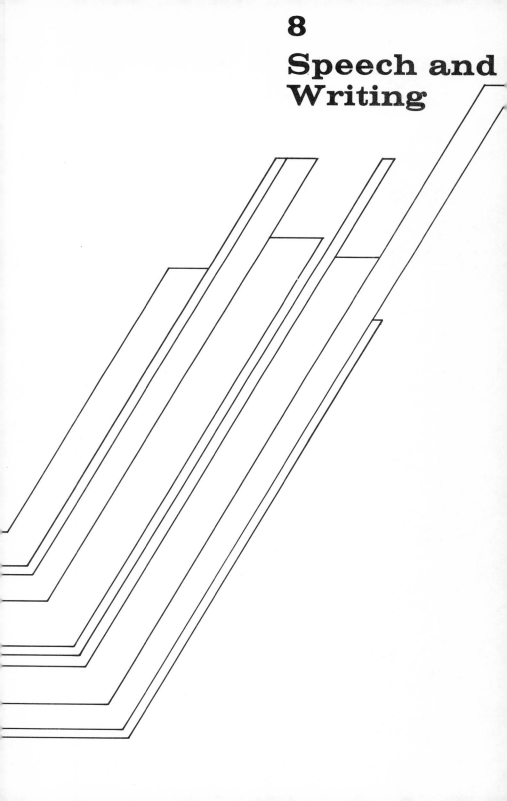

The trouble with modern English spelling is that it doesn't spell modern English.

(Harold Whitehall, *Structural Essentials of English*, New York.)

Writing designates two quite different things: (1) the system of graphic marks designed to represent certain features of speech, and (2) written composition. Our primary focus in this chapter will be on the former.

The purpose of writing is to memorialize speech. Speech is ephemeral, writing is more or less permanent. Prior to the invention of writing, the knowledge and wisdom of the society had to be passed down from generation to generation by word of mouth. Writing allows man to store vast quantities of information and makes possible the development of complex technologies. On the other hand, an oral tradition produces certain skills that are soon lost in a print culture—notable among them, the prodigious memory of the tribal story teller *cum* historian. Indeed, the oral arts tend to die in a print world. Where are the arts of conversation and declamation? Who but a rare few can read aloud with skill, ease, and effect? Of course, we do today have the tape recorder to capture speech as speech, and there seems to be some movement in the direction of an aural-oral culture. Further, there seems to be less need now to store data as print. Nevertheless, the quantity of printed material in circulation today is prodigious. Anyone who works in an office of any kind can testify to that! The print-copier business is booming. We are afloat on a sea of letters, brochures, directives, memoranda, data sheets, pamphlets, books, newspapers, magazines, handbills, forms, etc., etc. Despite Marshall McLuhan, we are still very much awhirl in the Gutenberg Galaxy.

Most importantly, literacy is still the prime "visible and outward sign" of the educated man. Despite the growing significance of aural and visual techniques in education, we anticipate no time when we shall rely on them to the exclusion of print. They will always be contributory, not primary.

Because European culture, which of course includes our own, is an *alphabet* culture, we are inclined to think of the alphabet as synonymous with writing. There are, however, other forms of writing than the alphabetic; nor is the alphabet the archetypal writing system. The fact is that any systematic use of graphic devices to preserve any message of a kind that can be expressed in speech constitutes "writing." One quickly dis-

170

covers that this view of writing admits of a variety of manifestations quite unlike our alphabetic system. Indeed, upon close examination, our alphabetic system proves not always to be purely alphabetic; that is, so structured that one graphic mark represents one bit of phonetic information. For example, the common abbreviation, Xmas, pronounced /krísmɨs/, uses X to represent "Christ-." The X, therefore, is not an alphabetic device here but a *morphographic* device very much in the manner of the Chinese character (*e.g.*, 川 , *chuan*, "river"). (Incidentally, there is nothing "sacrilegious" in the spelling Xmas, for not only was it widely used during the Age of Faith, but it is properly contrived from XP (*Chi-Rho*), a conventional symbol for Jesus (*XRistos*) and one still officially sanctioned by the Church.) The *ampersand* (&) is another common *morphograph; i.e.*, a symbol for a unit of meaning rather than for just a sound. When we see &, we read the word, *and*. Other examples are numerals, mathematical and other symbols, and even the letters of the alphabet when they are used as the *names* of the letters (Z = "zee," etc.), the meaning in the last example deriving from the naming function. It may, in fact, be possible to write a passage purely in English morphographs.

Though alphabetic writing is a latecomer to writing (indeed, the latest comer), it is by far the most efficient of currently used writing systems. Unfortunately, this efficiency has been vitiated somewhat in English (as well as in French and in Irish) by marked deviations in pronunciation from the original values of the written symbols and by inconsistencies that have crept into the system over the years. As examples are not difficult to find, one or two will suffice here: the sound of *s* in *sugar*, which commonly requires two symbols in conventional spelling to render it (*sh*), but which can also be rendered as *t* (*nation*), *ss* (*issue*), *ch* (*cabachon*), and *c* (*fallacious*). And any example of homophony points up the waywardness of our modern alphabet (or our use of it, at any rate): *way*, *weigh*, and *wey-*, as in the name *Weymouth*. The actual issue here isn't homophony but *dysgraphia*. That is to say, all the homophones in a consistent alphabetic writing system should be spelled precisely alike, as they are in a transcription system like the International Phonetic Alphabet where the examples above would all thus be rendered [we].

Despite the failings of modern English spelling, however, the alphabetic system is the easiest to learn and to use. With a small number of arbitrary symbols one is able to render graphically every word of his language. In Turkey, where the Roman alphabet was introduced fairly recently to replace the Arabic, there is a nearly invariable relationship between sound and symbol; and once one has mastered the correspondences, he is able to transcribe any word of Turkish whether he knows the word or not. All he need do is hear it clearly. Hence there is no such thing as "spelling" as a subject for study, and there is virtually no such thing as a spelling mistake. If there is a "mistake," it is chargeable to mis-hearing or mis-speaking, but not to vagaries in the graphic system.

Of course, even an alphabetic system with a perfect "fit" between sound and symbol, like Turkish, cannot render every detail of speech. For example, most of the intonational information of speech is lacking in writing. Punctuation and other graphic devices (italics, boldface, and various typographical arrangements) are of some use in suggesting the writer's intended intonation, but most of the subtleties are necessarily lost. This fact requires of the writer special skill in trying to convey the tone of the writing without the availability to him of the actual "tone of voice." Sarcasm, for instance, which in speech can be expressed so exquisitely by intonation must, in writing, be suggested in other ways. Thus the demands of writing are rather different in certain important particulars from those of speaking. Writing isn't *just* speech in graphic form. There is a "naturalness" to speaking that is alien to writing. We learn to speak from infancy, and it requires little or no *conscious* effort on our part to "learn" it. Writing is altogether different. We must go through a more-or-less structured learning program to get it. We must learn to use a set of muscles far removed from those involved in speech. Hence, we must train new nerveways in other parts of the brain. But it must be stressed here that writing is neither anterior to speech nor more "important." We do far more speaking than we do writing, and the average person out of school can get by without having to write much more than his signature. Whole cultures to this very day are without literacy and most of man's time on earth has been spent without it. Speech is absolutely necessary for the development and growth of human society and its attendant culture, but writing certainly is not. It *is* useful all the same!

A detailed historical study of English orthography is beyond our scope. It will suffice to say that from its beginnings in the seventh century A.D. at the hands of monks using the Latin alphabet in its Irish form, English spelling has been plagued by a variety of problems of fit. Actually, Old English (Anglo-Saxon) orthography is in many ways a good deal more successful in achieving a fit than that of modern English, which is, as we well know, an orthographical nightmare. George Bernard Shaw was right in wishing for a better way but wrong in thinking that much could be done to accomplish it. There are simply too many people speaking too many dialects to make any broad rectification possible. We are pretty much stuck with the system. The problems it affords are, after all, not insoluble; and it stands as a common convention to all literate users of the language in much the same way as Chinese writing does for the Chinese, who speak a number of mutually unintelligible dialects but use a common writing system. Thus, any person literate in English, regardless of his dialect, can read what any other literate user of English has written. Dialect differences are not reflected (except in unimportant ways) in the writing. It doesn't matter that a Britisher may say 'strawn'ry and an American may say extraordinary for the word spelled extraordinary. Likewise, the Chinese morphograph, 人 , will sound several quite different ways (chin, ren, lun, etc.), depending on the individual speaker's dialect.

A deadly combination of our "national mania for correctness" and the disparities of our spelling system guarantee that much valuable time will be spent in learning how to spell, but we are probably well advised not to invest so much emotional energy on the problem. (A particularly useful project is to explore with the student the vagaries—as well as the consistencies—of the system. Such a project will combine reading, pronunciation, and spelling, as well as the learning techniques of inquiry, discovery, and problem-solving. One product of such an exploration might be a chart of regularities and irregularities and a statement of principle regarding their operation. We listed above six spellings for the initial sound of sugar. There are eight more, at least! On the other hand, there are twelve sounds that correspond with considerable regularity with their graphic symbols on a one-to-one basis.)

In the history of the development of the alphabet, the syllabary is the alphabet's immediate ancestor, though the advent of the alphabet proper did not mean the demise of the syllabary. The syllabic system uses symbols that stand not for individual sounds, as in the case of the alphabet, but for syllables, either single-peak vowels or various consonant-vowel combinations. Syllables are to be understood as units of sound only, not as units of meaning, though single syllables (in English, for example) frequently are coextensive with words. Our alphabet derives ultimately from the Semitic syllabary from which the Hebrew alphabet (in some ways itself still a syllabary) derives. But the modern syllabary par excellence is the Japanese kana system, called the "Fifty Sounds," which is capable of accurately representing the language graphically since Japanese phonotactics require that every consonant (except n) be followed by one of the five vowels; vowels can occur in immediate sequence because each vowel is, of course, a syllable. Thus, a typical Japanese sentence might be

Anata wa Oeyama no oni hanashi wo go-zonji desu ka.

In the Japanese syllabary, anata wa, for example, would be rendered by four symbols: a あ , na な , ta た , wa わ . The fit between sound and symbol is generally good. But when foreign words are taken into Japanese, they must be phonotactically restructured in order to match the phonological and, therefore, the graphological habits of the language. Hence, the English word misprint, which has been borrowed into

Japanese, is modified to *misu-purinto*, following the normal Japanese phonotactical pattern precisely. Other examples: *contrast/kontorasuto; control/kontrōru; staple fiber/sutēburu faiba; dress/doresu.* Wherever English uses a consonant cluster, Japanese must open the cluster with vowels. Phonologically it is impossible for a Japanese to create a mono-syllable like *strength* out of native materials, as it were; and it is impossible to write it with the Japanese syllabary. Of course, a Japanese can learn the English word *strength*, just as an American can learn to pro-nounce Japanese words properly; but the Japanese would have to write *strength* in the Roman alphabet, for his syllabary will allow only some-thing like *suturengusu.* (The *su* substitutes for *th*, a sound that is non-existent in Japanese and for which, naturally, there is no syllabary symbol.)

Both the alphabet and the syllabary are comprised of *arbitrary* symbols. That is, the letter *k* (for example) and the syllabic symbol for *ka* (𝄇) represent nothing but *sounds.* The Chinese morphographic writing system likewise represents specific phonological information but clearly suggests its origins in an *ideographic* (ultimately *pictographic*) system. The *character* is a stylized picture. Thus, the character for "big" derives from a simple picture of a man with his arms outstretched. Of course, the modern Chinese reader does not think of a man with his arms outstretched when reading the character for "big." He simply sees the character for "big." The system is called *morphographic* because each character stands for a *unit of meaning*, a *morpheme.* Thus 女 stands for "woman" (*nü*) as a *free word* (i.e., free morpheme) but "female" (女的 , *nü tê*) as a *bound word* (bound morpheme). In an alphabet or syllabary it is true that there are some words or mean-ing units that are single sounds or syllables (English, *I*, first person singular pronoun); by no means all of them are. In the case of a morphographic system, every character is either a full word or a bound word. There are virtually no symbols just for sounds, though it is pos-sible to turn a character into an arbitrary symbol by using its phonolog-ical value and ignoring its meaning, as is done for foreign words. Indeed, it is this technique that historically led to the alphabet. The presumption is that the alphabetic system of writing derives ultimately from the Egyptian hieroglyphic system, which was essentially morpho-graphic but which in time gave way to the more efficient syllabary sys-tem (whence then the Semitic syllabaries and finally the alphabet). Incidentally, the alphabet was "invented" once and once only, and its many modern forms—Roman, Greek, Cyrillic, East Indian, Hebrew, etc.—are developments of the single original concept. Likewise, the *idea* of writing seems to have had a single origin and to have spread through-out the world thence. Thus, the Chinese system probably owes a debt to the Egyptian, though there never was *direct* contact between the two (or so we assume) and the two *look* a good deal different one from the other.

Thus far, we have looked at writing systems that convey specific phonological information. Such systems have been styled "true" writing systems. With the earliest Egyptian and Chinese systems, however, we are in a transition between true writing and pre-writing, for hieroglyphs and Chinese bone writing (a hieroglyphic type of incised symbols probably for hieromantic purposes) were, or so it seems, concerned not to convey specific sounds but, rather, *ideas*. A simple drawing of the sun would mean in such a system, "sun," "light," "warmth," "brightness," etc. This means that a decipherer would not be able to reproduce from the writing a particular set of sounds but only a more or less accurate explanation of what the symbols *mean*. The highway signs that indicate various curves and bends in the road are analogous. The "reader" of these signs does not pause over whether the signs provide phonological information: "curve" or "bend" or "twisting road," etc. It suffices that he get the *idea* implicit in all of these and clearly signaled by the curved line on the sign. (This pictographic/ideographic system is ideal for conveying certain kinds of useful and necessary information from country to country, hence the new international standardization of highway signs.)

But the severe limitations of a writing system dependent solely on "idea pictures" very quickly becomes apparent. Among the small, exclusive priestly class, the system was useful as a kind of secret code, the knowledge of which both marked one's status and helped to preserve it. (*Hieroglyph* means "priest writing," and connotes secretiveness.) But as the uses of writing broadened beyond priestly hocus pocus, it was forced to change. In the West, the change continued until the emergence of the alphabet proper. In the East (*i.e.*, China), the changes took the original pictographic system only as far as the present morphographic system, still well short of an alphabet. It was the Japanese who moved closest to the alphabet with their syllabary, a specialized simplification of certain Chinese characters that was forced upon the Japanese as they entered literacy by way of the Chinese system. Chinese and Japanese are unrelated languages, and a system that suited the one proved inadequate to the other. Chinese has no inflections; Japanese has an elaborate system of inflections. The Chinese characters work well enough for the word roots, but the inflections must be supplied by some other means. Hence, the syllabary—a clear instance of necessity giving birth to invention.

Among the less sophisticated, though useful, systems for preserving and/or transmitting information are the Inca *quipu* or *knot records* (a mnemonic system based on the size, number, color, and placement of knots in a bundle of vines), North American Indian *smoke signals*, Indian and African *drum talk* (based to a certain extent on the intonation contours of speech), and early *petroglyphs* and *petrographs* (rock and cave carvings and drawings done in connection with rituals of "sympathetic magic"). Though these primitive precursors and analogs of writing are relatively unsophisticated, they did, and do, serve their purposes and mark a major step in man's intellectual development.

The descriptive study of a writing system is called *graphics* or *graphemics* and is to writing what *phonemics* and *morphemics* are to speech. (But while we do use *phonology* and *morphology* as variants of phonemics and morphemics, the term *graphology* is denied us because of its preëmption by handwriting analysts, though we do use *graphological* on occasion. A *graph* is a visual symbol, written, drawn, or printed, meant to represent an isolate of speech. When such a graph has been categorized, it is an *allograph* of a *grapheme*. Thus all of the forms of *b* (upper and lower case, italic, script, etc.) are called the allographs, "alternate" or "variant graphs," of the grapheme *b* and are cited within ⟨ ⟩. Likewise, the punctuation and diacritical marks: ⟨.⟩ ⟨,⟩ ⟨;⟩ ⟨:⟩ ⟨" "⟩ ⟨?⟩ ⟨( )⟩ ⟨[ ]⟩ ⟨'⟩ ⟨`⟩ ⟨/⟩ ⟨*⟩ ⟨··⟩ ⟨^⟩, and so on.

Each writing system, like each phonological system, has its own rules. Because writing is meant to represent at least some features of the phonology, there will of course be parallels between the two systems. However, it is important not to confuse the two. In English, for example, in certain contexts letters occur that directly represent no sounds. These "silent letters" do, nevertheless, occasionally play a kind of displaced phonological role: *bit/bite* and *lit/light* illustrate the phonological signaling role of the silent letters. The role is a fairly complex one, for if we take *e*, for example, to have a certain sound value (actually, in English it has several: *equal, bet, litter, new*, etc.), how are we to classify it in a word like *bite?* The issue is further clouded when we add an *r* to produce *biter* ("one who bites"), where the *e* then takes on one of its usual sound values. At any rate, the occurrence of the final *e* can serve to signal the sound value to be given to the medial vowel. In *house*, the *e* is wholly functionless, though in the plural it does take on a sound value: *houses*. A word like *disheveled* adds more confusion, for according to the principle that a postconsonantal *e* influences the preceding vowel, where the preceding consonant is not doubled, the sound value of the preconsonantal vowels (*viz.*, -evel-) should be pronounced as the vowel of *beet:* "disheeveeled." They aren't.

We have studiously avoided saying that the silent *e* causes the preceding vowel to be *lengthened*, for the term *length* is irrelevant in a study of English phonology. It is true that some sounds take longer to say than others, but length—duration—is not a distinctive feature in English. Here is a quick proof: The vowel of *bad* takes longer in ordinary pronunciation to say than the vowel in *bat*. Yet both are the low front vowel /æ/. If one stretches the vowel in *bat* to match the length of the vowel in *bad*, nothing happens except a small non-contrastive change in pronunciation. We have not produced a different word, as would be the case in, say, Latin, where vowel length *is* a contrastive feature. Most of the so-called long vowels in English are in fact *diphthongs*, but contrast on the basis of *quality* not *length*. The pure (*i.e.*, undiphthongized) vowel of *bid*, /i/, has as much length as the diphthong of *beat*, /iy/, and the latter is shorter than the diphthong of *bead*, also /iy/. Yet the school "phonics" textbooks teach that the vowel of *bid* is "short" and the vowel of *beat* is "long." Further, the "short" vowel is called *i* and the "long" vowel *e*. As the phonemic transcription clearly shows, they both contain the nuclear vowel *i*—that is, high front. We reserve *e* for the mid front vowel, as in *bet*. These and other orthographical confusions are why the teacher must understand the precise relationships between sound and spelling and be able to translate the sounds first into a consistent notation. Any of the currently used phonemic notational systems is suitable. The Initial Teaching Alphabet is an attempt to accomplish the same end, though it is probably not necessary to use such a system to the total exclusion for a time of conventional spelling as ITA partisans urge.

We are faced in our description of the graphemic habits of English with (1) grapheme *distribution* and (2) *role*. As we have seen, the role of *e* is a complex one. The role of *k*, for example, much less so. *Distribution* embraces (1) *frequency of occurrence* in randomly chosen samples of running text and (2) *allowable tactics*. Just as we allow certain sound combinations and disallow others, so we allow certain grapheme combinations and disallow others. Initially, we cannot write *kk-*, though medially it occurs in *bookkeeper*. Actually, the occurrence of double letters initially is statistically almost nil in English and can be stated as a graphotactical rule. (There is a rarely occurring family name, *ffrench*, that exhibits two graphemic peculiarities: initial consonant doubling and initial lower case. To our knowledge, the word is unique in its graphemic habits.)

The letter graphemes are analogous to the segmental phonemes, the punctuation graphemes to the intonational and junctural features. The twenty-six letters of the English alphabet comprise the letter graphemes of English; but the number of punctuation and other non-letter graphemes is indeterminate, for in addition to various amounts of blank space (*i.e.*, for separating segmental graphemes, graphic words, and perhaps graphic paragraphs, chapters, and the like), we have a huge inventory of graphic symbols beyond the usual punctuation marks and letters: 1234-567890, $+@\#\$\%\not\subset=$, etc., so that any number we might offer would be arbitrary and only a part of the total.

A great deal can be learned about our system of punctuation simply by a close study of the distributional patterns of the marks. Some of this can be done without reference to meaning. (Thus, capital letters commonly follow a blank space wider than that separating the letters of a word; periods commonly precede such blank spaces.) But the limits of this method are fairly severe. Punctuational strategies like using commas to set off non-restrictive modifiers can be understood only by appeal to meaning.

Such meaning is evident from the intonational differences between an utterance with the commas in opposition to one without. The following graphic strings must be spoken to illustrate the point:

1. The students, ⁽⟶⁾ who were absent last week, ⁽⟶⁾ have a good deal of work ahead of them.
2. The students who were absent last week have a good deal of work ahead of them.

The full stop marks the end of intonational clauses, a fact that can help to cure the "run-on" sentence, a graphemic not a grammatical error. If the student will read his "run-on" aloud, he will put the intonational full stop (falling clause terminal) where it belongs regardless of his punctuational failures. Where his voice drops (the usual signal of the clause terminal), he should be directed to mark a period. Once he understands this simple equation, he will have overcome the run-on problem. The "comma splice" can be similarly overcome. The pedagogical beauty of this approach is that the student acts as his own informant.

We must not, however, push the punctuation-intonation analogy too hard. There is much in punctuation that is arbitrary and conventional and not tied to intonation (e.g., dates), and there are many intonational features for which we have no commonly used graphic devices. One "correspondence" taught, it would seem, by nearly every English teacher, is that between the *question mark* and a *rising pitch* at the clause terminal. The fact of the matter is that except in a few special cases, the intonation of the *wh*-question and the noun-verb inversion question is precisely the same as that of the declarative; that is, the pitch drops and the voice trails off. Try these:

1. $\overset{2}{\text{Are}}$ you going away for the $\overset{3}{\text{holidays}}$ $\overset{1}{\text{?}}$↘

2. $\overset{2}{\text{I'm}}$ going away for the $\overset{3}{\text{holidays}}$ $\overset{1}{\text{.}}$↘

3. $\overset{2}{\text{Where}}$ are you going for the $\overset{3}{\text{holidays}}$ $\overset{1}{\text{?}}$↘

   Then contrast:

4. $\overset{2}{\text{You're}}$ going away for the $\overset{3}{\text{holidays}}$ $\overset{3}{\text{?}}$↗

Only in (4), which is not structured like a question, does the pitch level normally rise at the clause terminal. Of course, the pitch can rise in examples (1) and (3), if the conversational context warrants. For example, (3) with a rising pitch at the clause terminal could signal incredulity ("You don't mean to tell me that you're going to *that* tiresome place!"), but such a meaning represents, as it were, a deviant kind of question (as over against the normal request for information).

A variety of orthographical problems arise when we undertake to *transliterate*; that is, to find graphemic equivalence from writing system to writing system. Thus the Greek Ψ is transliterated to *ps*; one symbol becomes two (*e.g., psyche*). But in the case of *borrowings* (as opposed to *renderings*), the *p* is lost in pronunciation (though retained in spelling) because English does not use these *sounds* in initial combination. (The *s* rather than the *p* might have been the sound lost but for the fact that the high energy continuent, /s/, overshadowed the weaker stop, /p/, causing the preceding sound to be "absorbed" by the following one. As it happens, the *ps* when fully pronounced with the regular English values for the two sounds does quite acceptably approximate the Greek pronunciation. But when we transliterate the Japanese ら as *ra*, we are much wider of the phonological mark, for the Japanese *r* (so-called) is quite unlike the English /r/. (It resembles a /d/ made by flicking the front—not the apex—of the tongue against the gum ridge.) And if we read Romaji (transliterated Japanese) with the values that the letters suggest, we will sound like nothing so much as Americans reading a set of English syllables. The Russian (Cyrillic) alphabet, like the Greek, is cognate with our own, but the sound values which it signals are quite unlike ours. Hence: Dostoevsky, Dostoievski, Dostoyevsky, etc. (German transliteration from Russian: Dostojewskij; French: Dostoïevski.) None of the transliterations quite does the job, though a Russian would recognize the name from an American's reading of any of the transliterated versions. The point to remember in sounding transliterations is that while they use familiar alphabetic symbols, these symbols do not truly represent the sounds of the original languages.

In brief, we may trace the development of writing from primitive drawings or carvings (on rocks, bones, and trees), designed to pictorially memorialize some important event or convey some significant information, to the various modern alphabets, the symbols of which are purely arbitrary (having, that is, no pictorial value). Against the evolution of man, the evolution of writing occupies but a moment. Yet this moment marks one of the giant steps of civilization. Not that man cannot manage without writing (most of mankind today does), but that the development of writing is a brilliancy of the highest order. If nothing else, it made possible the development of literatures far vaster than could have been committed to memory by even the most skilled of the tribal storytellers. And, of course, without writing we could have developed no *polis* beyond the small tribal community, and no industrialization.

Our task as teachers is to understand how writing works and to contrive ways of teaching literacy that accord with that understanding. And while we have attempted in this chapter no exhaustive study of writing, we trust that such observations as we have made will provide sufficient background to contend with the projects that follow.

Implications for Teaching

Like anything else that we undertake to teach, writing is a legitimate subject for exploration. By this we mean that it is not enough simply to teach the child to write; that is, use the coding system. He must *understand* what it is we are teaching him. This understanding can be had only through exploration. Teacher and class should work these projects through together. And, as always in good education, each question should raise others, each thread should interconnect with the whole complex of language—and beyond.

1. There are two general types of alphabetic writing: *print* and *script*. Using sizable samples of each, make an inventory of all the different graphic symbols you can find. Determine the frequency of each letter. Try building a *code* or *cryptographic* system based on frequency. Why would such a code be easy to break? Can you modify your code to make it less easily analyzable without the key? Try to explain the function of each of the non-alphabetic symbols in the English writing system. Which of these seem absolutely necessary? There was a time when no marks beyond the letters themselves were used. Indeed, there are some texts extant in which every letter of the text is equally spaced from every

other, *ratherlikethis*. Try writing a paragraph without any punctuation. Then add just enough to make your meaning acceptably clear. See if you can find out how the comma, period, semi-colon, etc., came to be. What do the names tell you? Check the etymologies in your dictionary. Is it necessary to use punctuation in a code? How can it·be indicated without using it directly? How is a coding system like the Morse Code similar to and different from alphabetic writing? What are the advantages of a system like the Morse Code? Disadvantages?

2. Writing itself is a coding system. It involves turning one thing (speech) into something else (writing) and back again. Write a report explaining how this is done in English. Base your report on your own examination of writing. Can you think of an efficient way of teaching the English coding system to a child? To a person who didn't know anything about writing? What points would that person have to understand before he could really *learn* the system (as opposed to merely committing it to memory)?

3. English writing goes from left to right on the page. This seems to us "normal." But the Chinese write from top to bottom (starting at the right side of the page), and Arabic and Hebrew are written from right to left. For a time in ancient Greece, writing went "as the ox plows" (*boustrophedon*), that is, from right to left on one line, then left to right on the next, and so on. And on Crete archeologists have found inscriptions that wind in spiral fashion from the outside to the inside of a disc. Try writing in each of these ways. Does any one seem "better" than any other? Does each system have any special advantages over the others? Do we ever use the Chinese plan? Where? Do we generally have any difficulties with it in those contexts? Can you think of any other ways in which writing might be done? Do those ways have any special advantages (or disadvantages)? A number of contemporary poets have experimented with typography, E. E. Cummings notable among them. Do these experiments serve any useful purpose? Discuss. Try writing some poetry (or even a story) using some other than "normal" way of setting up the page. Explain how you changed the typography and what you accomplished by it.

4. In both print and script we use *capital* (*upper case*) and *small* (*lower case*) letters. On the basis of an example of several samples, try to formulate some rules for the use of each. Under what circumstances are these rules broken? In the case of handwriting (script), the graphemes vary (to greater or lesser degree) in shape. Which variations are governed by *position* or *environment*, and which seem to be *freely variable*? Make a collection of *a*'s, *b*'s, *c*'s, etc., culled from the handwriting of several people. What seem to be the limits of what one can write and still have it read as an *a, b, c,* etc.? What allows all of these variations in a letter to be read as that letter?

5. The biblical Hebrew writing system has been called more truly a *syllabary* than an *alphabet.* Try to discover why. One interesting feature of biblical Hebrew is its non-use of vowel symbols. Rewrite a paragraph (from any source) by omitting the vowels. Can the paragraph still be read? Now replace the vowel symbols and strike out the consonant symbols. Can any of the paragraph now be read? What does this tell you about the structure of English words? And what does this possibly tell you about the problems of reading a Hebrew text without the vowel points marked? (Vowel markings—*points*—do exist in Hebrew, but they were not used in biblical times. The consonants were considered the "body" of a word, the vowels the "soul," breathed into the word when it was spoken.) A type of shorthand can be contrived by eliminating most vowels (*i.e.,* vowel *symbols*). It is easy enough to determine that *vwls* stands for *vowels,* for example. Try developing such a shorthand that you can put to practical use in taking notes, etc. What difficulties arise in the project? Where *must* you maintain vowels? Why? (N.B. The English alphabet has five vowel and two semi-vowel symbols: *a, e, i, o, u; y, w.* English speech has several times that number of vowel *sounds.* Whenever we are speaking of the *alphabet,* we are speaking of the *symbols.* Teachers, unfortunately, often confuse the two, or at least fail to prevent the confusion from arising in their students.)

6. What seem to be the weaknesses and irrationalities of the English writing system? How might the present system be improved? Can you formulate any rules for English spelling that can be consistently applied, without exception? Try starting from scratch to develop a wholly rational spelling system for English. Might it be useful to regularly include symbols for intonational features now not generally marked? Which ones would you choose to mark? Why? Might we make greater use of morphographs such as &, %, etc.? What could be more efficiently expressed morphographically? What problems arise when one attempts to reform our spelling system? Which of these problems seem possible of solution and which seem insoluble? Explain.

7. How does our system of abbreviations work? Is it in fact a *system* at all? What common words would we be just as well off writing as abbreviations all the time? (*Mr.* and *Mrs.* are two such. Rarely does anyone write *mister* and *missus.*) Try working out a convenient system of abbreviations. Explain the principle involved.

8. Though a "true" writing system is one designed to carry specific phonological information, it can be argued that it is not the primary purpose of a spelling system to represent *speech.* Can you offer any evidence in support of this argument? (Clue: compare "What are you doing?" with "Wotchadoin.") And if it is not the primary purpose of writing to represent speech, then what would the primary purpose be?

9. For each of the English consonant symbols, determine the sounds ordinarily associated with it. Exemplify these pronunciations in words. Do the same for the vowel symbols. Can you develop these data into a set of spelling rules? Much criticism has been leveled at English spelling for its irregularity. Just how irregular is it? What are, for you, the principal confusions of English spelling? Make a list of the words you commonly misspell. Study the misspellings carefully and see if you can devise some system, other than rote memory, for avoiding them.

10. The pronunciation of what kinds of words seems to be wholly uninfluenced by spelling? On the contrary, the pronunciation of what kinds of words seems to be strongly influenced by spelling. Compare the spellings of names, particularly surnames, with the expected pronunciation of those letter sequences. The name *Campbell*, for example, is given a *spelling pronunciation* by many—*campbell*—but its normal oral tradition pronunciation is *camel*. Does there seem to be any orderly relationship between the spellings and pronunciations of names? What is a complicating factor here?

11. Try to track down the origin of the "silent letters" in the following words. (Can you add to the list?)

aisle	calm
could	phlegm
debt	rhyme
foreign	subtle
mortgage	thumb
receipt	thyme

Is there any advantage in retaining these unsounded letters? Rewrite a passage of prose by striking out all of the silent letters. Ask several people to read the new version back to you. Did they have any difficulties in doing so? What, if any, were they? Try to diagnose the difficulties, if any; that is, try to determine what the silent letters (now missing) signal in each case.

12. Try turning a paragraph from anything you are reading into a rebus. (E.g., dogwood = + ; dance = d + , etc.) Discuss the problems you had in trying to make the rebus. Can you develop any rules or principles for rebus-making? Does the rebus have any advantages as a writing system? Disadvantages? Discuss.

13. Try to develop a simple picture-writing (*pictographic*) system that would adequately serve your everyday (non-school) written communication needs. Explain your thinking in respect to working out the system. What problems arose? What types of meanings can your system readily convey? What types can it convey only poorly or not at all? Write a few messages in the system. To what degree is the system *self-explanatory;* that is, not requiring special study in advance of its use? Try your communications out on someone who doesn't already know what you intend the pictographs to mean.

14. Try to develop a "memory jogger" (*mnemonic* device) by tying knots in string (in the Indian *quipu* fashion). What kinds of information can be handily stored by such a system? How complex can the information be? Make an actual knotted-string message and explain how it is to be decoded. How does this system differ in principle from (1) a pictographic system, and (2) an alphabetic system?

15. Early graphic symbols took their particular shapes because of the tools used to produce them. The Sumerian *cuneiform*, for example, was made with a *cuneus* or wedge-like tool which was pressed and scribed into soft clay tablets. The symbols reflect the tools and materials:

And the character of Chinese calligraphy is dependent upon the soft brush, ink, and paper (or similar surfaces). Try to develop sets of alphabetic symbols reflective of tools and materials other than pen (or pencil), ink, and paper. (*E.g.*, punch, chisel, knife, etc.) Explain how the characters relate to the tools used for making them and the surfaces upon which they are to be made. Write a short communication in each alphabet.

16. Try to develop a *program* (*i.e.*, a programmed learning program) for teaching a fairly complicated task to an illiterate who speaks a different language from you and whose language you don't speak. No interpreters are available, and he is just as intelligent as you are! Discuss the problems of developing such a program. Don't assume that a given picture will mean the same to him as it does to you. Or even that a left-to-right linear presentation will necessarily do the job.

> "Literacy gives people the power to focus a little way in front of an image so that we take in the whole image or picture at a glance. Non-literate people have no such acquired habit and do not look at objects in our way." (Marshall McLuhan, *The Gutenberg Galaxy*, p. 37.)

17. In what ways do advertisers use *typography* to attract the eye? Make a catalogue of common typographical devices (type faces, special kinds of lettering, other graphic symbols) and try to determine what kinds of meanings or feelings are meant to be associated with each. How do we "learn" these meanings? How can you test the accuracy of your set of presumed correspondences between symbol and effect? In this project try to concentrate exclusively on the *graphics*; that is, ignore the *overt* messages they are being used to spell out. Work up some advertising layouts for a range of products. Concern yourself primarily with typographical effects. Explain how the typography and related graphic material reinforces the message (namely, "Buy X!!") for each type of product. Try your hand at designing a personal letterhead. Justify your design as truly representative of your personality.

18. *Graphology* (handwriting analysis) has achieved sufficient respectability that it is being used in criminology, and its findings are admissible in a court of law. Make a collection of handwriting samples from a variety of people (different ages, sexes, backgrounds) and see if you can arrive at an orderly description of handwriting types. Explain your procedure. When you have finished, do some reading on the subject and compare your descriptive findings with what the experts say. Does it seem reasonable that aspects of one's personality, character, and even health can be "read" in handwriting? Explain the basis for such reading. Handwriting experts claim to be able to detect forgeries—even expert forgeries. What is there about handwriting that would seem to allow of such detection?

19. Write a dialogue (or even a short play) in which you indicate the proper intonation for each speech. To do this you will have to work out a system of graphic devices to show *pitches*, *stresses* (degrees of loudness), and *pauses* of various lengths; and the notation for these features will have to be simple and easily readable. To what extent can you rely on existing punctuation and other graphic marks (commas, dashes, italics, bold-face type, etc.) to do the job? Are there utterances whose vocabulary and grammatical structure are in themselves adequate signals of intonation? Examples? Have someone read a poem or paragraph aloud to you and see if you can use your system to indicate the reader's intonation. Try to teach someone the system and see if he can render to your satisfaction the dialogue you have written and marked with intonational symbols. (A tape recorder will be very useful for this project.)

20. Though primarily utilitarian, writing has an *aesthetic* dimension (touched on in exercise 17). Indeed, *calligraphy* is a major art in China and Japan. What evidence can you find of this aesthetic dimension of writing? Closely examine type designs in several printed works. How do they differ from each other? Attempt to evaluate them aesthetically as "attractive," "dull," "poor," etc. Try to formulate some principles of evaluation. Try designing a new type face according to these principles.

Is there any aesthetic value in attempting to relate in some way the type face to the work it is being used to render? (A book like S. H. Steinberg, *Five Hundred Years of Printing*, may give you some guidance.) Examine the type and graphic design of various magazines. (Include magazines that deal with the arts, e.g., *Art in America*, and advertising, e.g., *Graphis*.) Assume that your class is going to put out a magazine. Design an appropriate type face for it and do a *dummy; i.e., a layout,* of the magazine. You will have to imagine the kinds of articles, stories, pictures, etc., the magazine might include. Having done this, your class should perhaps go ahead and actually do a magazine. Of course your design will have to be modified to suit realistic limitations. (Unless, for example, you have a sizable budget—not likely!—you will probably have to "print" with a mimeograph machine, a spirit duplicator, or a hektograph. But this doesn't mean that the magazine must be graphically dull.)

9
Linguistics, Composition, and Literature

The tight little society that constitutes most departments of English stands in serious danger of solipsizing itself. The typical English department, with a perversity almost unimaginable, systematically excludes from its ranks all those who admit to any aspect of human discourse but the literary—and that narrowly defined. Linguists are suspect, and by and large they have escaped to happier havens outside departments of English (where, it might be added, the linguists can solipsize themselves).

(W. Ross Winterowd, *Rhetoric: A Synthesis*, New York.)

Syntax is the inner dynamics that makes literature.

(Harry R. Warfel, *Language, A Science of Human Behavior*, Cleveland.)

Literature and composition are two of the traditional divisions of "English." The third is "grammar," which traditionally has been (mis)-studied as an isolated discipline that was nevertheless supposed to prove somehow useful.* That there should have been divisions at all is a great pity, and that textbook grammarians so early lost themselves so thoroughly in that benighted intellectual backwater called "grammar" is an even greater pity. What we are saying is that the several manifestations of language *are* language, that literature, composition, and anything else that we subsume under "English" or "language arts" are linguistic phenomena. This means that linguistics (of which grammar is a part, but grammar in a new key, not the "grammar" of the traditional school textbooks) is the core discipline, for it addresses itself to the whole world of language experience. This means, further, that the methodologies and insights of linguistics will inform and illuminate both the "doing" of language (e.g., speaking and writing) and the examination of language (the study of literature, among other matters). Indeed, thought itself is a language-rooted behavior. Our concern in this chapter will be to explore some of the operational relationships among language study, composition, and literature, and to suggest ways of making these explorations in the classroom.

A composition is an intellectual construct. The compositional process thus takes place in the mind and not on paper. A written composition is merely an archival form of the mental construct. A tape recording is

---

* On its proven uselessness in all the areas in which its partisans have touted its usefulness, namely, those of disciplining the mind, aiding in the study of foreign languages, helping one to use better English, helping one to read better, and aiding in the interpretation of literature, see Neil Postman and Charles Weingartner, *Linguistics: A Revolution in Teaching*, 1967, pp. 63–66.

another. The construct is a linguistic one if it is manifested as speech or writing. If it is manifested as a painting or a piece of music, its mental "language" is something other than a linguistic one, although it can trigger a linguistic response.* *Composition* as we use the word in the English classroom labels the visible *result* of the compositional process. This means that in addition to the necessity of the student to control quite narrowly the operations of the mind upon a particular subject, he must control the graphic conventions of writing. More, he must articulate those conventions with what he is doing in his mind. It is a complex process indeed. And we should not be surprised that it is not easily mastered. Though the student would be better served were he earlier involved in its mastery.

A paragraph is a series of interlocked predications. And while no one has yet worked out an adequate "grammar" of the paragraph, we sense that there is an underlying structure of some sort. Although we can, on the basis of existing paragraphs, categorize the several usual structures (according to various principles), we do not produce paragraphs with these structures consciously in mind, perhaps not even sub-consciously. This simple truth underlies the failure of the common practice of "teaching the paragraph" by having students write paragraphs that by turns are "structured" by "particulars and details," "comparison and contrast," and the like. It makes as much sense to ask a student to do this as it does to make him write sentences and label the parts of speech as he writes. We do not require conscious knowledge of these entities in order to construct sentences either for speaking or for writing. Sentence composition like paragraph composition is a mental process that proceeds according to deeply internalized programs. Just as the initial one-clause sentences of the young child soon expand to multi-clause sentences, so the initial one-sentence paragraphs soon expand to paragraphs of lengths necessary to do whatever job the writer has in mind; and the strategies of paragraph construction develop to meet ever-increasing subtleties and complexities of thought. Of course, the paragraph has not the "natural" dimensions of the sentence and is not so easily got in hand, but we teachers haven't helped a great deal.

There is unquestionably great value in examining a student's paragraph to determine the logic of its structure. But this is quite a different matter from imposing an order *a priori*. The latter approach is rather like writing a paragraph before writing a paragraph. Such an approach is not to be confused with the technique of *imitation*, a technique that can be used most effectively in helping the student develop an ear for *style*. Style, of course, is rooted in the ordering of syntactic elements within the sentence (and in the choice of vocabulary). What we are suggesting here is that a paragraph grows organically. The early growths

---

* Any reflection on a non-language composition is done via language. Thus the meta-language of music is not music but language.

may be grotesque, but copious experience will work the desired change. Plainly put, the student will slap down a sentence, which "generates" another, which in turn generates another, and so on until the generative process limits itself either by *repetition* or *discursion*. When the next sentence merely repeats the substance of an earlier sentence, the paragraph is complete. Or when the next sentence parts company with those that precede it, the paragraph is complete.

The kind of intensive outlining that many teachers ask their students to do prior to writing is disastrous. The student is in effect being asked to write his paper before he writes it. Far more useful to the student is abstracting an outline from the piece he has already written. This formulates for him the logic (or lack thereof) of his work and will clearly show him what he must do to more effectively organize the piece. (Further, this is a fine exercise in inductive thinking. The composition is the data, the outline is the generalization he draws from the data.) A valuable pre-writing exercise is a written brief discussing the proposed project. By this means, the student focuses his attention but does not lose the delight in surprise that should mark the experience of writing. We deny this delight when we demand that the student pre-write his composition through an outline. Indeed, we seem to leave the student little to discover in writing but its drudgery (compounded as he tries to "fill in" his outline). No wonder he comes to think of writing as a painful bore and finds the teacher's professed enthusiasm over the "values" and "pleasures" of writing unfathomable.

There is no denying that various paragraphs make use of "particulars and details" and the rest, but these strategies spring naturally from the substance of the paragraph and the nature of the generative process that has been set in motion. Of course, a paragraph can be revised, and there is no question but that many professional writers do a great deal of revision, but the revision is worked upon a thing already created. With the creation before us, we can discover its shape and its internal makeup, the articulation of its parts, its gross and local anatomies, so to speak. What we discover will in turn suggest what changes might be fruitfully made. We are saying that it is far easier for the writer to work upon an existing entity than upon one that is not yet born. Let us not, therefore, impede the birth. Outlining and most of the rest of the "guides to better composition" that fill the textbooks merely impede.

Part of the difficulty for the student in his writing classes is the insistence of the book or teacher upon "subjects" (*i.e.*, to write about), "topic sentences" and the like. Let the student write a sentence. Let him follow that with another, related sentence, and let him keep writing until he runs the vein dry. Enough of this kind of writing experience and he will learn more that is genuinely useful to him about writing than he will learn from any schoolbook on the subject of writing. The human mind by its nature imposes form and order, but any reality upon which the mind works can be ordered in a variety of ways. There is no absolute order insofar as human perception is concerned. The simplest of objects may be described in many ways. Some descriptions will, of course, be more apt or more revealing than others. But the fledgling writer (and we mean writing to start in the first grade or earlier, with tape recorders as the first "writing" tools) must make these explorations on his own. The teacher cannot compose for the student if composition is going to be mastered by the student.

As the student grows more sure of himself in his writing and thus more willing to really write, he can be given sentences from which to generate paragraphs or longer compositions. Any sentence that will trigger a chain of related sentences is a "topic" sentence. Instead of worrying about inductive and deductive paragraph structures, the student should be examining the sequential relationship of sentences within the paragraph. He should understand how sentence 2 follows sentence 1. And how the last sentence of the paragraph is related to the first. He should, in fine, understand the thought process that produced the paragraph. He should write a dozen or more paragraphs each built upon the same first sentence. He should try to discover order based upon grammatical signals, lexical signals, phonological signals, logical signals. He will thereby not only learn a great deal about how a paragraph "works" but how his own mind works.

Consider this famous paragraph by James Joyce:

> A few light taps upon the pane made him turn to the window. It had begun to snow again. He watched sleepily the flakes, silver and dark, falling obliquely against the lamplight. The time had come for him to set out on his journey westward. Yes, the newspapers were right: snow was general all over Ireland. It was falling on every part of the dark central plain, on the treeless hills, falling softly upon the Bog of Allen and, farther westward, softly falling into the dark mutinous Shannon waves. It was falling, too, upon every part of the lonely churchyard on the hill where Michael Furey lay buried. It lay thickly drifted on the crooked crosses and headstones, on the spears of the little gate, on the barren thorns. His soul swooned slowly as he heard the snow falling faintly through the universe and faintly falling, like the descent of their last end, upon all the living and the dead.

(*"The Dead," Dubliners,* pp. 287–88.)

Can we imagine that Joyce set himself the task of building this paragraph by "particulars and details," that he pondered over whether the paragraph should be inductively ordered or deductively ordered, and the like? The careful orchestration of grammatical elements built around *falling* within a phonological universe dominated by /s/, the sound that both begins the word *snow* and (by virtue of that fact) suggests the sound of "snow falling faintly through the universe," provides the formal linguistic structure of this paragraph and give depth and dimension to its cognitive meaning. It is likely, of course, that this paragraph wasn't written off "automatically." Joyce unquestionably tinkered with it (he was a sedulous tinkerer) until it sounded as he wished it to sound. But first there was the underlying "ur-paragraph," that sprang from the inner necessity of each succeeding sentence. And we must never underestimate the value of the "happy accident." W. B. Yeats tells us that much that happens in the construction of a poem is after all accidental. Of course, the successful accidents happen to those who have the experience to recognize the value of an accident and to let it stand. A close study with the student of the Joyce paragraph will yield considerable riches. Such a study should focus on, for example, the chiasmus ("crossing") of ". . . falling softly . . . softly falling . . . ," the incremental repetition of "It was falling . . . falling softly upon . . . softly falling into. . . . It was falling, too . . . ," and so on. The incantatory quality of the passage and the heavy reliance upon repetition are not only most appropriate to the dirge-like quality of the whole story but are suggestive of the type of generative paragraph we have been discussing. Listen to children at play. If a particular word or phrase strikes their fancy, they will pick it up, chanting it, ringing changes on it, generating, in short, a ritual out of it. The production of a piece of writing and of the elements within the piece of writing has a ritual dimension. As teachers, we must take advantage of the mind's innate urge toward order and rhythm. And in the case of language, the order is well established (else the child could not communicate via langauge), the potential for ritual ready to be realized, for language is, after all, our most elaborate ritual.

Thus practice in paragraph generation is of paramount importance in the student's learning to control language compositionally. (Specific projects will be found in the Implications section.)

Once the student develops a degree of fluency in paragraph generation, as he inevitably will if he is allowed to, and has subjected his and other paragraphs to fairly intensive examination, he should begin to grasp the art and logic of the paragraph and should, therefore, be able to reconstitute his own work to bring it closer to the ideal synthesis of structure and sense that characterizes the best writing. This cannot be done, as we have said, according to formula. Writing, to be sure, has its conventions, but it cannot be formulated like a medical prescription. The conventions are networks of language and logic (or metalogic) within which the writer has ample room to move according to his own lights. (We are not speaking of the exceedingly narrow conventions of, say, technical writing, which comes as close to mechanical formulation as writing can come.)

This is not to say that statements resembling formulas cannot be abstracted from any piece of writing. Indeed, any discussion of style that lacks a statistical foundation lacks seriousness. But a rigorous description is quite different from an attempt to write according to that description.

To be rigorous, the formula-produced piece would match the original in every particular—paragraph construction, syntactic construction, lexical choices—and would, in fact, be identical with the original. Stylistic *imitation* (*i.e.*, writing *in the manner of*) has great value to the novice writer. This, however, is rather different from what would amount to a *copying* of the original. At any rate, *style* is primarily sentence-involved.

At the point of actually writing, we are only remotely or sub-consciously aware of the grammatical system, that system having been programmed into us when we were learning to speak. The precise causes of the occurrence of any particular structure (taken as stylistic choice) can very probably not be known. What we can do consciously, however, is to manipulate the structures that we have already fed into the paragraph. Thus we are back to the issue of revision and the conscious effort to improve or polish our writing. This can best be done by a kind of cross-referencing between the piece of writing as it stands and all that we know about writing, which in turn is the result of our own past experience as writers and our appreciation of the operations (*i.e.*, potentials) of the language as we know it from understanding how other writers (and speakers, of course) have used it.

Implications for Teaching

In learning to write, there is no substitute for writing; and in learning about rhetoric and style, there is no substitute for examining writing. That is, *doing* is better than *reading about* doing. The real weight of this chapter, then, lies in the projects that follow.

1. A good warm-up exercise in writing is to rewrite by reordering the syntactic components of a sentence of some rhetorical distinction. This one from Thoreau's *Allegash and East Branch* will do nicely for a start:

> It was a dense and damp spruce and fir wood in which we lay, and, except for our fire, perfectly dark; and when I awoke in the night, I either heard an owl from deeper in the forest behind us, or a loon from a distance over the lake.

A sentence of this complexity will allow of a considerable number of versions. After the student has produced as many as he can (there is incidentally, a game element here that the teacher shouldn't overlook), he should be asked to select two or three different favorite versions. These should be dittoed and distributed. Whatever discussion can be drawn from their study in common will be useful in sensitizing the class to the *art* of writing. The student should be encouraged then to attempt this intensive revision of a few sentences from various compositions he has already written. There should be a good deal of rumination in the classroom over the merits and defects of these various sentences and their various versions. If possible, the class should sketch the beginnings of a kind of rhetorical guide for the evaluation of sentences. All evaluative principles, however, must be defensible (and defended) by those who formulate them. (The tone of these discussions must, of course, be both pleasant and impersonal!) The teacher will continue to provide examples of well-written sentences from a variety of sources—but only as a stimulus to writing and discussion. The approach must not be either explicitly or implicitly to draw invidious comparisons between student work and the work of "great" writers. Such an approach will do little more than intimidate, and probably antagonize, the student.

2. Because any sentence can generate a paragraph (hence, be a "topic" sentence), some or all of the sentences experimented within the preceding exercise should be taken as paragraph-initial sentences and the student should be asked to write a suitable paragraph for each. Again, results should be compared and discussed. For those sentences that were taken from outside sources, the student (after he has done his paragraphs) should be given the original source for comparison. What the student discovers by making the comparison is in itself a useful subject for a composition. Writing about one's writing, about what one has discovered about the process of writing as one attempted to work out a writing problem, is a valuable technique in self-education.

3. Much writing (student and otherwise) lacks both a *sense of audience* and a *distinctive voice*. Yet any piece of writing that conveys these qualities has a perceptible character. That is, we somehow feel the writer in the writing. And since we do, we should be able to identify those elements in the writing that prompt the feeling. The student, therefore, should be asked to subject a variety of writing samples (from various books, magazines, and newspapers) to analysis for the authors' sense of audience and distinctive voice. Let the student define the terms to his own satisfaction. Let him devise his own analytical techniques and his own terminology, and question him relentlessly, though pleasantly. Then ask him to write essays, reports, news stories, etc., for a variety of clearly defined audiences (adult, high school, suburban, etc.). Ask him to discuss the basis for his definition of this or that audience. Discuss the lexical and grammatical strategies pertinent to each audience and each voice. Often it takes but a few seemingly minor changes in a passage to radically change its "feel." The student should subject a variety of passages, his own and others', to this kind of revision. And he should be asked to discuss the results. He should now begin to appreciate the delicacy and subtlety possible in verbal expression. He will, therefore, be on the way to developing an "ear," without which no amount of guidebook rules will be of any real use. (*All* writing projects should, where possible, be done within the framework of some purpose other than just writing because the teacher wants the student to do writing. One such framework is the class newspaper or magazine.)

4. As we have seen, the utterances of our language are built by combining and manipulating a small number of simple elements. Thus, a sentence like *Merwin decided to go* is said to derive from *Merwin +
decide + PAST + [something]* and *Merwin + PRESENT + goes*. The student should attempt to recover the predications of a passage of prose (or poetry), and to describe the processes whereby the surface structures were produced, and to rewrite the passages by producing different surface structures from the same base structures. The following sentences, for example, derive from the same bases:

1. The fact that Quentin smoked pot angered his parents.
2. Quentin's parents were angered by the fact that he smoked pot.
3. Quentin's smoking of pot was what angered Quentin's parents.
4. Quentin's pot smoking angered his parents.

A variation of this exercise is to recover the base predications of, say, the infinitive constructions culled from a piece of writing. Another dimension is to compare the findings for one piece of writing with those for another piece by a different writer. Or compare/contrast two distinctively different publications like *The Atlantic* and *Variety*. The varying uses of the feature (in this case, the infinitive) should be identified and characterized. (But this is *not* the game of "find the infinitive." If the student has any difficulty in finding them, the teacher should simply point them out.) Doing this kind of study over a wide range of grammatical features results in a stylistic profile of the writing.

5. To test the assertion that "poetry is syntax," reorder the syntax of a selection of short poems (preferably from several periods of literature) to make it conform to "normal" syntax. (To determine what "normal" syntax is, do a survey of randomly chosen prose samples. Make a count of the various sentence types—S-V-O; S-V$_{INTR}$; S-V-O-O, etc. —and of the positioning of movable elements—adverbs, etc. The norms will be the arrangements that occur most frequently.) Compare the originals with your revisions. What differences do you note in effect, impact, tone, feeling, and aesthetic value? Describe the grammatical strategies of each of the original poems and try to explain how they lend to the totality of the poem. How, for example, is the "message" enhanced by the "medium" (*i.e.*, by the poet's use of language)?

6. Diction (word choice) is ultimately a grammatical issue. Each word lives, as it were, in a semantic universe that is subtly keyed to the grammatical habits of the language. This is another way of saying that grammar has a semantic component that must be taken into account when choosing one's lexicon. Test this notion by substituting presumed synonyms for key words in a few pieces of writing (some poetry and some prose). Describe what happens. Attempt to *explain* precisely (for

each word) what happens. You will find that in some cases the "synonyms" are reasonable alternatives and in others they are unreasonable in varying degrees. Account for these results as well as you can. Try to determine to what extent grammatical choices demand certain lexical choices and forbid others. Try to determine how certain lexical choices demand certain grammatical choices and forbid others. Can you organize your findings in a way that will be illuminating to someone interested in this issue?

7. Choose passages from two writers with clearly different styles (e.g., Melville and Hemingway) and write the content of the one passage in the style of the other and vice-versa. Describe how you prepared yourself to do the job, what problems you ran into, and what you learned by doing it. Do more such projects using different pairs of writers.

8. Read several issues of *The New Yorker, New York Magazine, The New York Daily News, The National Review, True Confessions* (or any other magazines with distinctive styles and audiences) and try to write a brief news item or article in the style of each. Discuss the problems you had and how you attempted to solve them.

9. A given sentence . . . can be subjected to four kinds of changes. We may suppose, if we like, that the sentence in question is a norm and that the changes effected in it are deviations. Or we may simply think of it as a sentence that a writer has written and is now revising. He can *add, omit, transpose,* or *substitute.*
   1. *Addition:* a word, phrase or clause is added ("The Poem is complex" = "The poem, I think, is complex").
   2. *Omission:* a word, phrase or clause is omitted ("The poem is very complex" = "The poem is complex").
   3. *Transposition:* the elements are rearranged in different order ("On first reading, the poem is complex" = "the poem is complex on first reading").
   4. *Substitution:* an element is replaced by another ("The poem is complex" = "The poem is complicated").
   (Louis Milic, *Stylists on Style,* p. 11.)

Take several randomly chosen passages, including some of your own work, and subject the sentences to one or more of these changes. Explain what you did and how it affected the impact of the passage. Did any of your changes improve any of the sentences? How? Did any of your changes worsen any of the sentences? How?

10. To grasp the purely stylistic choices made by a writer, one can subject a passage to a process known as *proposition reduction.* This process strips the passage bare of anything but its basic propositions (the cognitive meaning stated wherever possible in simple declarative sentences). The pruned material represents the *style* of the passage. Here are the instructions for proposition reduction given by Milic (pp. 18–19):

1. Each sentence yields one proposition. No sentence is left out and none subdivided.
2. Word order is restored to normal if inversion occurs.
3. All connective links are omitted and all pronouns and similar words which refer to items in other sentences are replaced by their referents.
4. Subordinate ideas and non-essential modifiers are deleted.
5. Figurative language is replaced by literal equivalents.
6. The diction is made neutral and commonplace.
7. Normal ellipsis is used: repetition within a given proposition should be avoided.
8. Quotations are omitted or preserved but not paraphrased.
9. Statements disguised as questions are reworded as declaratives.

Using this guide, perform proposition reduction upon a selection of passages of poetry and prose. Then do the following:

a. Identify the style markers of each passage and attempt to write a passage of your own using the same markers.

b. Discuss the problems you had in performing the reductions and try to account for the fact that you had these problems. Then explain how you resolved them.

c. Discuss what you learned about writing, communication, and style by working on this project.

11. It has been suggested (J. P. Thorne, "Stylistics and Generative Grammars," *Journal of Linguistics*, Vol. 1, 1965, pp. 45–59) that the language of poetry is a congeries of unique languages and that it is better to develop a grammar for each poem than to try to expand the grammatical statements of the matrix ("parent") language to include such deviances as we find in nearly any poem we may choose to examine. This is an arguable point of grammatical theory, but there is nonetheless much to be gained by attempting to develop a grammar for each poem or for the canon of the particular poet, for each poet tends to fall into a set of linguistic habits that repeat throughout his work. Try doing this for works by Donne, Pound, Eliot, Thomas, E. E. Cummings, Ginsberg, and/or any other poets whose work intrigues you. Discuss your findings, compare the results from one poet to the next, and compare the special grammars of the poets with the general grammar of the language. What did you learn about poetry (and your language) by working on this project?

12. Language theory has concerned itself largely with the sentence. It has been said indeed that grammar ends with the sentence. But a few linguists are attempting to develop a grammar of rhetoric (or, at least, a grammar of the paragraph). A piece of writing is, after all, not merely a set of discrete sentences. These sentences stand in some sort of relationship to each other and perhaps follow some definable principles analogous to the grammatical principles associated with the sentence. Can you find any basis for such a "supra-grammar" ("meta-grammar")?

Gather a collection of paragraphs that will serve as the raw material for such a grammar. Then attempt by detailed comparison and contrast among these paragraphs to determine some "paragraph-grammatical" principles. Consider such matters as sentence beginnings and endings, sentence types, etc. Don't be disappointed if the project causes you a certain amount of frustration. Ignore the frustration and concentrate on what you will be learning about paragraph structure. And remember that the writers were very likely not *conscious* of the structure. They felt it and recognized it when they saw it. This is the writer's "instinct." It is in fact learned, and one way of learning it is to work at projects like this one.

13. Implicit in every piece of writing are the author's assumptions regarding his presumed audience. Examine a diversity of writing samples and attempt to determine what in each case those assumptions are. Develop a model for each of several different audiences and write a paragraph or two for each on any subject in a style that you feel appropriate to each. Explain how you developed your models and discuss the stylistic characteristics that you feel effectively serve each audience.

14. Make an anthology of styles, using paragraphs from various samples of writing ranging from literary "classics" to journalism. Drawing on all that you know about style and about English grammar, attempt to characterize each style. Test your characterizations out on others to determine whether they truly convey your intentions. Discuss the problems you have in discussing style.

15. After a sufficient experience of reading, one can begin to make value judgments about the quality of writing; *i.e.*, it is apparent that some writers are more skillful, more artful, more craftsmanlike than others. What specifically leads you to these judgments? What constitutes being "more skillful," "more artful," "more craftsmanlike"? (It may help you if you practice first on, say, *musicianship*, for it is not at all difficult to tell the difference between one who plays an instrument ineptly and one who plays competently. Sports offers another analogy. A beginner at basketball looks quite different from one who has been playing for a while. Of course, making judgments among performers— musicians or sportsmen—who are at least competent is far more difficult and requires far more experience. Thus it is with writing.) Clues: look for *overwriting* (pomposity), *overloaded writing* (wordiness), *cloudy writing* (words without substance), *imprecision* (wrong or inexact words), *insensitivity to sound and rhythm*, etc. You might want to set up a matrix of parameters (such as those just listed) to use as a guide in judging writing quality. The more examples of any of these flaws, the poorer the writing. (Remember, we are *not* worried here about the *subject matter* of the writing.)

10
Non-Standard English

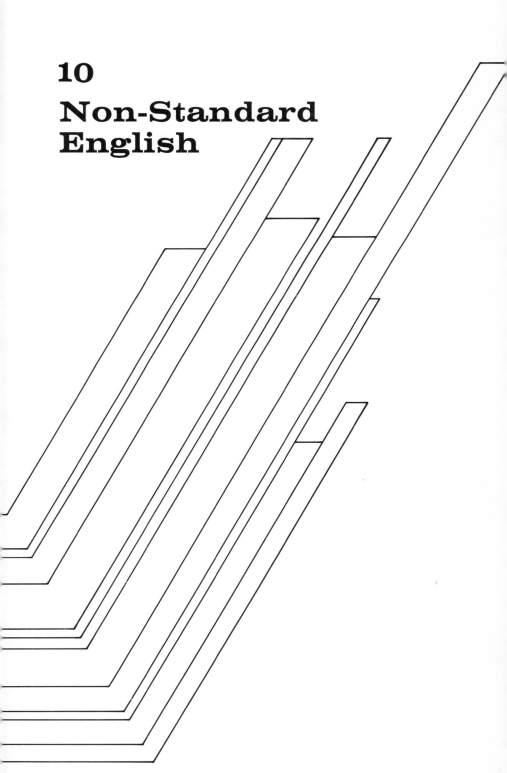

Here in the United States, there are a number of English teaching situations which appear to involve a quasi-foreign language relationship between a standard variety of English and some English-based pidgin or creole or nonstandard, natively spoken dialect of English. It is primarily in the densely populated and more fluid and competitive social environment of the larger cities, however, that the resultant problems are likely to have the most serious consequences for the nation as a whole.

(William A. Stewart, "Urban Negro Speech: Sociolinguistic Factors Affecting English Teaching," *The Florida Foreign Language Reporter: Special Anthology Issue*, Vol. 7, No. 1, 1969.)

In English, "standardness" has never been clearly defined nor universally acknowledged. At the supra-national level, there is clearly no standard, though certain forms of British English are sentimental favorites. At lower levels, the standards are local; that is, it is possible to speak of "standard British English" with some expectation that the British will recognize its existence and use it as an educational model. Though it is not possible to speak of "standard American English," at least as a *spoken* dialect, schoolbook written English comes as close to a national standard as we have in this country. At lower levels ("lower" here not meant to be pejorative) still, standards are merely the speech norms of the various dialects. At the lowest level, that of the individual, the idiosyncratic dialect, *idiolect*, of the individual is his "standard."

The traditional schoolbook standard was derived from earlier literary English. But, of course, the living language changes while the literary language of the past is "frozen" and not really relevant to present reality from the standpoint of linguistic standards. And although the United States has over the years been relatively free in its use of the language, we have nonetheless long been obsessed with the notion of "correctness" in language. Lacking any sort of central authority over linguistic matters (cf., *l'Académie française*), American English has never settled on a single standard. As it turns out, most dimensions of "correctness" are bound up with *social* rather than *linguistic* issues, which is to say that they are *sociolinguistic*. The use of *ain't* (as an example) thereby becomes a shibboleth. Its use marks the speaker as a member of a certain class or group (or at least denies him membership in other classes or groups)—in America, that is. In Great Britain, there is a different standard, and *ain't* enjoys the company of noblemen, or at least the old-line provincial aristocracy; and this neatly demonstrates the arbitrariness of "standards of correctness." One can speak, therefore, of a linguistic norm *only* in terms of a particular group. It is at this point that the concept of norms and standards comes into conflict with communicative competence. Most people have multiple social memberships fulfilling several social roles and will develop their greatest linguistic competence in the social group (or context) most important to their everyday existence. What constitutes competence and is, therefore, "standard" in one group, may be considered extreme deviation by another group. Hence, we cannot speak of an inherently "right" or "wrong" linguistic performance but only of *contextually appropriate performance*. What might be called *absolute grammatical incompetence* is virtually impossible, for a native speaker would have in his social context no model for such deviance. This is to say, if one speaks English, one speaks English. Thus, personal and social values, goals, status, etc., are implicated in pronouncements about language. In a culture with a social hierarchy, the speech habits of the upper strata comprise a "prestige" dialect that speakers from the lower strata tend to feel, or are made to feel, is somehow "better" or more nearly "correct" than their own dialects. In our own language, for example, a locution like *I don't want no spinach* is considered by many to be "bad" English or "incorrect" English. Why? Until the great normative movement of the eighteenth century, double negation (indeed, *multiple* negation; compare Chaucer: He *never* yet *no* vileinye *ne* sayde) was normal in English, as it still is, for example, in French. On the foolish grounds that one negative "cancels out" another, the prescriptivists ruled against its use. Because this "logic" had the force of authority, it became "good" English while multiple negation (still widely used) became "bad." The fact is that single negation was made a status dialect shibboleth. Intrinsically, it is no better (or worse, though less expressive perhaps) than multiple negation. And so it goes.

Non-standardness appears not only in the "social" sense, but also as a marker of linguistic foreignness. The deviations in this area, however, are the result of attempts (albeit often subconscious) to impose a non-English grammar or phonology or lexicon onto the newly acquired English, and are easily recognized as "foreign" mistakes. Such deviations are not truly "dialects" of English but rather imperfect renditions highly colored by the speaker's native tongue.

The most striking examples of non-prestigious social dialects in the United States are Black English (BE) and Puerto Rican English (PRE), often pejoratively labeled "sub-standard." Both dialects are not only spoken by millions of native Americans, but are being perpetuated as a "mother tongue." Of the two, Black English has been the most intensively studied and has as well been the focus of much educational controversy. Although the dialect constitutes a field of study in its own right, we feel that the goals of this book will be served by inclusion of a brief survey of Black English. The following descriptive analysis, therefore, is intended to provide a quick overview and is limited to a few points where there are major or contrastive differences between Black English and Standard English (SE). These differences occur at all levels of analysis—phonological, morphological, and semantic.

And while it is true that relatively few non-blacks speak Black English, it is not true that all blacks do speak it. Black English is the distinctive dialect of a particular culture, that of the inner city or the rural South and of lower socioeconomic status. History and circumstance have seen to it that the majority of such speakers are black, though very few blacks speak "pure" Black English. Most use dialects conflated in various ways from Standard and Black English. Black English thus can be thought of as a dialect continuum that at its most attenuated is barely distinguishable from Standard English. To the extent that social mobility enables some speakers to move into other classes, the dialect will penetrate those classes, and, in the absence of counter-pressures (strong personal motivation, etc.), may perpetuate at least some of its features.

PHONOLOGY

In most languages (perhaps all languages) vowels are relatively less stable or "fixed" than are consonants. The contrast is one of less easily defined locations in space (vowels) as over against more easily defined locations fixed by the cross references of *articulator* and *point of articulation; i.e.*, the placement of some part of the tongue against some part of the mouth. In Standard English not all speakers make the same vowel contrasts, and some dialects do not distinguish between certain pairs of vowels. These situations obtain *a fortiori* in Black English, and, combined with other phonological differences, can create serious problems not of understanding only but of spelling and reading when these Black English speakers are put into a Standard English school environment.

For example, *pin* and *pen* may both be pronounced identically, either both as *pin* or both as *pen*, which is to say that *pin* and *pen* are homophonic in this dialect. Likewise *hear* and *hair*. *Poor*, *sure*, and *door* frequently form a vocalic triplet, in which all are pronounced to rhyme with *door*. In an *r*-less dialect (where final and pre-consonantal *r*'s are modified to vowels as in eastern New England and large parts of the South), the vowel will be lengthened to [o] or [oə]. Diphthongs, which in SE are usually up-gliding, tend to lose the up-glide portion of the vowel and what is left merges in the vowel system with [a], [o], and [ɔ] (e.g., *oil* > [ɔːl], similar to SE *all*.)

Initial unstressed vowels are often lost in BE:

alarm   > [la:m]

fire alarm > [fa: la:m] or [fa:ə la:m]

expell   > [spɛl]

Although BE consonants generally follow SE patterns, the BE tendency is toward a weakening or loss of finals. In contrast, initial dentals, /t/, /d/, tend to be more forcibly articulated and aspirated than in SE. Final /r/, /l/, /t/, /d/, /s/, /z/, and sometimes /n/, all tend to be lost. SE final clusters are diverse, but the most frequently occurring clusters have /t/, /d/, /s/, or /z/ as the second element. These also happen to constitute most of the inflectional phonemes left in English (with the choice of a voiced or voiceless phoneme almost invariably predictable). In BE the final consonant cluster undergoes extensive simplification even when the final phoneme is grammatically significant. This is to say that most inflections are dropped (*He talks > He talk*). Three-consonant clusters are rare in BE and usually reduce to two-consonant clusters or, occasionally, to a single consonant. The most frequently lost consonants are /t/, /d/, and /s/, with /n/, /k/, /g/, and /p/ following in frequency of loss.

In the initial position, /ð/, and /θ/, are commonly replaced by /t/ and /d/, respectively (e.g., *them/dem; think/tink*). In the final position, they become /v/ and /f/ (e.g., *bathe/bave; bath/baff; truth/trufe*, etc.)

Many SE speakers speak an *r*-less dialect which means that the characteristic r-lessness of BE is not unique to BE, though its occurrence in a Standard English dialect area that does not exhibit this feature will make the BE speaker stand out for that feature alone. Analogous to the *r*-less habit in BE is the loss of the final /l/; e.g., *ball/baw; sell/seh*. This is distinctively BE and more widely noticeable than *r*-lessness.

GRAMMAR

Verbs

Present Tense. The Black English verb system with respect to tense differs from that of Standard English in several important ways. In SE the present tense retains an irregular suffix, s, to mark the third person singular (*he talks*). This irregularity is *not present* in the BE verb system; i.e., it is not overlooked or deleted in some way; it simply is not part of BE's regular verb system (*I talk, you talk, he talk*, etc.). This regularity is maintained in the negative (where *do* is frequently used as an auxiliary) and in the verb *have*, thus:

BE	SE
He don't talk much	He doesn't talk much
He don't go	He doesn't go
He have to go	He has to go
He have a new car	He has a new car

This is the general pattern in BE and includes without exception all present tense verbs in the third person singular.

Past Tense. The regular past tense marker in SE is marked by an inflection in -ed, variously pronounced /t/, /d/, or /ɪd/ according to the final phoneme of the base verb. This marker is often absent from BE because BE phonological rules differ from those of SE. Actually, the suffix is "grammatically" present, but is automatically deleted by pronunciation rules comparable to deletions in SE contractions (*I'll* = *I*[wi]*ll*; *he'd* = *he* [coul]*d*, etc.). With some verbs, viz., those ending in dental sounds, /t/, /d/, the phonological rules in some cases can even work back and eliminate the final dental sound as well as the suffix. (See above, *Phonology.*)

In SE, a few irregular verbs have no form to distinguish present and past tenses (e.g., *hit, bet*). In BE there are a few additional verbs of this class (e.g., *come, say*). As a rule, tense intention is signaled adverbially (e.g., *He say that yesterday*).

Perfectivity. The SE perfective contractions of the auxiliary *have/has* (*i.e.*, *-'ve/-'s*) are further contracted in BE. The elimination of the *-'s* form (*He'*[ha]*s gone*) is analogous to the BE treatment of the present tense suffix, but the leveling of both forms to zero often leads to the erroneous interpretation that BE has *no* perfective tense. This false claim is buttressed by the fact that *stylistically* BE uses a past perfect tense form (*had* + a participle) more frequently than does SE, especially for narrative purposes. As with the past tense in -ed, the contracted suffixes of the perfective are present grammatically but deleted phonologically.

Past Participle. The existence of a past participle has been questioned by some linguists, as the participial form in -ed is identical with the regular past tense form and suffers the same phonological fate. There are of course irregular verbs in SE that have a distinctive past participial form (e.g., *do/did/done; take/took/taken; ring/rang/rung*, etc.). In BE the distinction is often not made, some speakers electing to use the SE past form as a BE participle, and others using the SE participle as their past form. Thus, it may very well be that BE contains only one past form, which doubles as either preterite or participle:

He taken the book.
He have taken the book.
They came yesterday.
They have came yesterday.

Temporal Aspects. SE distinguishes two perfective tenses for which it uses *have* or *had* plus a participle. BE, however, uses not only these two aspects but two others in *done* and *been*. Like the perfective tenses, these constructions are formed with the "past participle" (if, as we have noted, such exists):

I done came to fetch her.
I done forgot about the party.

This construction in BE denotes a *completive* aspect and can be expressed only paraphrastically in SE. The construction in *been* means that the action of the verb took place in the *remote* past:

She been had that picture there a long time.

Future Tense. Black English like Standard English uses the auxiliary *will* to indicate future time. Like SE, too, BE usually contracts this auxiliary to *-'ll*. As with *-'ve* and *-'s*, *-'ll* can be deleted phonologically, especially when preceding an /l/ or a bilabial sound (/m/, /b/, /p/). This deletion of the contracted portion of *will* gives the impression that BE future is sometimes accomplished by using the main verb only, especially when an adverb of time is also present. This is particularly likely when the verb following the *-'ll* form is the verb *be*, which begins with a bilabial sound. The same process occurs in constructions in *would* and *be*. The contraction results in *-'d* followed by a bilabial, and deletion occurs. These two forms of invariant *be* also occur phonetically in SE despite their orthographic presence. In the following sentence, the main clause (underlined) is often pronounced as [hi: bí hɪr] or [hiʔ bí hɪr]:

If you would've invited him, <u>he'd be here.</u>

The skeptical reader can experiment for himself by pronouncing the complete sentence in a normal tone of voice, with *'d* deletion, to the average listener and ask him if the sentence is "correct" or "grammatical." An overwhelming majority of listeners will insist that they distinctly heard the *'d*.

Auxiliaries: Going to/Gonna. The Standard English construction *going to . . .*, often contracted to *gonna . . .*, occurs frequently in Black English though almost never with the associated form of the verb *be* as in SE:

BE: She gonna work today.
     He gonna bring some more.
SE: She's gonna work today.
     He's gonna bring some more.

The BE form of *gonna* has become so standardized that it is accepted as a full form and, in consequence, is often further reduced phonologically (as it is not uncommonly in SE). Thus:

I'm gonna go > I'ŋ gna go.

To Be. In addition to the *be* forms derived from the contraction of auxiliaries plus deletion, Black English has several distinctive uses of *be* as a main verb. It has been argued that *be* is a tenseless verb in BE (see R. W. Fasold, "Tense and the Form 'Be' in Black English," *Language,* Vol. 45, No. 4), but there is as yet no agreement on the linguistic nature of the invariant *be* in Black English. The use of the copula *be* in Black English differs substantially from its uses in Standard English both in respect to those syntactic patterns in which it is *absent* as well as those in which it is *present.*

The absence of *be* in present-tense statements is not peculiar to BE but occurs also in Hungarian, Russian, Hebrew, and other languages. The question arises whether the copula is truly absent, for it might be present grammatically in deep structure and undergo deletion before it reaches the surface. As Chomsky and others have noted, the underlying representations of dialects of the same language are not likely to be very different one from the other despite marked differences in surface manifestations. The presence of *be* forms in other environments (*e.g.,* first-person contractions, past tense, modal constructions, emphatics, yes/no questions, etc.) supports the view that Black English has high level rules that introduce the copula. Labov has found that "wherever Standard English can contract, Black English can delete *is* and *are,* and vice versa; wherever Standard English cannot contract, Black English cannot delete *is* and *are* and vice versa" ("Contraction, Deletion, and Inherent Variability of the English Copula," *Language,* Vol. 45, No. 4, p. 722).

Among the grammatical environments preceding which the copula can be absent in Black English are these:

1. Noun Phrase
2. Predicate Adjective
3. Locative
4. Negative
5. Present Progressive form in *-ing*
6. Construction with *gonna*

The presence of the invariant *be* may be attributed to several other sources because of a difference in semantics between Standard English and Black English. In Black English, invariant *be* indicates *repeated* but *not continuous* occurrence (*i.e.*, the subject or the predications are distributed or occur over points in time). This distribution can be intermittent. *Be* in Standard English never being used this way, it is often misunderstood by SE speakers as a deviant or non-standard form of *am*, *is*, or *are*. This of course is not the case, and this special Black English use of *be* can be expressed only paraphrastically in SE. Thus:

SE: I'm good = a permanent attribute of·goodness
BE: I'm good = the goodness is intermittent

Negation. Historically, the contracted negatives of *am*, *are*, and *is*, and *have* and *has* (as auxiliaries) developed into *ain't*, a locution much fussed about by prescriptive grammarians and self-styled guardians of our linguistic "purity." Yet, despite its designation as a marker of low social status, it has continued to be used at all social and educational levels (and is, as we have noted, strictly an upper-status form in certain aristocratic circles in Britain). From a linguistic point of view, it makes at least as much sense as the (curiously) acceptable, *aren't I* (which is the question form of *I are not*, certainly unacceptable to the habitual users of *aren't I!*)

In Black English, *ain't* is used extensively and without social stigma. In addition to its SE equivalent usage, it is used in double negations and, in some dialects, as a replacement for SE *don't* or *didn't*:

They ain't never seen me.
They ain't nobody seen me.
They ain't seen me.

Again, despite its "official" disapproval, double negation is not at all uncommon in SE, though some types are less disapproved than others (e.g., *I can't hardly see the goalie*). In BE the grammatical rules for negation *require* that negation be marked both in the main verb (regardless of following negative adverbs) and in all subsequent indefinite noun phrases. The latter leads to multiple negation in some instances:

1. It don't hardly pay to go
   (SE: It doesn't pay to go, or, it hardly pays to go.)
2. We ain't never had no beef about none of us not showing up.

Double negation occurs even when the auxiliary is preposed in sentences with a negatively marked indefinite noun phrase:

1. Didn't no cop catch him.
2. Wasn't nothing wrong.
3. Can't nobody beat me.

(These are all intoned as declaratives, though their syntax suggests a rising final pitch.)

NOUNS AND NOMINALS

Genitive

Common Nouns. Unlike SE, which uses -'s (in its various pronunciations) to mark the genitive, BE commonly uses word order alone (e.g., *the boy hat = the boy's hat*), although there is considerable dialect variation according to geography. In constructions, however, where the -'s ends the clause, the standard form seems to occur more often (e.g., *The hat is the boy's*).

Proper Nouns. BE follows the SE pattern, but occasionally uses the genitive marker redundantly by adding it to both surname and given name in the same context.

Pronouns

One of the most characteristic features of Black English is pronominal apposition to the noun subject of a sentence:

1. Jack, *he* a cool cat.
2. My brother, *he* in the Army.
3. That girl, *she* giving me the eye.

The construction is superficially like SE cross-referencing (*That kid of mine, he sure is getting out of hand*), but is more pervasive and obviously a regular grammatical feature. Thus far, its precise distribution, restrictions, etc., have not been formulated.

In the absolute possessive final position, the Standard English *mine* often becomes Black English *mines*, by analogy to the other pronominal possessives, *his, hers, its, ours,* etc. This regularization of the form does not occur in attributive constructions, where *my* is used. Occasionally (especially in the South), the standard nominative or accusative pronouns are used throughout all attributive constructions (e.g., *him house, he boat, you book*).

The expletive *there* of SE is often replaced in BE by *they* or *it:*

SE: Is *there* anybody here?
BE: Is *they/it* anybody here?

Plurality. Although most BE speakers have the plural in their grammar, the marker (-s) is sometimes omitted. In certain cases, BE simply does not have a differentiated plural (*cf.*, SE *sheep/sheep; deer/deer*). On the other hand, BE regularly pluralizes with -s, words which in SE have irregular (usually internal replacive) plurals such as *foot* (BE plural, *foots*). It may even "pluralize" words (of this irregular type) that are already plural in SE (BE *mices, childrens, mens,* etc.). Of course, SE has done the same thing with *children,* which was first properly pluralized from *child* to *childer,* then double pluralized by adding the plural marker from another class of nouns.

A study of the semantics of Black English is beyond the scope of this book and the competence of its authors. Suffice it to say that while SE and BE share a large vocabulary and semantic universe, there are equally large areas of semantic isolation. It is easy to be misled. From our shared vocabulary we may assume shared meaning. But if, for example, a BE speaker uses the term *mama,* he probably doesn't mean what a Standard English speaker means (BE *mama,* "a pretty black girl"). Much work remains to be done in Black English, perhaps the most fascinating in rhetoric and stylistics, for BE has developed its own rhetorical modes and its own styles, rhythms, metaphors, and so on, to say nothing of its own world of meanings.

PUERTO RICAN ENGLISH (PRE)

The study of the non-standard Puerto Rican variant of English has lagged far behind other dialect studies, and there is, accordingly, a paucity of both data and theory. Although some attempts have been made to establish a phoneme inventory for PRE, no comprehensive and methodologically sound piece of work has come to our attention. (The field of published research was recently surveyed by George M. Williams, Jr., for the *Language Research Foundation,* Cambridge, Mass.). According to one worker surveyed, four SE phonemes (/θ/, /ŋ/, /ɛ/, and /ɔ/) normally absent from the phoneme inventory of native speakers of Spanish are added by a large percentage of these speakers (70–85%) in acquiring English. The /æ/ and /v/ are acquired by 41–44%, and the remaining "foreign phonemes, /ð/, /â/, /ɪ/, /ʊ/, /z/, and /ž/, are acquired by from 7–26%. There thus appears to be a continuum of difficulty in adding new phonemes. The precise nature of the difficulties involved is not made clear in most of the studies (several of which disagree with each other).

Some of the studies showed a tendency on the part of PRE speakers to substitute [b] for SE initial /v/, or to unvoice /v/ in final clusters. Difficulties with other word-final consonants resulting from regressive unvoicing in Spanish represents an area of considerable trouble for Spanish speakers learning English. The resultant cluster simplification often resembles those of Black English. By and large it is impossible to predict PRE variations on the basis of Spanish-English phonological contrasts, for second-language learning produces certain phonological adjustments.

One of the more noticeably deviant patterns, however, is in the handling of intonational components. Spanish is a syllable-timed language as against English, which is stress timed. The lack of "marking" in English writing for those patterns makes them difficult to master where the learner is heavily dependent on written materials. Spanish uses only three pitch levels, all closer together than the four of English. The absence of a zero, or reduced, stress in Spanish results in the equalization of syllable length. In English, syllable length is variable (confusingly so for the Spanish speaker). The PRE tendency toward syllable equalization causes difficulty in handling pairs of words or phrases that differ primarily in stress (e.g., conTRACT vs. CONtract). Other dimensions of SE stress are reduced or missing in PRE.

Although very little has been thus far reported, syntactical differences lie mainly in

1. word order, especially adjective and adverb positions
2. article use, especially regarding definiteness vs. indefiniteness
3. varying prepositional uses
4. double negation
5. use of grammatical gender (as in Spanish); instead of English "natural gender" (thus a *table* will be referred to as *she*, following Spanish, *la mesa*, feminine noun).

As with Black English, semantic and related matters are wide open for exploration. A *contact vernacular* called "Spanglish" is beginning to develop, but little work has been done on it.

Implications for Teaching

Considerable controversy rages over the role (or lack thereof) of Black English in the classroom. Issues of this kind can only be resolved at the local level. There are blacks, for example, who reject Black English and feel that encouraging it in any way is educationally counterproductive. There are other blacks with precisely the opposite view. As linguists, the authors are interested in Black and Puerto Rican (and other) English. Language is infinitely fascinating and "studiable" wherever it is found. But we cannot make recommendations about the role of these dialects in a formal educational context (below the university and graduate school levels). We can, however, urge that the teacher who has in her charge students who speak BE, PRE, or any other non-standard dialect learn something about those dialects, recognize their legitimacy as a tool for communication, and overcome the destructive traditional attitudes toward non-textbook English. Teachers must first communicate (an obvious enough notion), but communication is impossible where the student is put on the psycholinguistic defensive. The teacher must appreciate that in no *absolute* or even *convincingly demonstrable* way is Standard English "better" than any other English. We are finally talking about social and cultural differences, social dominance, and other non-linguistic matters. The student has to feel at home with himself and his environment before he can concern himself with the business of the classroom. Where, then, there is a dialect problem, it is up to the teacher to manage the problem in ways not damaging to the student.

Where such work seems appropriate, the students can try their hand at these projects:

1. Compile a BE/SE dictionary. How do you begin? Where do you get your word lists and definitions?
2. Compile a "Spanglish"/SE dictionary. What problems are involved in both of these projects?
3. Try to develop a program for teaching BE to a speaker of SE. Part of the program might be stories, poems, or articles in BE to be "translated" into SE. Try writing a story in BE.
4. Black English often uses Standard English words and phrases but gives them different meanings. Make a collection of these and try to account for the different meanings.
5. What dimensions of culture can be perceived through language? What dimensions of the cultures that produced Black English, Puerto Rican English, Mexican-American English, etc., can be perceived through these dialects?
6. Can you develop a program for teaching SE to speakers of a non-standard dialect? What problems are involved?

11

Linguistics and Foreign Language Teaching

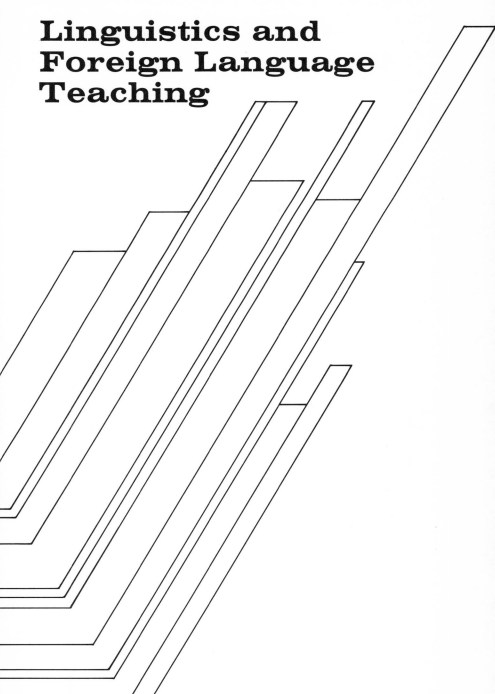

If there were as much failure in the secondary schools of the world in the teaching of mathematics, history or science as there is in the teaching of living foreign languages, education as a whole might be said to have broken down.

(E. V. Gatenby, "Conditions for Success in Language Learning," *English Language Teaching*, 6, 1950.)

$\mathbf{F}$oreign language teaching in America has not been an enterprise of notable success, though certain special (usually "crash") programs have been spectacularly successful (e.g., the Intensive Language Program of the American Council of Learned Societies, which served as the model for the U.S. Army language program of World War II and for later military and Department of Defense programs). But the selection of any foreign language at an early stage of the school program must be based on scant if not totally absent knowledge, since it cannot be foretold with any degree of accuracy what a student's future language needs will entail. Lacking such knowledge, it can only be *hoped* that such foreign language skills as may be acquired will readily transfer and facilitate that foreign language learning that the future may require. Thus, the learning skills must be emphasized on a level commensurate with achievement in any realistic assessment of educational goals. It is not, however, our purpose here to evaluate current (or past) efforts but to examine ways in which the science of language can be brought to bear on the various problems of foreign-language learning.

We would set the following goals for the learner:

1. Fluency or "translating" proficiency (*i.e.*, semantic control and authenticity in usage)
2. Grasp of social and cultural structures underlying the language
3. Recognition of linguistic structures involved
4. Development of specific perceptual and cognitive abilities
5. Development of foreign-language learning skills that will be transferable as needed

Definition of what constitutes an adequate degree of semantic control in a foreign language will vary with the particular objectives and the educational level. A science student might be concerned merely with a "translation" of written technical material; a student aiming for a diplomatic career will need to develop a sophisticated conversational skill as well as reading skill. The degree of semantic control necessary must reflect the purposes for which the foreign language is studied and, of course, be relevant to those purposes. Clearly, committing to memory locutions like *The pen of my aunt is on the table of my uncle* is worse than useless as is the ability to spout declensions that include *to or for the table* and *O, table!* Broadly, fluency subsumes the substance of the other goals in the tabulation above. Narrowly, it implies a conditioned recognition of and response to specific lexical items and syntactic constructions.

Proficiency in a foreign language means more than the ability to control the semantic content of the lexicon and grammar. Language is a social instrument and as such reflects the culture and societal structure of its community. Of course, some minimal knowledge of this is acquired with even rudimentary foreign language skills. But the development of any real proficiency must include a heightened sensitivity to and comprehension of the social (including intellectual) system that underlies the language. The character of language used in a particular discourse signals the level of communication in progress and the social or hierarchical relationships among the speakers involved (see M. Joos, *The Five Clocks*, pp. 11, ff.). These relationships vary from society to society and very often the social structure is revealed through the linguistic structures. (This dimension of language is dealt with in Chapter 2 above.)

It has been rumored from time to time that such Latin programs as are left in the schools have been spared the budgetary guillotine only because of the persistent (and wholly unsubstantiated) belief that studying Latin is really the only way to properly learn English grammar. The election of Latin to this unique tutorial role is, to be sure, a kind of compliment to the dedication of generations of long-suffering Latin teachers. The error, of course, lies in the conclusion that Latin grammatical structure can serve to explicate English grammatical structure. The key role, however, as most experienced foreign language teachers (should) recognize, is played by the logical processes of comparison and contrast (hence, any foreign language by this token can "explicate" English grammar). Man's knowledge of his world derives from his ability to categorize experience via these processes, though he may not be conscious at any given moment of the process in operation. A man is rich or poor only as his means stand in contrast to the means of others; he may seem tall to a midget and short to a giant. Man's *knowledge about* his language is no exception. Monolingual fluency does not automatically bring with it expertise on the nature of language any more than the ability to fly an airplane qualifies one as an aeronautical engineer.

The study of a second language, then, can be of value in the formal study of one's own language. Conversely, the study of English-as-language can contribute to success in learning a foreign language. The two areas touch and overlap in many fundamental matters. There is every reason, therefore, for English and foreign language departments to coordinate their activities. The benefits to be derived are many whether considered from the standpoint of culture, pedagogy, or linguistics. Anything that increases the student's (and the teacher's!) grasp of *materia linguistica* can only prove helpful in the total language program.

While one learns his native language with relatively little conscious effort, his later acquisition of other languages demands a conscious outlay of considerable intellectual energy. The abiding difficulty is that his first language is so thoroughly learned and assimilated into his very thought processes that it simply gets in the way. As the native language has been the medium of all instruction and learning, it acts as a "filter" through which foreign language learning must pass. Further, the first language has become efficient through development of a number of complex habits. Control of the phonology of a language involves the exercise of a highly refined control over many delicately adjusted muscles, a control that operates sub-consciously in most situations and with great precision. The number of neural patterns such feats require is mind-boggling to contemplate.

Since the phonemic structure of no two languages is identical, it is often necessary to develop a whole new set of neuromuscular controls. But for the late starter in foreign language learning, the native language habits are so deeply embedded that it is extremely difficult to take on the new pattern with any great accuracy. Even the most highly motivated of learners will not overcome his native phonological habits with ease. The language that can work so well for us in its own environment can just as easily prove a prison of sorts. Recent work in neurolinguistics has shown, however, that very early experience with a second language mitigates this "blocking" effect of the native language, *even if the second language is soon dropped and another not taken up until much later in life.*

The neuromuscular speech habits develop in the early years such that non-native sounds or sequences of sounds are automatically excluded. The average native speaker of English can usually identify an unknown word as being English so long as it *sounds* English to him (e.g., *rhizome, antidisestablishmentarianism, malvaceous, bosky,* etc.). "Nonsense" words, however, or foreign words, which contain phonotactical patterns not used in English are immediately recognized as being "foreign," i.e., non-English (e.g., *shrdlu, gde, zdrastvuite, mwalimu, mtu, mke, mzazi,* etc.). But a loan word in Swahili, *wiki* ("week"), containing acceptably English sound sequences does not sound "foreign" to the native English speaker. And the famous nonsense words of the "Jabberwocky Song" are less strange and foreign than the Russian and Swahili cited above, for Carroll built his words with standard English phonotactics.

One's linguistic habits provide one with a comfortable feeling toward his language. The speaker knows that he has a successful and effective adaptation to his linguistic environment and that he can communicate without effort and without embarrassment. This psychological set is lacking when he tackles a new language and can, at least at the outset, work against his efforts in acquiring the new language.

The foregoing problems in second language acquisition exist regardless of motivation, and where motivation is weak they constitute a formidable, perhaps insurmountable, barrier. Thus the first step in solving the language learning problem like any problem is to determine the nature of the problem. The "question" must be known before any kind of an "answer" can be found.

All foreign language methodologies stress the importance of authentic pronunciation; *i.e.*, one modeled accurately on that of the native speaker. But a fluent (even native) speaker is not necessarily aware of the particular phonetic and phonemic problems arising in the student's language acquisition, recognition, and production capacities. Only an accurate knowledge of the phonemic structures of *both* languages (native and target) plus a reasonable familiarity with the anatomy of the vocal apparatus will permit the required analysis of pronunciation problems. It is not enough to tell the student, "No, listen to me [or the tape recorder]." There are nearly ten times as many neural circuits going from the brain to the ear as the other way around. Consequently, one hears what one's "mind" wants heard. This preconditioning is a natural consequence of having the phonetics and phonemics of the native language imprinted at an early age. It is not necessarily either stupidity or recalcitrance that causes a student to persist in "mispronunciation." He may be imitating exactly what he "hears," but his hearing is simply not linguistically accurate. At this point, an explanation and illustration of both sound systems, their similarities and points of contrast, together with a few suggestions on how to produce the unfamiliar sounds, will do much to remove the stumbling blocks to accurate pronunciation. The satisfaction to the student of achieving rational and volitional control over the very first learning problem in an unfamiliar territory cannot be overestimated. With this behind him, the student *knows* that he is on the right track and knows how to stay there.

To illustrate the process we have just outlined, let us examine the consonantal systems of English and German as contrasted in the table below.

Consonantal Systems of English and German*

English

	Labial	Dental	Palatal	Velar
Stops	p b	t d	č ǰ	k g
Fricatives	f v	θ ð		
Sibilants		s z	š ž	
Nasals	m	n		ŋ
Other	l	r	j w	h

German

	Labial	Dental	Palatal	Velar
Stops	p b	t d		k g
Fricatives	f v		ç	χ
Sibilants		s z	š ž	
Nasals	m	n		ŋ
Other	l	r	j	h

* Adapted from Moulton, The Sounds of English and German, pp. 18, 23.

Since both languages are of Germanic origin, we can expect at least some agreement between the two systems. However, the charts clearly reveal that there are areas of marked disagreement. English lacks the German /ç/ and /χ/; German lacks the English /θ/, /ð/, /č/, /ǰ/ and /w/. The naïve English speaker who attempts to pronounce a German word containing the "new" phonemes /ç/ and /χ/ will not find them in his own phoneme inventory and will in all probability hear them as variants of the closest English phoneme—in this case, either /č/, /k/, or /š/. The /č/ substitution offends German ears because /č/ does not exist in German; the /š/ or /k/ substitution causes ambiguities because these phonemes fill other slots in the German system. For German speakers learning English, the same problem occurs with English /θ/ and /ð/. For these phonemes, the German speaker chooses either the /t/-/d/ pair from his own language or, often, the /s/-/z/ pair (preserving in both choices the voiceless-voiced contrast of the English pair). French speakers seem to favor the latter choice (/s/-/z/).

The basis for a solution to the manifold problems attendant on learning to pronounce a foreign language lies in a thorough exploration of the two phoneme systems from both an articulatory and an acoustic point of view. The student must learn, first of all, what features are contrastive in each language and, secondly, how the phonemes are physically produced. This, as one might say, theoretical background will make practical results far easier to achieve than they would be otherwise.

Beyond the phonological component, with its patterns and structures, lies the much more complex syntactic component. This is the truly "creative" part of language, with its open form classes and its infinite number of possible utterances. Yet this embarrassment of riches is by no means chaotic. On any level of analysis, from any point of view, we discover that any language is highly, even rigidly, structured. Language is polysystematic and complexly integrated. And despite the great variety of syntactic arrangements that languages have developed, certain universally basic things seem to be a part of all sentences. Human beings all share certain physical characteristics, environmental experiences, and inter-human relationships, and of necessity must communicate about similar fundamental realities. Despite surface differences, therefore, all languages are rooted in their common humanity. Again, as in the phonological systems, closely related languages (e.g., English and German) tend to maintain in common, with relatively little change, those syntactic and semantic structures they derive from a common linguistic ancestor (e.g., Proto-Germanic). Structural differences in the same language family (or branch of the family tree) are usually reconcilable via orderly linguistic principles.

One of the more difficult linguistic adjustments for the English-speaking learner is that of distinguishing between English "natural" gender and the *grammatical* gender that characterizes so many languages (notably in our own Indo-European family). If the student is given to understand that in contrast to English nouns (which are unmarked for gender except for a few in -*ess* and -*ette*—*waitress, majorette*), nouns in grammatical gender languages are considered for reasons that have little to do with sex and a lot to do with grammatical patterning to have a sex, so to speak (in German, masculine, feminine, and neuter). The transition need not be traumatic (even though one will in German have to consider a "young girl," *das Mädchen*, "neuter"), for one need only be reminded that the English language itself once used the self-same grammatical gender form grouping and that our present habit of substituting masculine, feminine, and neuter pronouns for various nouns is a remnant of the system. Of course, we have changed the ground rules a bit in that we require, say, *he* for a noun like *boy* because a real (*i.e.*, non-language) boy is male. Still, we use *she* for ships and airplanes and *they* (*no* gender designation) for plurals of any count noun (*the boys* . . . *they; the girls* . . . *they; the books* . . . *they*). So our "gender" system isn't all that "natural" or "biological." The point is that a little linguistic perspective can shed light and help overcome these cross-linguistic rough spots. The student will discover that, after all, one language is no more "sensible" than another, that they all do the job demanded of them though each by less or greatly different means.

All languages have the equivalent of "subject" and "predicate"; all languages interrogate, command, modify, etc. Where the linguistic devices for these operations are similar, the student may rely with reasonable certainty on his native language habits; where they are different the teacher should be able to provide some fairly sophisticated contrastive explanations. In English, for example, word order is a major device in signaling meaning; and while word order signals meaning in all languages, its role isn't necessarily as significant in every one of these languages as it is in English. Two languages may have similar word-order sequences in some constructions, and quite different ones in others:

English: I have something to do.
          I have to do something.
Spanish: Tengo algo que hacer.
          Tengo que hacer algo.

But, in contrast:

English: They want the book.
          They want *it*.
Spanish: Ellos quieren el libro.
          Ellos *lo* quieren

In English, the subject of a sentence must be specified (except in certain special cases); in Spanish it can be implicit in the context and thus explicitly omitted. Both languages rely upon the concept of a subject as necessary for a complete sentence; Spanish, however, contrasts with English in the grammatical means by which it signals the subject.

To develop potentialities into abilities—the overall educational goal —perceptual and cognitive flexibilities must be developed concurrently. The very fact that an *infinite* number of sentences can be subsumed under a small, *finite*, number of grammatical rules indicates that there are laws of great generality operating here. An understanding of the nature and operational principles of such laws can provide the student with the *how* of inquiry and learning.

The ability to produce speech rapidly (automatically, as it were) is the result of the native speaker's long and continuous exposure to his language. By the time a child reaches his early teens, he has had approximately 60–70,000 hours of such exposure, the result of which is considerable facility in the use of his native tongue. During a six-year secondary-school foreign language program (grades 7–12), a child would at best get 1000 hours of discontinuous exposure. A two-year high-school course adds up to about 350 hours of (classroom) exposure. Even if we assume, in the latter case, an additional 350 hours of out-of-class preparation for a total of seven hundred hours of foreign language "exposure," the disparity between that and the seventy thousand hours of native language exposure (and constant use) is so great that we can expect the student to accomplish little in the way of second-language competence unless he can be led to develop a cognitive awareness of the structure, patterns, and processes of his native language and to understand these in relation to the target language. Such cognitive activity serves as a "shortcut" in what would otherwise be a lengthy learning process (or, of course, the failure or near-failure it commonly proves to be).

The process of learning a foreign language suffers constantly from dilution, for a student (1) never learns *all* of the materials to which he is exposed and (2) his exposure is discontinuous and prey to native-language interference. If the student holds on to 50 per cent, the teacher has reason to be grateful. Only a substantial "overlearning" will firmly implant the desired language habits. But the quantity of material to be absorbed is simply too great to permit this kind of "leisure." (Besides, the student will balk at the concomitant tedium.) Many teachers who use manipulative materials are familiar with the Chinese proverb:

I hear and I forget;
I see and I remember;
I do and I understand.

To understand is to be able to "do." The student who can deliberately reconstruct the abstract edifices and procedures pertinent to a given subject or problem can cope with virtually all problems. Mathematics is the prime problem-solving tool (and thought process) of science. Linguistics is the mathematics of language.

The nature of the process by which the child first learns language is still largely unknown despite much investigation. Likewise the perceptual and conceptual processes. But it is clear that there must be some basic mechanisms (perhaps those involved in early motor-sensory development) that aid or participate in our ability to think and to relate to the world outside the mind. We certainly do not learn afresh with every new experience. We call, rather, on previously developed faculties and mechanisms, as well as a stock of memorized data, to categorize, interrelate, and evaluate. Like all human skills, they improve with use. But if a *skill* is desired, it should be isolated to whatever extent is possible and then intensively developed. A lexical rule, for example, is of great value in vocabulary expansion. Regardless of the exterior form of any individual language, *all* languages have the equivalents of nouns, verbs, modifiers of each class, and some way of nominalizing non-nouns in order to expand the stock of nouns. In English we can do this in several ways, one being a transformation of a predication (e.g., *He goes*) into a nominal (*His going*).

Our aim in this chapter has not been to offer a specific program designed to produce specific results but rather to convince the foreign language teacher that (1) there is a place in the foreign language classroom for the application of linguistics and (2) there is a place in linguistics for the foreign language teacher. In teaching language one cannot (nor should one) avoid teaching structure and pattern; linguistics is the formal discipline that attempts to reveal and explain the principles that underlie those structures and patterns. Although the foreign language teacher may think that he "knows" the grammar of the target language, some exploration of language through the objective rigor of the science of language is of immeasurable benefit. The teacher becomes aware of the inner processes of language, and his ability to help the student move gracefully from native to foreign language is thereby greatly enhanced.

> Grasping the structure of a subject is understanding it in a way that permits many other things to be related to it meaningfully. To learn structure, in short, is to learn how things are related.
> (Jerome Bruner, *The Process of Education*, p. 7.)

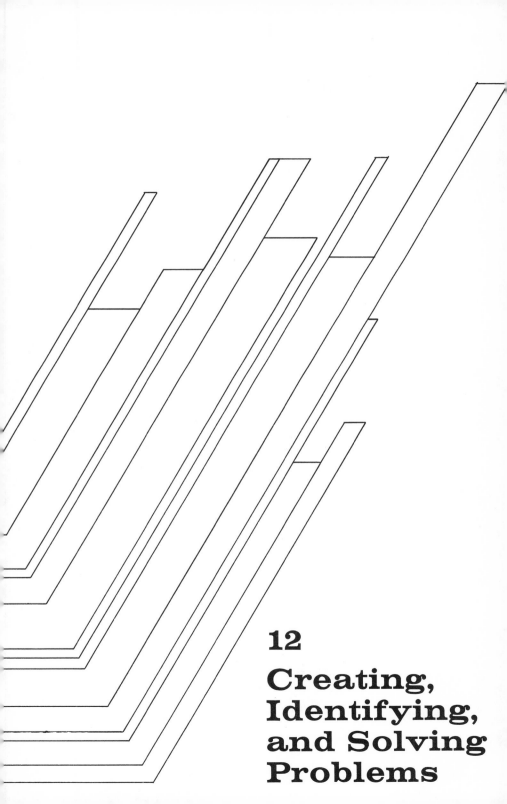

12

Creating,
Identifying,
and Solving
Problems

I always tell my students that I do not pretend and do not believe that what I am saying is the final truth. It is just the truth as I see it this morning. I hope some of my thinking will continue to be revised in the future as it has in the past.

(George V. Sheviakov, "Some Reflections on the Problem of Discipline," in Rudolf Ekstein and Rocco L. Motto, eds., *From Learning for Love to Love of Learning*, New York.)

Very generally, and at the risk of oversimplification, it is useful to distinguish two kinds of teaching: that which takes place in the *expository mode* and that in the *hypothetical mode*. In the former, the decisions concerning the mode and pace and style of exposition are principally determined by the teacher as expositor; the student is the listener. The speaker has a quite different set of decisions to make: he has a wide choice of alternatives; he is anticipating paragraph content while the listener is still intent on the words; he is manipulating the content of the material by various transformations while the listener is quite unaware of these internal options. But in the hypothetical mode the teacher and the student are in a more cooperative position with respect to what in linguistics would be called "speaker's decisions." The student is not a bench-bound listener, but is taking a part in the formulation and at times may play the principal role in it. He will be aware of alternatives and may even have an "as if" attitude toward these, and he may evaluate information as it comes. One cannot describe the process in either mode with great precision of detail, but I think it is largely the hypothetical mode which characterizes the teaching that encourages discovery.

(Jerome Bruner, *On Knowing*, New York.)

N o textbook, no curriculum, no lesson plan accounts for the bewildering multiplicity of life. Whatever is accounted for takes the place of all that isn't. "There is more in heaven and earth, Horatio, etc." In a proper classroom, exploration is the *modus operandi*. This means that the search for and identification of problems and the operation of the inquiry-discovery principle of learning should dominate. Our subject here is language, but the techniques of discovery are relevant whatever the subject.

The various questions and projects included in this book are meant merely to suggest the wealth of problems that attend an exploration of language. Each question is open-ended; that is, the student should be encouraged to ask many more. Indeed, any classroom situation can yield profitable explorations. For example, a teacher complains that her students use a great deal of unseemly and insulting language among themselves. This often breaks out in class and causes varying degrees of disturbance and disruption. What to do? Traditional discipline methods don't really solve problems, they merely repress them temporarily. Why not, then, raise the question publicly, *i.e.*, in class, of what this whole business of *insults* and *insulting* is all about. Such questions as these come quickly to mind:

1. What is an insult?
2. What do you do to a person when you insult him?
3. How do you feel when you insult someone? When someone insults you?
4. What kinds of insults are there? Are there special "formulas"?
5. What factors come into play during the insult process? Does, for example, *age* make any difference? What about age *differences* between the insulter and the insulted? Status differences? Sex differences? Economic differences? Educational differences? Racial differences? Other?
6. Are there *degrees* of insult? If so, describe them. Are there friendly (as opposed to unfriendly) insults? If so, describe them.
7. What circumstances must prevail in order for an insult to "work"?
8. Try to find out about the "art of the insult" in a language (or languages) other than your own. Write a report on "How to Insult People in. . . ."
9. Does the ability to insult people serve any useful purpose in a society?
10. Look up the word *curse* in the *Oxford English Dictionary*. Do we still use *curses*? How is a *curse* different from an *obscenity*? What are some curses in English? What can you learn about a culture from the kinds of curses it uses? Are curses and insults related? If so, how?

And so on. One question breeds another—if, that is, we allow it to. We must be willing to let the questions come and to face up to any line of inquiry that might open up. This way lies intellectual honesty and, of course, intellectual growth.

Problems and questions arise at any point at which we can detect a discontinuity; that is, at any interface between two realities. An obvious example is the broad philosophical question that springs from the discontinuity between the self and the non-self (*i.e.*, the world "out there"). "Who and what am I, and who and what are they?" etc. From a definition of self (*Cogito, ergo sum*), Descartes was able to construct a philosophical system. Given, therefore, any datum, one can generate a string of questions that will eventually tie that datum to the rest of existence. If we start with the given of *language*, we can easily raise such questions as these:

1. What does the existence of language imply about human beings? What leads you to these conclusions? What do we have to know in order to deal with the question at all, and how can we find what we need to know?
2. What human constructs and processes are dependent upon the existence of language? What role does language play in these constructs and processes?
3. In what ways (if any) does language enhance cultural processes? Impede cultural processes? How? Why?
4. In any particular language, which elements seem to be, as it were, local and arbitrary, and which seem to be universal and necessary? What do you need to know in order to deal with this question? What are some ways of finding out what you need to know?
5. A *definition* is a kind of explanation. What elements, dimensions, aspects, etc., of language seem to you to need definition? Why? Can you suggest ways to define them?

And so on.

A fruitful problem-identifying and problem-solving technique is that of *model building*. Any identifiable reality can be analogously projected as a model, which is a different reality but one that helps us to understand its subject. A model airplane is one type of model—the most obvious and the easiest type to construct. The scientist's theoretical model, which is mainly a set of mathematical analogs, belongs to the same class of things as the airplane model, but in some senses is rather more difficult to manage, its abstractness not the least part of the difficulty. A grammatical formula (e.g., $S \rightarrow NP + VP$) is likewise a model and is, like the mathematical statement, a highly abstract model. Nonetheless, these intellectual (as opposed to physical) models are powerful tools for discovery.

One of the characteristics of any model is its concern with *essentials*. That is, once the orientation of the model has been determined, the model is built with that orientation in mind. This means that in the case of an airplane model that is designed to reveal airflow characteristics (such as the actual models used in wind tunnel tests), nothing but those features of the actual (or planned) aircraft that bear on airflow will be included. Thus it will not be necessary to include interior decor, decorative paint, insignia and the like, for none of these has anything to do with airflow. On the other hand, if the intention of the model is to give the viewer an accurate impression of a certain airplane (the Red Baron's Fokker Triplane, for example), then all the visual detailing of which the model is capable of is in order. The models of various ships and boats at the Smithsonian Institution are marvels of the model-maker's art, but they do not include details that are not relevant to the purpose. They merely look outwardly like the ships and boats they are meant to represent, they are not *substitutes* for them, only the *actual* full-sized working ships and boats could be their own substitutes. In the case of the grammatical model, the *principles* of the operation of the language are what we want, not exemplifications of every possible utterance, which, of course, could never be managed anyway.

Valuable insights into the process of communication and understanding can be had through model building. In Chapter 9 we raised questions about the audience for a piece of writing and asked that the student attempt to construct models of various types of audiences. Here are a few more questions on this type of model building:

1. Though you may not be conscious of the fact, you carry around as a part of your intellectual-psychological-emotional furniture, a collection of models of beings, things, and experiences. For example, when you meet up with a baby, you deal with him according to your notion of what a baby is, even though a baby (and every other being) is, in fact, a "black box" that can be known only inferentially; that is, nobody can really "get inside" of anybody else intellectually, emotionally, psychologically. This means that you have somehow built a model of a baby in your head, so to speak, and deal with all the babies you meet according to that model. The interesting question that arises is what precisely that model is and how you came to build it as you did. Attempt to reveal and account for your model baby. How does this model square with actual babies you have known? With other people's models of babies? Do you ever modify this model? How and why? Now turn to models of more immediate import: parents, siblings, friends (and enemies), boys and girls, figures of authority (police, political leaders, teachers, officials of various kinds, members of various outgroups (e.g., races, ethnic groups, economic groups, etc.), pets (dogs, cats, etc.), and so on. Try to consciously build a model of a person of your own age, opposite sex, from a group quite different from your own. How is language implicated in the model? Now use this model as the basis of a written communication to him/her. Don't forget to take into account the very

problem of communication across the various lines that the society forces us to draw. Try to build his/her model of you. This may help to give you a needed perspective. What are the problems in (1) building the model of him/her, (2) building his/her presumed model of you, and (3) communicating?

2. Imagine that you are the teacher. Build a model of the class and a model of communication within the class. What do you need to know to build these models? How will you find out what you need to know?

And so on.

Among the most productive of classroom strategies is that of *game playing*. (See H. F. Beechhold, *The Creative Classroom*, 1971.) Indeed, a large proportion of the class year can be fruitfully given over to games. The best approach, of course, is to let the students themselves develop the games. The logical problems attendant on game making are formidable, yet at the same time appealing. These questions will get things going:

1. What is a game? What seem to be the principles behind the operation of a game?
2. What language elements seem to lend themselves to game playing? (Obvious example: spelling.) Why?
3. Try to devise some simple language games that are not merely copies of existing ones. Make believe your games will be manufactured and will need, therefore, to be described completely.
4. What can one learn by playing your games? How will he learn it?
5. Most of the existing language games are based on vocabulary and spelling. Can you conceive of games that are based on other dimensions of language? Can you, for example, devise a *grammar* or *sentence structure* game? (Don't get hung up simply on matters of "correctness," whether, for example, one can use *ain't* or not.) A *semantics* game? A *phonology* game? A *sociolinguistics* game, etc.?

And so on. Puzzles such as those contrived nearly every week by *New York Magazine* (e. g., modify a familiar phrase by changing punctuation and/or adding italic emphasis: "What are you giving up for, Lent?" "I love you. A. Bushel and A. Peck," etc.) and those in D. M. Borgmann's *Language on Vacation* (1965) can get the student started on the playful side of language. And language *should* be played with. One can argue that literature is a special type of playing with language.

As linguistics is a relatively young science and one that is growing rapidly, it is alive with new theories and suggestions for modifying existing theories. Many knotty problems exist and many viewpoints are in contention. All of which makes for a good deal of excitement as well as a certain amount of frustration and confusion. The questions and problems that follow touch on a number of current issues in linguistics and should stir up a considerable discussion. We need not be concerned to resolve any of the issues but merely to explore them. As Professor N. R. Cattell says of English grammar,

> Teachers and students must give up the expectation that a grammar book will provide them with a ready-made and complete description of English, and must rather try to follow with interest the partial knowledge that has been acquired by the science of linguistics.
>
> (*The New English Grammar*, p. 29.)

We can of course do more than just "follow with interest." We can dig in ourselves and make a contribution or two of our own.

1. From the following evidence, attempt to develop a theory of attribution. Test your theory by adducing additional evidence. (Hint: Concentrate on adjectives of measure and quality.) The starred (*) forms do not normally occur in native English speech in the contexts given.

    a. How tall is it?
       Very tall
       Very short

    b. How short is it?
       Very short
       *Very tall

    c. How good is it?
       Very good
       Very bad

    d. How bad is it?
       Very bad
       *Very good

Other dimensions of this project can include *negation*, thus:

    a. He is attractive, and she is not unattractive either.
    b. *He is attractive, and she is not attractive either.

Nominalization:

    a. She is *beautiful* (adjective)
    b. She has *beauty* (noun)

Adverbialization:

    a. He gave an *angry* refusal (adjective)
    b. He refused *angrily* (adverb)

And so on. The whole project is, of course, an excursus into the *semantic structure* of the adjective.

    2. *Figure* can occur in constructions like:

        a. I *figure* it to take about an hour.
        b. What do you *figure* him to do?

Gather several more examples of similar uses of *figure*. What does *figure* here seem to mean? Can you substitute a synonym for *figure* in the same context (without changing anything else)? If not, why not? Try to develop a set of frames for *figure* and a set of distributional rules governing the word's use. Would you conclude that *figure* here is a deep structure item or a surface structure item? Discuss.

    3. The question arises whether *idioms* are to be classed as analyzable utterances (like normal phrases and clauses) or as *set-piece constructions*, which are unitary and hence unanalyzable. Make a collection of English idioms (*e.g., How do you do*) and attempt to develop a "theory of idiom." Part of your task will be to determine how the idioms were derived; that is, to track down their deep structures. How does one know an idiom when he sees one? Are there *transitional* forms ("semi-idioms")? What functions do idioms perform in the overall operation of the language? Try writing an article on any subject that interests you, but *use no idioms*. Discuss the problems involved.

    4. *And, but, yet,* and *for* are traditionally called *coordinating conjunctions*. Yet in practice their *coordinating* function is often unclear. Consider the following sentences:

        a. Jules and Jim bought a sculpture by Smith.
        b. Sticks and stones may break my bones. . . .
        c. Broomis and Fala have fleas.
        d. Pierre, Pedro, and Peter met in Berlin.
        e. Lars and Kirsten met in Stockholm.
        f. And death shall have no dominion.

Examples (a) through (e) are ambiguous (hence the difficulty of determining coordination), that is, in (a), for example, did Jules and Jim *each* buy a sculpture, or did they pool their resources and buy one piece between them? Example (f) presents a different problem. Try to determine the nature of the ambiguities (and other problems) in these and in as many other sentences containing "coordinating" conjunctions as you wish to gather as evidence. Then try to work out a description of just how these conjunctions are used. In some cases, they will unequivocally coordinate, but not in all. Account for *all* the uses, however. The awareness of potential ambiguity can be useful in writing. How? What principles can you state that will guide writers in the unambiguous use of, say, *and?*

5. Attempt to develop a set of rules governing the normal use of re-flexive pronouns (*myself, herself, themselves,* etc.). But be certain that your rules don't allow such constructions as *He gave the book to themselves.* How will you go about developing these rules? How much and what kinds of data will you need? Be sure that your final rules are as simple and inclusive as you can make them. That is, it is scientifically preferable to have a few rules with wide application than a lot of rules each of which applies to only a very few cases. Why? The most elegant (scientifically speaking) rules or principles or generalizations usually have a high degree of abstractness.

6. Consider the following sentences:

a. The candle will burn for three hours.
b. The candle will burn for three hours, if that.
c. The candle will burn for a long time.
d. *The candle will burn for a long time, if that.
e. The building is 100 feet high.
f. The building is 100 feet high, if that.
g. The building isn't very high.
h. *The building isn't very high, if that.
i. The building is very high.
j. *The building is very high, if that.
k. Fifteen people attended the meeting.
l. Fifteen people attended the meeting, if that.
m. *Exactly fifteen people attended the meeting, if that.
n. *A great many people attended the meeting, if that.
o. He was bruised a bit, if that.
p. *He suffered a brain concussion, if that.

The problem here is to make some sense of the normal uses of the tag phrase, *if that.* And when you have contrived a set of rules for *if that,* you can go on to *if at all, if ever, if anywhere, if anything.* For these, gather your own sample sentences.

7. Consider the following sentences:

a. He gave his all to the cause, and then some.
b. He gave a lot to the cause, and then some.
c. *He gave $2.00 to the cause, and then some.
d. He worked beyond endurance, and then some.
e. He worked all day.
f. ?He worked all day, and then some.
g. He worked six hours.

    h. ?He worked six hours, and then some.
    i. *He worked five minutes, and then some.
    j. ?He gave his all to the cause, at least.
    k. ?He gave at least his all to the cause.
    l. *He gave a lot to the cause, at least.
    m. ?He gave at least a lot to the cause.
    n. He gave $2.00 to the cause, at least.
    o. He gave his all to the cause, and more.
    p. ?He gave a lot to the cause, and more.
    q. *He gave something to the cause, and more.
    r. *He gave $2.00 to the cause, and more.
    s. *He gave at least $2.00 to the cause, if that.
    t. ?He gave at least $2.00 to the cause, and more.
    u. *He gave more than $2.00 to the cause, and then some.

The problem is to develop a set of rules governing the use of what might be called *hyperbolic tags*. To do this, we must remember that the sentences given are *surface structures*. Hence the rules cannot deal with them directly. We must, for example, determine what deep structures are represented by the tags (which are surface structures). Thus, what can *and then some* be reasonably derived from? And how can these deep structures be transformed to produce the surface structures of the acceptable sentences above (and none of the unacceptable or questionable ones)? It will help if you gather additional evidence—particularly examples with verbs other than *give* and *work*.

    8. Most transformational descriptions of language give little attention to the phonological component other than to mention that the utterance is realized phonologically. This seems to suggest that phonological realization is strictly a surface manifestation. But there are cases that demand that we look into deep structure for phonology (perhaps we should say "deep phonology"). Consider the declarative sentence pattern that is given an interrogative meaning strictly through phonology:

    (a) The Captain has a pleasant personality.
    (b) The Captain has a pleasant personality?

Consider also the following, where the intonation (a phonological element) seems to precede certain syntactic movements:

    Q. Was she happy?
    A. a. Yes, surprisingly.
            [Yes, she was surprisingly happy.]
        b. Yes, surprisingly.
            [Yes, surprisingly, she was happy.]

With this evidence and as much more as you can gather, discuss the transformational implications of sub-surface insertions of phonological elements. (Don't fret if you can't find unambiguous answers. Exploring and raising pertinent questions is at this point far more important.)

9. Consider the following tag-question sentences:

    a. He has a lot of charm, doesn't he?
    b. He has charmed a lot of girls, hasn't he?
    c. He charms people, doesn't he?
    d. *He has charmed a lot of people, doesn't he?
    e. He is incapable of charming people, isn't he?
    f. He is capable of charming people, isn't he?
    g. He isn't capable of charming people, is he?
    h. He has the capability of charming people, doesn't he? (Hasn't he?)
    i. He hasn't the capability of charming people, ____?____ he?
    j. He may charm a few people, ____?____ he?
    k. He may not charm a few people, ____?____ he?
    l. He should have charmed a few people, ____?____ he?
    m. He ought to have charmed a few people, ____?____ he?
    n. He used to charm many people, ____?____ he?
    o. He was used to charming people in the old days, wasn't he?
    p. He dare not charm anyone, ____?____ he?
    q. It had been his practice to charm people, hadn't it?
    r. It hadn't been his practice to charm people, had it?
    s. His desire was not to charm people, ____?____ it?

The problem is to work out a set of rules for the tag question and to determine what grammatical features are implicated in the tags. Gather your own stock of examples, using other persons and numbers and other main verbs. For doubtful tags, resolve the doubts by trying the sentences on others. Show results statistically.

10. Though *vice versa* is commonly used to replace the second of a pair of conjoined sentences, its use is not always so straightforward, nor is it always clear precisely what *vice versa* is meant to represent. The first examples below are "normal" and easily interpretable:

    a. Harry insulted Herman and vice versa.
        [Harry insulted Herman + Herman insulted Harry.]
    b. How long has she loved you and vice versa?
        [How long has she loved you? + How long have you loved her?]

The examples that follow are less clear. Attempt to classify the uses of *vice versa* and to develop a set of rules for its use. The rules will have to preclude the use of vice versa in confusing and ambiguous ways. As usual, gather a good number of your own examples.

    c. Many Frenchmen are·anti-American and vice versa.
    d. Our pet alligator dislikes children and vice versa.
    e. Shakespeare said that all the world's a stage. I rather think it's vice versa.
    f. Airline pilots rarely travel by ship and vice versa.
    g. Chess players rarely play other games and vice versa.
    h. When I wish to relax, I play the flute, and vice versa.

And so on. Your first step will be to determine in each case what *vice versa* stands for. Then you should gather a collection of your own examples from conversational as well as literary use.

    11. Consider the following pairs of sentences.

      a. The climbers have already reached the top.
          *The climbers haven't already reached the top.
      b. I would rather spend the day in bed.
          *I wouldn't rather spend the day in bed.
      c. She could just as well have walked.
          *She couldn't just as well have walked.
      d. Merton is far brighter than Burton.
          *Merton isn't far brighter than Burton.
      e. Mr. Kreks still beats his wife.
          *Mr. Kreks doesn't still beat his wife.
      f. The twins don't play much.
          *The twins play much.
      g. The McCoys don't ever intend to end the feud.
          *The McCoys do ever intend to end the feud.
      h. They aren't all that happy.
          *They are all that happy.
      i. They don't give a hoot about each other.
          *They give a hoot about each other.
      j. Sturdley hasn't done a lick of work in days.
          *Sturdley has done a lick of work in days.
      k. Napoleon and Josephine don't care a thing about each other.
          *Napoleon and Josephine care a thing about each other.
      l. Desmond wanted some quiche lorraine.
          ?Desmond didn't want some quiche lorraine.
      n. Tillie didn't ask for any bread.
          *Tillie asked for any bread.
          (Did Tillie ask for any bread?)

What is happening here? Try to develop a clear description of the grammatical and semantic operations. Gather additional evidence.

12. On the general pattern of the preceding exercises, locate and describe as many features of the language as you can. Each set of data should exemplify one feature (or operation) and one only. Three areas that you might find productive are *negation*, *ellipsis*, and *word-group substitution* (e.g., *She accepted his proposal, and I was surprised that she did so; she did so* substitutes for what?)

13. Consider the following passage:

> If there is magic on this planet, it is contained in water. Its least stir even, as now in a rain pond on a flat roof opposite my office, is enough to bring me searching to the window. A wind ripple may be translating itself into life. I have a constant feeling that some time I may witness that momentous miracle on a city roof, see life veritably and suddenly boiling out of a heap of rusted pipes and old television aerials. I marvel at how suddenly a water beetle has come and is submarining there in a spatter of green algae. Thin vapors, rust, wet tar and sun are an alembic remarkably like the mind; they throw off odorous shadows that threaten to take real shape when no one is looking.
>   Once in a lifetime, perhaps, one escapes the actual confines of the flesh. Once in a lifetime, if one is lucky, one so merges with sunlight and air and running water that whole eons, the eons that mountains and deserts know, might pass in a single afternoon without discomfort. The mind has sunk away into its beginnings among old roots and the obscure tricklings and movings that stir inanimate things. Like the charmed fairy circle into which a man once stepped, and upon emergence learned that a whole century had passed in a single night, one can never quite define this secret; but it has something to do, I am sure, with common water. Its substance reaches everywhere; it touches the past and prepares the future; it moves under the poles and wanders thinly in the heights of air. It can assume forms of exquisite perfection in a snowflake, or strip the living to a single shining bone cast up by the sea.
>   (Loren Eiseley, *The Immense Journey*, pp. 15–16)

This is good writing. Our purpose here, however, is not to *evaluate* it but to try to understand how it works (hence, how any piece of writing works). The questions below should help:

a. How is each sentence related to the sentence preceding it? To every other sentence in the passage?

b. Are the first and last sentences related in any way? If so, how?

c. Are there any phonological, syntactic, and/or semantic patterns detectable in the passage? If so, describe them.

d. Does the linguistic structure of the passage reflect the thought structure of the passage? If so, how?

e. Are there any deviations from linguistic "norms" (e.g., syntactic deviations) in the passage? If so, what are they? If so, how do they serve the passage?

14. Upon a poem of your choosing (no fewer than fourteen lines), perform the following tasks:

a. Paraphrase it. Explain how you paraphrased it and how the paraphrase differs from the original. What did you discover about the craft of poetry by paraphrasing?

b. Summarize it. Explain how you summarized it and how the summary differs from the original. To what extent do you have to *interpret* the poem in order to summarize it? Explain what the word *interpret* in this context means.

c. Locate all the features of the poem (grammatical and otherwise) that lend unity to the poem. How do they lend unity?

d. It has been said that "poetry consists in getting the right words in the right order." What can you make of a statement like this? What does the phrase "right words" mean in the practical terms of this poem? How can you test the "rightness" of the words? Change some of the words to make them "wrong." How are they "wrong"? Are there different kinds of "wrongness"? Explain. What elements of the poem are susceptible to "ordering"? What does "right order" mean in the practical context of this poem? Reorganize some elements of the poem to put them into "wrong" order. How are they "wrong"? Are there different kinds of "wrongness" in ordering? Explain.

e. What role does *sound* seem to play in the poem? Explain how you go about coming to grips with this question.

f. It has been claimed that detailed analysis of a work of art (in this case a poem) "destroys" it. Do you think this is true? If you do, explain how. Does a detailed analysis of a chemical process or of an engine or the operation of an engine or even of a person "destroy" anything? If so, what? Are there useful analogies between a poem (or any work of art) on the one hand and processes, objects, and beings on the other? Explain. If a work of art truly "works," how can a close examination of it hurt it? What are some possible positive values in close examination?

Things never cease happening—especially language things. This means that questions are always around begging to be asked. The teacher should be guided by the minute by minute experience of life going on before his eyes. Pat lessons (per syllabi, etc.) are poor substitutes for genuine challenges to inquiring minds. We must create a climate in which challenge is the norm. No teacher has all the answers to all the questions—or even knows what all the questions are. There are no answers in the back of this book and no special teacher's guide because the authors feel that the problems and projects provided in the book should be explored by student and teacher together. There is something pedagogically specious about the rigged quiz game that characterizes so many classrooms. The teacher's attitude should not be "Guess what answer I have in mind," but "Let us tackle this problem together and see what we can find out."

The study of language is a science; teaching is an art. But science serves art well (consider the impact of science on the fine arts) if we allow it to. Indeed, it is only the teacher who understands the science of things who can raise the most perceptive and challenging questions about things. The teacher who lacks an understanding of language and its science will end by cheating his students, for language is, after all, at the heart of the human experience.

> Because no one questioned the importance of the contributions of the linguists, it was easy to overlook how revolutionary they are. They have profoundly altered not only the content of language study but attitudes toward language. They have demonstrated unmistakably that popular ideas about "good English" are trivial and shallow when not false. There remains the unanswerable question of just when, what, and how much to teach about the language, but the agreement of the seminar that English teachers need to have a sound, conscious knowledge of the language means that *most teachers need to be retrained and the English curriculum drastically revised*. [Emphasis added.]
>
> (Herbert J. Muller, *The Uses of English*, Guidelines for the Teaching of English from the Anglo-American Conference at Dartmouth College, pp. 73–74.)

Appendix 1

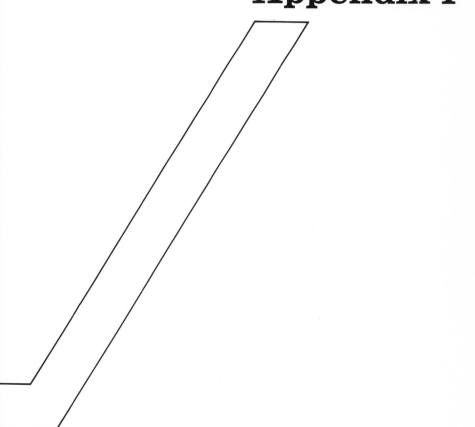

ARTICULATORY CLASSIFICATION OF CONSONANTS

Manner of Articulation	Bi-Labial	Labio-Dental	Apico-Dental	Apico-Alveolar	Apico-Palatal	Fronto-Palatal	Dorso-Velar	Pharyngeal & Glottal
Stop								
voiceless	p pʰ		t̯ t̯ʰ	t tʰ	ṭ ṭʰ		k kʰ	ʔ
voiced	b bʰ		d̯ d̯ʰ	d dʰ	ḍ ḍʰ		g gʰ	
Affricate								
voiceless						č čʰ	χ	
voiced						ǰ ǰʰ	ɣ	
Fricative								
Slit								
voiceless	φ	f	θ					h
voiced	β	v	ð					h ɦ (murmured)
Groove								
voiceless				s	š			
voiced				z	ž			
Lateral								
voiced				l lʰ				
Trill								
voiced				r̩̩ r̩̩ʰ	r r			
Flap								
voiced				r̦ r̦ʰ	r r			
Nasal								
voiced	m mʰ			n nʰ		ɲ n	ŋ n	
Semi-vowels								
voiced	w			r		y		

Diacritics for consonants:

    superscriptʰ = aspiration
        ∩ = *fronted* from hypothetical normal position
        • = *backed* from hypothetical normal position
        r̦ = single tap r
        r̩̩ = trilled r

Examples in English:

/p/	pill	/k/	kill	/h/	hill	/s/	seal	/ɲ/	inch
/b/	bill	/g/	gill	/f/	fill	/z/	zeal	/ŋ/	sing
/t/	till	/č/	chill	/v/	villain	/š/	plush	/w/	will
/d/	dill	/ǰ/	Jill	/θ/	thin	/ž/	pleasure	/y/	yell
/l/	Lill	/r/	rill	/ð/	then	/m/	mill	/n/	nil

ENGLISH VOWEL SYSTEM

Front	Central	Back
	Checked	

	Front	Central	Back
High	I		U
Mid	ɛ	ʌ	
Low	æ		ɑ (ɒ)

I	sit,	lift
ɛ	step,	head
æ	cap,	stack
ʌ	cut,	blood, double
U	push,	foot
ɑ/(ɒ)	stop,	warrant

Free

	Front	Central	Back
High	i		u
Mid	e	ɜ	o
Low		(aː)	(ɑː) ɔ

i	see,	seat
e	stay,	rate
u	brew,	food
o	go,	goal
ɔ	thaw,	forge
(aː)/(ɑː)	part,	hard; Shah, calm
ɜ	third,	fern

Diphthongs

	Front	Central	Back
High			
Mid			
Low		aI aU	ɔI

aI	fight,	sigh
aU	house,	now
ɔI	point,	joy

Unstressed

	Front	Central	Back
High	I	ɨ	
Mid		ə	
Low			

I, ɨ	for many speakers, -less, -ness, -es, -ed, etc.; others use [ə] or a vowel in between
ə	sofa, about, connect; for r-less dialects, mother, persuade

Appendix 2

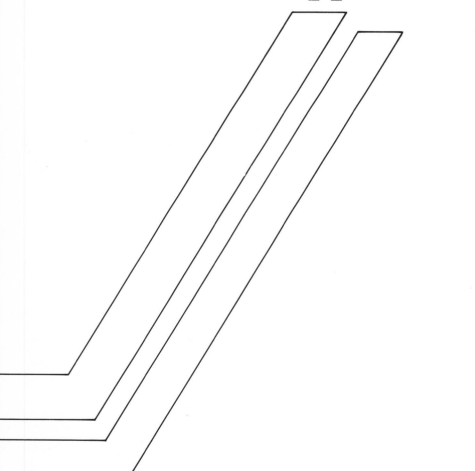

BASIC TRANSFORMATIONAL PROCESSES

The various transformational rules that operate on deep structures and introduce or create complexity in the sentence structure are derived from the following basic or elementary processes:

1. Deletion
2. Adjunction
    a. Permutation (the sum of deletions and adjunctions)
    b. Insertion (pure adjunction, or addition)
    c. Substitution (the sum of deletion and adjunction)

In *deletion*, some part of the deep structure Phrase-marker (P-marker), a partitioned sequence, is subtracted or removed, and any non-terminal symbols that do not themeslves dominate anything, are erased.

1. John didn't take the exam because he was afraid to take it.
2. John didn't take the exam because he was afraid.

In the underlying deep structure, the phrase that was deleted, *to take it*, was semantically redundant and therefore could be deleted transformationally from the surface structure, because the meaning was "recoverable"; *i.e.*, would not be totally lost. This is important to transformational theory since only those elements may be deleted (or added) that will not result in a change in meaning.

Adjunction is the addition of material at some particular point or node in the P-marker.

Permutation is the rearrangement of the elements in a P-marker, a reshuffling and change in the order, which produces change in the actual structure of the sentence. As such it is a more complex transformation than either deletion or addition, and is conceived of as being the sum of both these elementary processes. One element is temporarily deleted and another element (likewise "freed" by deletion) is inserted, and so on.

Insertion is pure addition or adjunction at some point in the P-marker of material that was not previously present. The inserted material may be quite diverse and will be specified in some way by the T-rule itself.

The passive transformation illustrates both permutation and insertion.

Melmoth struck Drusilla.
Drusilla was struck by Melmoth.

The NP's have been permuted (rearranged) and new material, *was* and *by*, has been inserted.

Substitution might actually be considered the result of a deletion plus an addition.

TRANSFORMATIONS

Quite obviously, transformations cannot be applied randomly or indiscriminately to any and all deep structures. Transformations are purposeful; *i.e.*, they seek to achieve certain linguistic goals of expression. As such, they are subject to numerous constraints and restrictions, and any less regimented procedure would result in communication chaos. As with other sets of rules in language, there appears to be a small, finite set of T-rules, capable of projection into an infinity of instances.

In order to determine *when* a transformational rule may be applied, we need to know its *domain; i.e.*, the classes or types of sentences to which it may be applied with grammatically acceptable results. Such a class of sentences can be economically described by an accurate structural description—SD. The change effected in the sentence structure by the transformation can likewise be represented by a new structural description, showing the structural change that has taken place—SC. Assuming a properly construed rule, then any sentences that do not conform to the rule may be further codified as exceptions, or *restrictions* on the rule. Thus, a T-rule will consist of (1) SD, structural description, (2) SC, structural change, and (3) restrictions.

The T-rule has been referred to here as "seeking to achieve certain linguistic goals of expression." This implies that the decision to use a particular transformation is by choice or option of the speaker. In many cases this is true, and those rules certainly can be designated as *optional* T-rules. Others, however, do not permit such choice but are *obligatory* in the grammar. Either the configuration of the SD or some *marked* condition of the deep structure will signal that a particular transformation *must* be applied. In the standard theory, such signals are considered to be semantic *markers*, attached to the underlying S node of the deep structure, e.g., NEG. NEG is a negative marker indicating that the negative of a certain statement proposition is meant, and the S must be transformed into a negative surface structure.

Given any input deep structure tree, a large number of transformations can or will be applied to produce surface tree structures. Evidence indicates that the transformational component of the grammar may be a "list" of T-rules. However, it also appears that the order of application of transformations from such a list cannot be random, and must at least be partially *ordered*. Ordering of rules may be of two kinds. (1) Simple linear ordering in which one can't return to a T-rule once it has been used. (2) Cyclic ordering, in which, given the rules of a transformational grammar with linear ordered rules, some continuous subset of these rules will be said to be cyclic. This means that the subset can re-apply, at successively higher levels of the input tree structure. In application, linear ordered rules are applied (only once) until exhausted and the cyclic subset is reached. The cycle is applied to the lowest level (the deepest embedded node) and then reapplied to the next higher, etc., etc., till exhausted at the top of the tree. Then, subsequent linear rules are applied as before. Thus, there are pre-cyclic, cyclic, and post-cyclic rules. Cyclic rules are restricted in their scope to a certain part of the tree structure at a time (except for the last pass); they start at the deepest S node and work up, re-applying at each S level.

A number of T-rules and examples follow; they are somewhat simplified in order to avoid unduly complicating the principles for the beginner. For technical details and treatment, see M. K. Burt in the Bibliography.

DATIVE, OR INDIRECT OBJECT MOVEMENT RULE
(optional)

SD: $X—V—NP_1—to—NP_2$
SC: $X—V—NP_2—\phi—NP_1$

The corresponding tree structures are

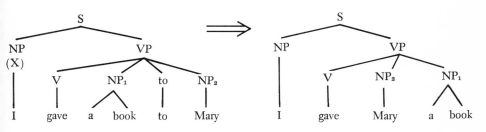

Restrictions

1. NP_1 may not be a pronoun.
2. NP_2 must be animate or a human institution.
3. V may not be a verb-particle combination.
4. V must be monosyllabic or bisyllabic with initial stress.
5. NP_2 may not be too complex in structure.

6. V + NP₁ may not be a "frozen" idiom.
7. Semantic restrictions on type of verb.

PASSIVE RULE   (optional)*

SD: NP₁—V $\left\{ \begin{array}{l} \text{particle} \\ \text{preposition} \\ \text{lexical item} \end{array} \right\}$ —NP₂

SC: NP₂—be+ -en—V (as above)—by—NP₁

The corresponding tree diagrams are

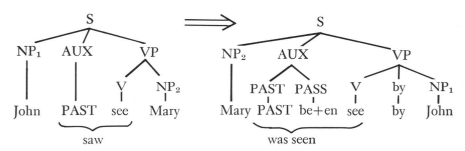

John PAST see Mary → saw

Mary PAST be+en see by John → was seen

Restrictions

1. Not all transitive verbs will passivize, only verbs that can take adverbs of manner.
   Verbs that are exceptions are such as: *cost, weigh, befit, suit, resemble, marry,* etc.
2. Only the first NP following the V undergoes passivization.
3. VP may not be frozen idiom.
4. Prepositions that are lexical and closely tied to the verb, e.g., *depend on, talk about, rely on, ask for,* etc. (There are, however, exceptions, e.g., *think of, strive for,* etc.)

**ORDERING (SEQUENCING) OF DATIVE AND
PASSIVE RULES.**

If T$_{\text{PASS}}$ is applied first, and then the T$_{\text{I.O.}}$, the structural description required for application of T$_{\text{I.O.}}$ will be lacking and that rule could not then be applied.

---

* If the SD is considered to be marked PASS, then the rule must be considered obligatory.

E.g., Mary gave a book to John.

$T_{PASS} \Rightarrow$ A book was given to John by Mary.

    X   V   to NP_1 by NP_2 (Incorrect SD)

But, if $T_{I.O.}$ is applied first,

E.g., Mary gave a book to John.
Mary gave John a book.
John was given a book by Mary.

This is *extrinsic*, or *independently motivated* rule ordering. This particular order allows one to generate *all* the sentences, without patchwork or *ad hoc* adjustments to the rules.

AGENT DELETION RULE (optional)

SD: X—PASS VP—by NP
SC: X—PASS VP—ϕ

Restrictions:

1. NP must be (a) unspecified (b) indefinite, or (c) irrelevant, with respect to major meaning.

Ordering

Agent Deletion must be placed after Passive, or there would not be any "agent" to which it could be applied without destroying the meaning of the sentence. This is *intrinsic* rule ordering.

REFLEXIVE RULE (obligatory)

SD: NP_1—X—NP_2 [where NP_1 and NP_2 are *co-referential*]
SC: NP_1—X—Pronoun + *self*

Restrictions:

1. NP_1 and NP_2 must both be in the same simplex sentence, S, not in the matrix sentence S and the embedded sentence S_1.

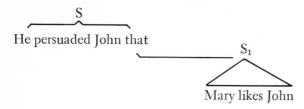

E.g., (a) *He persuaded John that Mary likes himself.
    (b) That John arrived before Mary pleased John.
        *That John arrived before Mary pleased himself.
2. The Reflexive Rule cannot cross over a conjunction:

E.g., John likes Mary and Harriet likes John.
     *John likes Mary and Harriet likes himself.

Ordering

Pronouns, as agents in Passive, are "weak" or "peculiar" in that they often become reflexives.

E.g., That paper was written by Mary and myself.

Thus, the reflexive should follow the passive rule.

THERE-INSERTION RULE (optional)

SD: NP_1 (AUX) *be* X
SC: There (AUX) *be* NP_1 X

The corresponding tree diagrams are

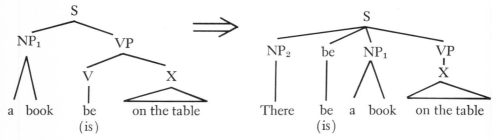

In this transformation, a constituent NP, *there*, has been introduced into the P-marker. *There* is considered a NP because both the Question Transformation and Nominalization can be applied to *there* as a NP.

The constituent following *be* is most typically a locative or past participle.

Restrictions

1. NP_1 is indefinite (except for enumerations).
2. AUX is not *dare*.
3. Not all passive sentences can undergo *there*-insertion.

Ordering

Only the Subject is involved in *there*-insertion. However, the Passive and Agent Deletion must precede, in order to generate sentences such as *There were some UFO's seen at midnight*. The Reflexive must also precede *there*-insertion, in order to preserve the co-referentiality.

RELATIVE CLAUSE FORMATION (obligatory)

Relative clause formation operates on a complex S with embeddings, to select a *co-referential* NP and move it to the front of its S, pronominalizing and attaching a WH- to it.

SD: $X—[_{NP} NP [_{S_1} Y—(P)—NP—W]_{S_1}]_{NP}—Z$
     1   2   3   4   5 6   7

SC: $X—[_{NP} NP (P) \begin{bmatrix} +PRO \\ + WH\text{-} \end{bmatrix}—Y—W —Z$
     1   2 4   5   3 6 7

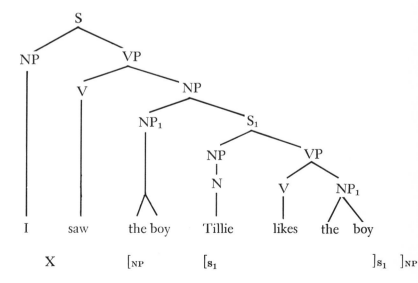

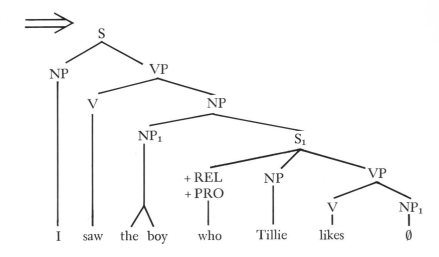

Restrictions

1. The NP to be relativized can not be dominated by another NP, *i.e.*, only dominant NP's can be moved.

Sequencing

1. The relative rule must follow the passive rule.

E.g., a. I saw the man the man helped Tillie.
⟹ I saw the man Tillie was helped by the man.
⟹ I saw the man whom Tillie was helped by.

b. I saw the man the man helped Tillie.
⟹ I saw the man who helped Tillie.
⟹*I saw the man Tillie was helped by who.

2. The relative rule must follow *there*-insertion. It appears that the example S must have the subject of the S as the thing that is *both* relativized and *there*-inserted.

QUESTION FORMATION RULE   (obligatory)

This rule is considered obligatory because of the presence of Q as an underlying marker attached to the sentence made at the highest level (in effect a PreSentence), and preclusion of Tag Formation because of introduction or presence of a *WH*-word.

Interrogatives, other than those formed intonationally, are of two kinds: (1) Those requiring a yes or no answer, and (2) Those requiring further information in the answer.

Yes-No Questions:

This transformation is also known as the Yes-No "Switch," because it reverses (permutes) the subject NP and certain parts of the AUX— the left-most IC carrying the tense.

SD: NP—T—$\left\{ \begin{array}{cc} M & V \\ V_{aux} \end{array} \right\}$—X

SC: T—$\left\{ \begin{array}{cc} M & V \\ V_{aux} \end{array} \right\}$—NP—X

E.g., John may come. $\Rightarrow$ May John come?

Do-insertion:

Whenever tense is carried solely by the verb form, and tense must be separated from the verb as in *laughed* = PAST + *laugh*, where no AUX or Modal is available to carry the tense, a form of the dummy verb *do* is inserted to carry the tense.

E.g., Q—Tillie gurgled delightedly.
      Q—Tillie PAST gurgle delightedly.
      Q—PAST Tillie gurgle delightedly.
      Q—Do PAST Tillie gurgle delightedly.
  $\Rightarrow$ Q—Did Tillie gurgle delightedly?

WH-word Questions:

The input sentences have V followed by an adverb of place, description, etc., or of a "thing" or "one" about which further information can be requested with a WH-word.

E.g.,	
My pen is somewhere.	Where is . . .
My pen is silver.	What color is . . .
My pen is one of those two.	Which one is . . .
My pen has purple ink.	What color ink has . . .
My pen is a fountain type (kind),	What kind of . . .
etc.	

In such sentences, the adverb, etc., following V is replaced by an appropriate WH-word, which is then preposed, and the Subject NP switch with the tense carrier is carried out as before.

Restrictions

1. Co-occurrence Restriction.
The presence of a WH-word in the S prevents application of the transformation.
E.g., I wonder *where* Melmoth is.
I question *whether* he can see Drusilla.

2. Adverb preposing constraints.
The presence of *sentence adverb, if,* etc., prevents preposing.
E.g.,   See if Melmoth is going.
*See where if Melmoth is going.
*See where Melmoth is going. (Not in the same sense)

3. NP's can't be moved out of relative clauses. (This is similar to relative clause restrictions.)

4. Some two-word idioms do not form questions.

TAG FORMATION RULE (obligatory)

This rule is obligatory because of the Q and NEG markers in the PreSentence, and the absence of a WH-word in the sentence. The tag usually agrees with the subject, which may, as in the imperative, have been deleted and is understood.
The tag is the *negative* of the first polarity.

$$\text{SD:} \left\{ \begin{matrix} Q \\ IMP \end{matrix} \right\} \left\{ \begin{matrix} NEG \\ \phi \end{matrix} \right\} - NP_1 - (T)\ (M) - V - X$$

$$\text{SC} \left\{ \begin{matrix} Q \\ IMP \end{matrix} \right\} \left\{ \begin{matrix} NEG \\ \phi \end{matrix} \right\} - NP_1 - (T)\ (M) \left\{ \begin{matrix} \phi \\ NEG \end{matrix} \right\} ProNP_1$$

E.g., a. Q NEG Tillie doesn't like petunias.
   b. Q ϕ Tillie does like petunias.
   ⇒ a. Q NEG Tillie doesn't like petunias, does she?
   ⇒ b. Q ϕ Tillie does like petunias, doesn't she?

Sequencing

Tags must follow the passive. The reverse order would generate the ungrammatical sentence:

E.g.,   Beowulf threw a spear.
    Tag   ⇒ Beowulf threw a spear, didn't he?
    Passive⇒ *A spear was thrown by Beowulf, didn't he?

IMPERATIVE RULE   (obligatory)

Traditionally, the imperative is of the form

((you) will) V_{inf}—X

Actually, the imperative is both a *form* and a *meaning* (command).
Command meanings may be couched in forms other than the imperative.

E.g.,   1. Stop!
      2. I order you to stop!
      3. I'd appreciate it if you'd stop!
      4. How about stopping!
      5. Would you please stop!
         etc.

The imperative *form* has other uses besides command.

E.g.,   1. Commands, as above.
      2. Requests: Help (me, please).
      3. Conditionals: Quiet down (and you'll get . . .).
      4. Wishes: Get well. Be happy.
      5. Advice: Leave now (before . . .).
      6. Threats: Quiet down (or I'll . . .)
      7. Epithets: Damn you. Go to . . . .
      8. Pleas: Don't hit me again.
      9. Incredulous Questions: Marry a co-ed?
    10. Yes-No Question: Want a beer?
    11. Permission: Stay home (if you wish).

Thus, there are imperative forms that are not commands, and commands
that are not infinitives (imperative form).

The verb *will*, if preserved in the S through the transformation,
equals the sense of *must, have to, are going to*, etc., and is imperative in
nature. It is not a "future" form. If a modal, it is a modal of obligation.
Imperatives that are to be carried out in the future are expressed differently.

E.g., Have the children ready for bed when I come home tonight.
For purposes of this section, the imperative transformation is considered
to be:

SD: IMP—NP—M—V_{inf}—X
SC: IMP—V_{inf}—X

Restrictions

1. On Subject NP. *You* equals the subject of the S. The subject may take a variety of forms:

   a. Reflexive: Wash yourself! *Wash himself!
   b. Own: Find your own spot! (You find . . .).
   c. Tags: Wash up, $\begin{cases} \text{will} \\ \text{won't} \end{cases}$ you.
   d. Final Vocatives: Come here, you.
   e. Indefinites: Don't anybody move.
                        One of you stand up.
   f. Proper Nouns: John, come here.

2. Verbs must be those of voluntary action, *i.e.*, the S cannot order that which can't be done.

   E.g., *Metabolize! *Digest your food!

3. No first person subjects in imperative sentence.

4. No sentence adverbials (does not apply to appositives).

   E.g., *surely, *certainly

5. No "evaluation" adverbs.

   E.g., *hardly, *scarcely, *almost

6. Please forms. These are requests, not commands.

7. Future modal, since future is implied in any command.

Sequencing

1. The imperative must follow Tag Formation, as otherwise there would be no subject NP for the tag to repeat; it would have been deleted by the imperative.

   Since Tag Formation follows the Passive, this sets the sequence as at least Passive—Tag—Imperative.

2. Imperative must also be sequenced after the Reflexive: Imperative reflexive commands, such as *Wash yourself!* would have no co-referentiality available for the reflexive, as *you* (subject NP) would have been deleted.

BIBLIOGRAPHY

General and Theoretical Linguistics

Anderson, Wallace and Norman Stageberg, eds. *Introductory Readings on Language*, 3rd. ed. New York: Holt, Rinehart & Winston, Inc., 1970. 492 pp.
An extensive and interesting collection of articles covering many fields of language and linguistics. Exercises and assignments are appended to each section. Very useful for the beginning student.

Bach, Emmon and Robert Harms, eds. *Universals in Linguistic Theory.* New York: Holt, Rinehart & Winston, Inc., 1968. 210 pp.
A collection of important papers presented at the Texas Conference on Linguistics. For the more advanced student, and includes papers setting forth theories on case grammar (Fillmore) and generative semantics (McCawley).

Bloomfield, Leonard. *Language.* New York: Holt, Rinehart & Winston, Inc., 1933. 564 pp.
Although many parts of this book are now out of date, it remains one of the great and comprehensive treatments of language. Clearly and lucidly written, it has much of value to the beginning student of language and linguistics.

Bolinger, Dwight. *Aspects of Language.* New York: Harcourt, Brace & World, Inc., 1968. 326 pp.
A readable, informative, and accurate account of language, language acquisition, and language structure from the transformational-generative point of view. A companion workbook is also available.

Burt, Marina K. *From Deep to Surface Structure.* New York: Harper & Row, 1971. 255 pp.
A thorough treatment of the syntactic structures and rules of transformational grammar, in particular, the ordering of about thirty transformational rules. Requires student motivation, but not necessarily sophistication.

Cattell, N. R. *The New English Grammar.* Cambridge: The M.I.T. Press, 1969. 162 pp.
A short introduction to phrase structure grammar and transformational-generative grammar. Clearly and concisely presented.

Chomsky, Noam. *Syntactic Structures.* 'S-Gravenhage: Mouton & Co., 1957. 118 pp.
A rather technical first presentation of the transformational theory that was to radically change the aims, goals, and thinking of linguists in our time. Although since modified in many respects by the author, it is a landmark in linguistic theory.

————. *Aspects of the Theory of Syntax.* Cambridge: The M.I.T. Press, 1965. 251 pp.
A major modification and recodification of transformational-generative theory by its founder. Although still technical in presentation, it is more readable than the earlier *Syntactic Structures.*

Cook, Walter. *On Tagmemes and Transforms.* Washington: Georgetown University Press, 1964. 67 pp.
A short but lucid presentation of the newer tagmemic-transformational model.

Dinneen, Francis. *An Introduction to General Linguistics.* New York: Holt, Rinehart & Winston, Inc., 1967. 452 pp.
A scholarly yet readable college-level text covering various concepts of linguistics and language from the early Greeks to Chomsky. Includes extensive biographical and historical background for the various linguistic philosophies treated.

Francis, W. Nelson. *The Structure of American English.* New York: Ronald Press, 1958. 614 pp.
A linguistically oriented college textbook containing a very useful chapter on dialect geography.

Fries, Charles C. *The Structure of English: An Introduction to the Construction of English Sentences.* New York: Harcourt, Brace & World, Inc., 1952. 304 pp.
The innovative techniques of an early structuralist, emphasizing spoken language as the criterion and the basis for any adequate linguistic analysis.

Gleason, H. A., Jr. *An Introduction to Descriptive Linguistics,* revised ed. New York: Holt, Rinehart & Winston, Inc. 1961. 503 pp.
A college textbook giving a detailed presentation of the principles of linguistic analysis. The emphasis is on structural descriptivism, although some theory is discussed. A workbook and record to accompany is also available.

————. *Linguistics and English Grammar.* New York: Holt, Rinehart & Winston, Inc., 1965. 519 pp.
This book ranges widely over general grammatical theory in reference to English, and has an extensive and well annotated bibliography.

————. "The Organization of Language: A Stratificational View." *Monograph Series on Language and Linguistics,* No. 17. Washington: Georgetown University Press, 1964.
A brief and concise presentation of the theoretical base and philosophy for stratificationalism.

Hall, Robert A., Jr. *Introductory Linguistics.* Philadelphia: Chilton Books, 1964. 508 pp.
A systematic presentation of results rather than of either theory or method.

Harris, Zellig. *Structural Linguistics.* Chicago: University of Chicago Press, 1951. 384 pp.

A strict development of discovery procedure and methodology, based on co-occurrences.

Hathaway, Baxter. *A Transformational Syntax.* New York: Ronald Press, 1967. 315 pp.
A largely discursive treatment of English syntax, primarily from a structuralist view of predications, but with some treatment of transformations.

Hockett, Charles F. *A Course in Modern Linguistics.* New York: The Macmillan Co., 1958. 621 pp.
A college level and strongly theory-oriented treatment of language and linguistics. Essentially structuralist and descriptive in approach.

Jacobs, Roderick A. and Peter S. Rosenbaum. *English Transformational Grammar.* Waltham: Ginn & Co., 1968. 294 pp.
A readable presentation of transformational-generative grammar for the uninitiated reader. The grammar is developed step by step in easy stages.

————, eds. *Readings in English Transformational Grammar.* Waltham: Ginn & Co., 1970. 277 pp.
A book of readings for the more advanced student. Includes papers by the leading theorists of the divergent transformational schools that have arisen since Chomsky (1965).

Lakoff, George. *Irregularity in Syntax.* New York: Holt, Rinehart & Winston, 1971. 207 pp.
Publication of Lakoff's Ph.D. thesis, "On the Nature of Syntactic Irregularity." Many of the ideas expressed in this work became the basis for the new school of generative semantics. The similarity of verb and adjective is closely examined, and the distinction between stative and nonstative verbs is also studied. For the more advanced student.

————. "The Role of Deduction in Grammar" in C. Fillmore and D. T. Langendoen, *Studies in Linguistic Semantics.* New York: Holt, Rinehart & Winston, 1971. 299 pp.
One of a collection of articles by leading theorists, dealing with the connection between linguistics and semantics generally, and particularly with the area and concept of presupposition in grammar. For the student with some background in current theory.

Lamb, Sydney M. *Outline of Stratificational Grammar.* Washington: Georgetown University Press, 1966. 109 pp.
A revised and expanded version of an earlier paper (1962), plus an analysis of an English text. Sets forth the stratificational view of grammar and presents its distinctive notational system for a network structure.

Langacker, Ronald W. *Language and Its Structure.* New York: Harcourt, Brace & World, Inc., 1967. 260 pp.
A concise, readable introduction to the nature and structure of language, largely from the transformational view, although some traditional material on language change and history is also included. Written for the beginning student.

Langendoen, D. Terence. *The Study of Syntax.* New York: Holt, Rinehart & Winston, Inc., 1969. 174 pp.
An introductory interpretation of the M.I.T. transformational-generative grammar of English. Has a useful glossary for the uninitiated, and a series of grammar problems as appendix.

Lazarus, Arnold, Andrew MacLeish, and H. Wendell Smith. *Modern English, a Glossary of Literature and Language.* New York: Grosset & Dunlap, Inc., 1971. 462 pp.
Clear definitions of most literary, rhetorical, and linguistic terminology. Many entries include bibliography of key works. Grammatical items generally well explained and illustrated. Does nothing, however, with grammatical theory beyond Chomsky's *Aspects of the Theory of Syntax* (q.v.)

Lester, Mark. *Introductory Transformational Grammar of English.* New York: Holt, Rinehart & Winston, Inc., 1971. 335 pp.
An excellent presentation of the rules of transformational grammar for the student with limited background in linguistics.

Longacre, Robert E. *Grammar Discovery Procedures.* The Hague: Mouton & Co., 1964. 162 pp.
Procedures for discovering and developing rules of grammar on a tagmenic base from a strange corpus, for word, phrase, clause, and sentence levels. Technical, and not for the beginning student.

Lyons, John. *Introduction to Theoretical Linguistics.* Cambridge, England: Cambridge University Press, 1968. 518 pp.
A comprehensive introduction to current linguistic theory, giving a rigorous and technical treatment of a wide range of topics, yet written in a clear and lucid style. It includes a sizable section on semantics as well.

Marchand, Hans. *The Categories and Types of Present-Day English Word-Formation.* Munich: C. H. Beck-Verlag, 1949. 545 pp.
A massive assault on compounding and other types of word-formation in English. Detailed, thorough, and not at all technically demanding.

Onions, C. T. *The Oxford Dictionary of English Etymology.* New York: The Oxford University Press, 1967. 1025 pp.
The best recent etymological dictionary of English. This or W. W. Skeat, *An Etymological Dictionary of the English Language,* Oxford University Press (first published 1879–1882, reissued periodically and currently available) should be in every English classroom.

Robins, R. H. *General Linguistics: An Introductory Survey.* Bloomington: Indiana University Press, 1964. 390 pp.
A short, easy, and literate account of the mainstreams of linguistics today, with inclusion of the British position. Generally Bloomfieldian in approach, but not strictly orthodox.

Sapir, Edward. *Language.* New York: Harcourt, Brace & World, Inc., 1921 (reprint 1955). 242 pp.
Although out of date in some respects, it is a stimulating and readable introduction to language and linguistics. The influence of language in

the shaping of thought, and the relation of culture to language are discussed.

de Saussure, Ferdinand. Trans. Wade Baskin. *Course in General Linguistics.* New York: McGraw Hill, 1966. 240 pp.
A classic presentation by an eminent Swiss linguist that provided a new theoretical foundation for linguistics in the beginning of the twentieth century. His ability as an Indo-Europeanist is evident throughout, but without detracting from simplicity and clarity.

Warfel, Harry. *Language: A Science of Human Behavior.* Cleveland: Howard Allen, Inc., 1962. 188 pp.
A structuralist introduction to the study of language. Particularly valuable for its comments on language and literary style.

Whitehall, Harold. *Structural Essentials of English.* New York: Harcourt, Brace & World, Inc., 1954. 154 pp.
An explication of the principal types of headed groups, based on Fries' structuralism, plus material on suprasegmentals and punctuation. Written for the beginning student.

Psycholinguistics

Bruner, Jerome S. *On Knowing.* New York: Atheneum, 1965. 165 pp.
Ten sensitively written essays on creativity, art, myth, mathematics, discovery, etc., but all basically concerned with how we learn, know, and perceive. Civilized and civilizing.

Chomsky, Noam. *Language and Mind.* New York: Harcourt, Brace & World, Inc., 1968. 88 pp.
Elaboration of three lectures on (1) past contributions to the study of mind, (2) contemporary developments, and (3) speculation on future research and developments. Ranges from Descartes to Locke to Piaget. Non-technical.

Deese, James. *Psycholinguistics.* Boston: Allyn & Bacon, 1970. 149 pp.
A small but excellent work on contemporary topics in experimental psychology as related to language. It outlines modern linguistic theory as it applies to psycholinguistics and is written with the beginning student in mind.

Emig, Janet A., James T. Fleming, and Helen M. Popp, eds. *Language and Language Learning.* New York: Harcourt, Brace & World, Inc., 1966. 301 pp.
A revision and expansion of the 1964 Special Issue of the *Harvard Educational Review.* Well-known linguists examine verbal learning, teaching techniques, and curricula. Grammars and their roles in learning and teaching are covered, and there is a section on English in World Literatures.

Hörmann, Hans. *Psycholinguistics, An Introduction to Research and Theory.*
New York: Springer-Verlag, 1971. 377 pp.
Perhaps the best available overview of this important and rapidly develop-
ing field. Full appreciation requires some linguistic sophistication.

Lenneberg, Eric H., ed. *New Directions in the Study of Language.* Cambridge: The M.I.T. Press, 1964. 194 pp.
Collection of papers presented at the 17th International Congress of
Psychology, 1963, covering new and unsolved problems and speculations
thereon. A strong biological orientation, but not overly technical, of animal communication and language acquisition and growth in children.

McNeill, David. *The Acquisition of Language.* New York: Harper & Row,
1970. 183 pp.
Developmental psycholinguistics. Good introduction to language development in children. Not overly technical.

Najam, Edward W., ed. *Language Learning: The Individual and the Process.*
(Part II, *International Journal of American Linguistics,* Vol. 32, No. 1,
Jan. 1966, Publ. 40). Bloomington: Indiana University Research Center
in Anthropology, Folklore and Linguistics, 1965. 273 pp.
Collection of papers on psychology and language learning, individualized
learning, and foreign language teaching.

Slobin, Dan I. *Psycholinguistics.* Glenview: Scott, Foresman and Co., 1971.
148 pp.
A highlighting of the major issues in psycholinguistics, especially those
in pedolinguistics. A brief but excellent survey of the field for the beginning student, with a good bibliography.

Smith, Frank and George A. Miller, eds. *The Genesis of Language: A Psycholinguistic Approach.* Cambridge: The M.I.T. Press, 1966. 400 pp.
A book of readings for the more advanced student interested in psycholinguistics. Contains papers presented at a conference on "Language
Development in Children," 1965, sponsored by the National Institutes of
Health, on stages in acquisition of grammar and phonology by children
and their innate capacities for this acquisition.

Foreign Language Teaching

Hughes, John P. *Linguistics and Language Teaching.* New York: Random
House, 1968. 143 pp.
An explanatory manual for the foreign language teacher, covering several
theories of grammar and the development of the Army method of teaching languages into today's school techniques.

Kufner, Herbert L. *The Grammatical Structures of English and German.*
Chicago: University of Chicago Press, 1962. 95 pp.
An analysis of structural differences between the two languages with
emphasis on the problems of German syntax. The treatment is on selected

topics where it is felt problems are most likely to occur for English speakers.

Moulton, William G. *The Sounds of English and German.* Chicago: University of Chicago Press, 1962. 145 pp.
A systematic analysis of the contrasts between the sound systems of the two languages, describing the similarities and differences, and including the suprasegmentals of stress, pitch, juncture, and intonation.

————. *A Linguistic Guide to Language Learning.* New York: Modern Language Association, 1966. 140 pp.
A clear and direct introduction to the principles of language and contrastive linguistics, and an elementary treatment of some transformational principles.

Politzer, Robert L. *Teaching French: An Introduction to Applied Linguistics.* Waltham: Blaisdell Publishing Co., 1965. 181 pp.
The principles of linguistics applied directly to the French language and related directly to problems experienced by English-speaking learners. Especially good in the area of phonetics and pronunciation.

————. *Teaching German: A Linguistic Orientation.* Waltham: Blaisdell Publishing Co., 1968. 178 pp.
The principles of linguistics applied directly to the German language and related directly to problems experienced by English-speaking learners. Especially good in the area of phonetics and pronunciation.

————. *Foreign Language Learning: A Linguistic Introduction.* Englewood Cliffs: Prentice-Hall, Inc., 1970. 164 pp.
An excellent beginning text, covering language, language learning, linguistics, and its application to foreign language learning. Examples include material in major languages taught in public schools.

———— and Charles N. Staubach. *Teaching Spanish: A Linguistic Orientation,* revised ed. Waltham: Blaisdell Publishing Co., 1965. 198 pp.
The principles of linguistics applied directly to the Spanish language and related directly to problems experienced by English-speaking learners. Especially good in the area of phonetics and pronunciation.

Rivers, Wilga M. *Teaching Foreign Language Skills.* Chicago: University of Chicago Press, 1968. 403 pp.
A thorough treatment of the objectives, methods, testing, and physical facilities involved in foreign language teaching. Handles material on both student and teacher level, and assumes no previous technical training.

Stockwell, Robert P. and J. Donald Bowen. *The Sounds of English and Spanish.* Chicago: University of Chicago Press, 1965. 168 pp.
A systematic analysis of the contrasts between the sound systems of the two languages, describing the similarities and differences, aimed at developing an awareness of obstinate persistence of English speech habits.

———— and John W. Martin. *The Grammatical Structures of English and Spanish.* Chicago: University of Chicago Press, 1965. 328 pp.

An analysis of structural differences between the two languages with emphasis on the problems of Spanish syntax. The treatment is on selected topics where it is felt problems are most likely to occur for English speakers.

Valdman, Albert. *Trends in Language Teaching.* New York: McGraw-Hill, 1966. 298 pp.
Presents the strengths and weaknesses of current theory and practice in foreign language teaching and learning, while stressing the current thinking of linguists, psychologists, and language teachers in exploration of improvement in educational practice.

Applied Linguistics

Borgmann, Dmitri A. *Language on Vacation.* New York: Charles Scribner's Sons, 1965. 318 pp.
A treasury of word games, puzzles, brain teasers (with answers). Goes far beyond the crossword puzzle level of word play. There should be much activity of this kind in the language arts classroom.

Fraenkel, Gerd. *Writing Systems.* Boston: Ginn & Co., 1965. 134 pp.
An excellent and concise history of the development of alphabetic and writing systems, and of attempts, successful and unsuccessful, at spelling reform throughout the world.

Fries, Charles C. *Linguistics and Reading.* New York: Holt, Rinehart & Winston, Inc., 1933. 265 pp.
Applications of linguistics to the teaching of reading by a leading structuralist. Offers a number of valuable insights into language and into the problems and process of reading.

Muller, Herbert J. *The Uses of English.* New York: Holt, Rinehart & Winston, Inc., 1967. 198 pp.
A trenchantly written report on the 1966 Anglo-American Seminar on the Teaching of English. Touches all bases lightly but precisely.

Postman, Neil and Charles Weingartner. *Linguistics: A Revolution in Teaching.* New York: Dell Publishing Co., 1966. 209 pp.
A popularly written overview of linguistics and some of the applications to teaching. Non-technical.

Roberts, Paul. *Patterns of English.* New York: Harcourt, Brace & World, Inc., 1956. 314 pp.
A structuralist grammar based on Fries' work, developed for public school use as a textbook.

Thomas, Owen. *Transformational Grammar and the Teacher of English.* New York: Holt, Rinehart & Winston, Inc., 1965. 240 pp.
An early, but clearly written sketch of a transformational-generative grammar of English.

Sociolinguistics

Burling, Robbins. *Man's Many Voices: Language in Its Cultural Context.* New York: Holt, Rinehart & Winston, Inc. 1970. 222 pp.
An anthropological linguist looks at the way language is affected by culture, and the way in which language structure is affected by and dependent upon things other than language. Anthropologically oriented and delves into cultures in remote parts of the world.

Fishman, Joshua A., ed. *Readings in the Sociology of Language.* 'S-Gravenhage: Mouton & Co., 1968. 808 pp.
A substantial collection of articles by sociolinguists, linguists, and anthropologists for those interested in social behavior of the language determinants. It views society as being broader than language and strives for an interdisciplinary approach.

Hall, Edward T. *The Silent Language.* New York: Doubleday & Co., Inc., 1959. 192 pp.
An anthropologist writes about culture and cultural structures that are reflected in human language and behavior—often non-vocally. The difficulties of cross-cultural communication are explored.

Hall, Robert A., Jr. *Linguistics and Your Language.* Garden City: Doubleday and Co., Inc., 1960. 265 pp.
A book intended for the general lay reader, which brings linguistics to bear on many everyday problems of language—local, national, and international. Depicts how prejudices and ignorance about language block efforts at effective communication.

Hymes, Dell, ed. *Language in Culture and Society.* New York: Harper & Row, 1964. 763 pp.
A collection of readings in linguistics and anthropology, providing extensive coverage to all divisions of both disciplines.

Labov, William. *The Social Stratification of English in New York City.* Washington: Center for Applied Linguistics, 1966. 655 pp.
An exhaustive and thorough linguistic analysis of one speech community, showing the highly systematic structure of our social and stylistic stratification.

Stewart, William A. "Urban Negro Speech: Sociolinguistic Factors Affecting English Teaching," in *The Florida Foreign Language Reporter: Special Anthology Issue,* Vol. 7, No. 1. North Miami Beach: Florida FL Reporter, Inc., 1969.
An examination of the educational implications where a non-standard dialect conflicts with the standard dialect.

Whorf, Benjamin Lee. *Language, Thought, and Reality.* Cambridge: The M.I.T. Press, 1956. 278 pp.
An illuminating account of the relation between language, perception, and thought. A study of cross-cultural values for the general reader.

Historical Linguistics

Buck, Carl Darling. *A Dictionary of Selected Synonyms in the Principal Indo-European Languages.* Chicago: University of Chicago Press, 1949 (reprint 1965). 1515 pp.
This book is subtitled "a contribution to the history of ideas," and so it is. The arrangement is according to categories (e.g., mankind, animals, food and drink, etc.) and represents a compendium of the linguistic raw material for thought of Western (Indo-European) man. A fascinating (albeit expensive) source book.

Lass, Robert. *Approaches to English Historical Linguistics.* New York: Holt, Rinehart & Winston, Inc., 1969. 484 pp.
An anthology of essays on the major aspects of the history of the English language. Not overly technical, but a glossary is provided. An excellent resource book.

Pedersen, Holger, trans. John W. Spargo. *The Discovery of Language.* Bloomington: Indiana University Press, 1962. 360 pp.
A treatment of the discoveries made in language relationships and of the philologists of the eighteenth and nineteenth centuries. Provides interesting biographical and historical backgrounds.

Pyles, Thomas. *The Origins and Development of The English Language.* New York: Harcourt, Brace & World, Inc., 1964. 388 pp.
A college-level textbook, with emphasis on the history and evolution of Old English (Anglo-Saxon) and Middle English.

Waterman, John Thomas. *Perspectives in Linguistics.* Chicago: University of Chicago Press, 1963. 105 pp.
A small book, limited in coverage, providing a moderate treatment of the history of linguistics and major achievements in diachronics.

Stylistics

Crystal, David and Derek Davy. *Investigating English Style.* Bloomington: Indiana University Press, 1969. 264 pp.
A fairly technical though readable and practical introduction to stylistic analysis. Detailed demonstrations are extremely helpful. Deals with style in both literature and other types of writing (legal, advertising, etc.).

Freeman, Donald C. *Linguistics and Literary Style.* New York: Holt, Rinehart & Winston, Inc., 1970. 491 pp.
An exceptionally good collection of essays on the study of style with the tools of linguistics.

Gibson, Walker. *Tough, Sweet and Stuffy.* Bloomington: Indiana University Press, 1970. 179 pp.
"Identifying three dominant styles in modern American prose, [the author] persuasively argues that all writing is an adjustment or compro-

mise among three ways of presenting oneself to an audience. By analyzing examples drawn from novels, essays, journalism, and advertising, he traces rhetorical-grammatical patterns that create these manners of expression, and examines the implied relationships between author and reader" (jacket copy). An eminently successful attempt at rhetorical analysis. A valuable resource book.

Joos, Martin. *The Five Clocks.* New York: Harcourt, Brace & World, Inc., 1961. 108 pp.
A linguistic excursion into the five styles of English usage, recognizing and analyzing the complex ways in which every speaker adjusts his language to various contexts and situations.

Leed, Jacob. *The Computer and Literary Style.* Kent: Kent State University Press, 1966. 179 pp.
Stylistic analysis through computer technique. Louis T. Milic's essay, "Unconscious Ordering in the Prose of Swift," is particularly useful, for it provides a sound theoretical framework for stylistic analysis via computation. Readable and reasonably non-technical.

McLuhan, Marshall. *The Gutenberg Galaxy.* Toronto: University of Toronto Press, 1962. 294 pp.
A seminal study of the meaning and impact of print culture (*i.e.,* the "Gutenberg Galaxy"). A mosaic of probes and illuminations. Excellent resource book for class discussions.

Milic, Louis. *Stylists on Style.* New York: Charles Scribner's Sons, 1969. 527 pp.
'This book is an attempt to construct a handbook of stylistics, something that will provide between two covers what is needed to pursue the study of English prose style: theory, method, practice" (p. 1). Excellent introductory essay; selections from diverse writers and comments thereon. Very useful.

Morse, J. Mitchell. *Matters of Style.* Indianapolis: Bobbs-Merrill Co., 1968. 318 pp.
An excellent practical (as opposed to theoretical) rhetoric. Superb writing assignments. Brilliant introductory essay.

Vinay, J. P. and J. Darbelnet. *Stylistique comparée du français et de l'anglais.* Montreal: Beauchemin, 1967. 331 pp.
Clearly written, linguistically sound, and copiously provided with illustrative examples. An indispensable guide to inter-language study. In French.

Winterowd, W. Ross. *Rhetoric: A Synthesis.* New York: Holt, Rinehart & Winston, Inc., 1968. 228 pp.
An attempt to build a new course in rhetoric, synthesized of traditional (*i.e.,* classical) and contemporary approaches to the art of writing. Theoretical and pedagogical materials. Demonstrations. Could be a useful resource book.

Education

Beechhold, Henry F. *The Creative Classroom: Teaching Without Textbooks.*
New York: Charles Scribner's Sons, 1971.
Education from Kindergarten through Thirteen based on inquiry/discovery/problem-solving techniques. Mainly, though not exclusively, concerned with language arts. Anti-textbook, but not anti-book.

Bruner, Jerome S. *The Process of Education.* New York: Vintage Books, 1963. 97 pp.
An important contribution to educational theory and practice. Should be required reading for all teachers and prospective teachers.

Philosophy

Aarsleff, Hans. *The Study of Language in England, 1780–1860.* Princeton: Princeton University Press, 1967. 279 pp.
The philosophical backgrounds of language study from Horne Tooke to the final plan of the *Oxford English Dictionary.* An essay in the history of ideas with particular reference to philological matters.

Beardsley, Monroe C. *Thinking Straight,* 2nd ed. Englewood Cliffs: Prentice-Hall, Inc., 1956. 332 pp.
A comprehensive and clearly presented introduction to logic. Well provided with exercises, many of which are imaginative and challenging.

Black, Max. *The Labyrinth of Language.* New York: Frederick A. Praeger, 1968. 178 pp.
A philosophically oriented exploration of language. Lively and stimulating.

Langer, Susanne K. *Philosophy in a New Key,* 2nd ed. New York: The New American Library, 1948. 256 pp.
A study in the symbolism of reason, rite, and art, with a large section devoted to language. An excellent treatment of the probable origins and development of symbolic behavior.

Reichenbach, Hans. *The Rise of Scientific Philosophy.* Berkeley: University of California Press, 1953. 333 pp.
An energetically written introduction to scientific (*i.e.,* anti-speculative) philosophy. Readable and thought-provoking.

Index

A

Aarsleff, Hans, 90
Abstract syntax theory, 151–52
Accretion, 160
Accusative case, 147
Adjectives, 87, 89, 110, 142
  definition of, 92, 102
Adjunction, 243
Adverbs, 50, 79, 87, 110
  definition of, 92
Allograph, 176
Allomorphs, 87
Allophones, 87
Alphabet systems, 170–72, 179–81, 182
  graphemes and, 177
  ideographs and, 174–75
American Indians, language of, 76, 84, 86
Analogist-Anomalist controversy, 78, 80, 90
Anaphora, 159
Anglo-Saxon language, 18, 58, 172
Antonyms, 71
Arabic language, 20, 181
Argumentation, 25–26
Aristotle, 68
  linguistic theory of, 78
Articles, 79, 118
"Artificial" languages, 40–41, 42
Associative references, 49

Attributive phrases, 133
Autonomous syntax hypothesis, 140
Auxiliaries
  in Black English, 205–6
  dummy, 23

B

Bach, E., 165
Balto-Slavic languages, 13
Basic English, 40
Beechhold, H., 4, 228
Behaviorism, 87–88
Bella-Coola language, 86
Black, Max, 7
Black African languages, 13
Black English, 201, 210–11
  grammar of, 203–9
  phonology of, 202–3
Bloomfield, Leonard, 4, 85, 91, 105
  behaviorism and, 87–88
  on morphemes and phonemes, 153–54
Boas, Franz, 84, 85
Borgmann, D. M., 228
Brand names, 39
Browne, Sir Thomas, 82
Bruner, Jerome, 222, 224